Magazine Editing

John Morrish

A BLUEPRINT book
published by Routledge
London and New York

First published 1996
by Routledge
11 New Fetter Lane, London EC4P 4EE

Simultaneously published in the USA and Canada
by Routledge
29 West 35th Street, New York, NY 10001

Typeset in Times by Datix International Limited, Bungay, Suffolk
Printed and bound in Great Britain by T.J. Press (Padstow) Ltd, Padstow, Cornwall

British Library Cataloguing in Publication Data
A catalogue record for this book is available from the British Library

Library of Congress Cataloguing in Publication Data
Morrish, John,
    Magazine editing / John Morrish.
        p.   cm.
"A Blueprint book."
    Includes bibliographical references and index.
    1. Journalism—Editing. I. Title.
PN4778. M67 1996
070.4' 1—dc20
96–7410

ISBN   0–415–15263–1 (hbk)
ISBN   0–415–13672–5 (pbk)

Contents

Foreword

Where was John Morrish's book when I slipped into my first editor's chair almost a decade ago? It would have saved me time and grief.

Slipped is the wrong word. There was nothing timed or effortless about my entrance. I left the crash bang wallop world of newspapers on a Friday as a 'been there, done that' features editor and became the eleventh editor of a national institution on the Monday. No one had prepared me for this.

I could vaguely remember my patter and promises at the interview six months before. I had the leaving party advice of my old editor [Charles Wilson] still ringing in my ears – 'Slam a few doors, rip up some layouts and fire someone before eleven.'

I found a broken squash racket in my bottom desk drawer and a piece of research that showed *my* magazine trailed its principal competitor 19–1 on a list of appreciation questions asked of readers of both titles.

I dabbled with some cover lines, shuffled some copy and mooched about the place like a lost soul, acutely aware that all eyes were on me. You learn loneliness on the first day as editor. John Morrish has clearly been there, too. This book describes the two contradictory impulses of any new editor – the urge 'to make your mark quickly' and the equally natural one 'to freeze'.

For me, and it sounds like for John, too, the thaw began with the chilling realisation that 'most colleagues have a vested interest in leaving things the way they are. They will not, however, be the ones to take the consequences when this course leads to disaster.'

These are relatively modern times in our industry that I'm recalling but it was still a time when our craft was learnt through anecdote and example, instinct and experience. A time when debate still raged as to whether journalism was a trade or a profession. And a time when the majority of the hoary-handed ones in charge believed with all their hearts that journalism couldn't be taught. It probably still is that time.

Whether or not it's a peculiarly British belief I'm not sure, but in the best traditions of amateurism we do still seem to believe that the bright and gifted will swim like fish in any water with the minimum of tuition. For instance, I have no idea why we believe that a teacher who's good in the classroom and relishes chalk on their hands is the best equipped to sort out the broken boiler, manage the budget and handle awkward parents as a school's head.

Our expectations of editors are much the same. They're laid out here in all their splendid awesome breadth. But John's real contribution is a brilliant piece of dissection. He parades the modern magazine editor in the round, then takes the beast apart, component by component. Here we have the editor as visionary, motivator, marketeer, accountant, manufacturer, canapé king and some-time ad. salesman. If, as is often said, the journalist knows a little about everything, then the editor described here is the consummate all-rounder.

This book is a brave undertaking. Editors are a cynical bunch not given to showing generosity towards their peers – it isn't a requirement of their rounded make-up. Perhaps that's why so few editors have taken the textbook plunge. One who did, of course, was Harold Evans and when I agreed to write this foreword I was reminded of what Hugh Cudlipp wrote of Harry's definitive five-volumes, *Editing and Design*. 'He is living denial of the saying: "Those who can, do: those who can't, teach."'

John Morrish was a class act as an editor, too. You'd have to be to stay on top at *Time Out*, the London listings title where a right-on veneer masks the business imperative. The advice and insights in this book smack of someone who's walked the tightrope with a measured step, a sense of balance and an instinctive feel for what the readers want.

'No one ever learned to be an editor from a textbook.' John Morrish wrote that and, as he admits, this book can never hope to replace experience. It can only encourage and inspire. It can't express the gut-churning, adrenalin rush of nearly falling from the tightrope or, on a good day, the thrill of hearing the readers roar their appreciation. What I really like about this book is that while laying bare the awesome magnitude of what's expected and required of the modern magazine editor, it never loses sight of the fact that editing is sheer joy. It beats hewing coal.

Nicholas Brett
Editor, *Radio Times*

Acknowledgements

Many people helped me in the preparation of this book. I would like particularly to thank the following editors, who talked to me about the way they work: Lewis Blackwell of *Creative Review*; Iris Burton of IPC's South Bank Group; George Darby, deputy editor of the *Telegraph Magazine*; Paul Finch of *Architects' Journal*; Maggie Goodman; and Robin Wood of Miller-Freeman. I would also like to thank the following for taking the time to explain to me the rudiments of on-line publishing, here and in the US: Chip Bayers of *HotWired*; David M. Cole of the Cole Group; Chris Feola of *Quill* magazine; and Julian Marszalk of *PowerPC News*. Thanks also to Debbie Beavor for explaining picture editing. Nick Voss Bark of *The Last Word* talked to me about editorial systems. Razi Mireskandari of Simons, Muirhead & Burton and Nick Braithwaite of Clifford Chance helped me through the new Defamation Bill. Any inaccuracies, omissions and misunderstandings in the book are, of course, my responsibility.

David Longbottom and Joanne Butcher, past and present directors of the Periodicals Training Council, offered valuable encouragement with the project. I should also like to thank Vivien James, formerly of Blueprint, for commissioning the book in the first place, and Rebecca Barden and Vivien Antwi of Routledge for seeing it through to publication.

I also owe a debt of gratitude, not always acknowledged at the time, to those magazine editors for whom I have worked and written over the years: Don Atyeo, Tony Bacon, Paul Colbert, Paul Finch, Simon Garfield, Howard Griffiths, Ian Hislop, Nigel Horne, Richard Ingrams, Sutherland Lyall, Adam Murza, Emma Soames and John Walsh. In their different ways they have all taught me a great deal about what it is to be an editor.

Most of all I would like to thank my wife, Deborah Thorp, for her help, advice and support through the writing of this book – and everything else.

John Morrish
February 1996

Introduction

The last few years have seen great technological changes in the way magazines are produced. If anything, those changes are accelerating. Already, most of us work in the 'digital domain' when we create material. Our words, pictures and graphical elements are produced, stored and manipulated by electronic means. In the next few years we are likely to turn to digital electronics for the delivery of that material.

In these exciting times, the instinct, judgement and skills of the editor will be more important than ever. This book examines those attributes in a way that should be helpful for aspiring editors, new editors and even experienced editors, who may on occasion need to be reassured that they are not alone.

At the same time, it discusses the other side of magazine editing: the managerial and leadership role that editors have, in the past, been expected to learn by trial and error. The aim is to ease the difficult transition from being 'one of us' to being 'one of them'.

The technological transformation of recent years is obvious enough, but there has also been a change in the way senior journalists, and particularly editors, think and work.

Many of us have learned to understand commercial realities, and business philosophy and language, in away that our predecessors would never have imagined. The disciplines of business are a powerful force in our society. Not to try to understand them is to shun full participation in our industry: indeed, in our democracy.

Business itself is changing, however. These days profit and loss are complemented by talk of responsiveness, flexibility and service. While some magazines and publishing houses stick to the old philosophy of mass production – produce something you consider acceptable and pump it out in volume – those which will survive and prosper in the new era are making ever greater efforts to serve their readers. If they continue to do so, they will continue to be attractive to advertisers. The virtuous circle by which editorial success and commercial strength reinforce one another will be maintained.

Knowing our readers and their interests has always been fundamental to editorship. As our industry takes its first steps beyond ink and paper, editorial quality will once again be revealed as the essence of periodical publishing.

The magazine will survive. It may not always be made out of crushed trees and processed mineral deposits. It may not always consist of still pictures and written text. But as long as human beings require a convenient, accessible, portable and self-renewing source of information, explanation, provocation, inspiration and amusement, the magazine idea will prosper.

As magazine editors we are working in an area of publishing that inspires great loyalty and affection. Since the end of the seventeenth century, when they first appeared in London and Paris, magazines have become part of the lives of most people on earth, or at least of that half of the world fortunate enough to live beyond subsistence level.

In those three centuries, the way magazines have been created and read has changed as radically as society itself. In the eighteenth century magazines were an adornment to an elite society built on elegant conversation. Printed to be read in coffee houses, they came into being simultaneously with the City institutions that financed the Empire and the Industrial Revolution. After the migration to the towns and industrial work came mass literacy, and the magazines grew with it. In our own century, the magazine has faced the challenge of radio, cinema and television and, with some exceptions, thrived.

Today, the magazine publishing industry continues its relentless search for new markets, a search built on finding new ideas and exploiting old ones more effectively. At the same time, every significant magazine publisher in the developed world is thinking about the longer term. How do we apply what we know, how do we use our skills, how do we protect our investment, in an era of technological development that promises to be unlike anything we have seen before?

This book takes as its starting point a consideration of the skills and personal qualities necessary in an editor. It moves on to discuss each of the areas in which an editor will need to apply those assets: in knowing the reader; in working with an editorial team; in dealing with money; in dealing with content; in presenting and organising content through design; in managing production; in adapting to new technology; and in dealing with the wider world.

It is important to remember what an editor actually does, the common thread of purpose that makes such a person essential for everything from the production of a house journal to the creation of a useful World Wide Web site.

In the first instance, the editor's task is one of selection. This might seem too passive, as if the editor were merely someone who opens the post and prints what looks interesing. It is more a question of selecting from life, from the mass of human activity, that which is of interest to a publication's readers. Only then does the process of selecting descend to the choice of writers or individual pieces of material. In the electronic age, when information in various disorganised forms is all-pervasive, the task of selection will grow in importance.

The second task of the editor, which is often overlooked, is acquisition. Few magazines have their own staff reporters, writers or photographers, which means that most of the material an editor uses will have to have been acquired. The art of buying editorial material is becoming central to editorship. The new electronic media will make it even more important.

The third task is authentication. One of the things editors promise their readers is that the material they are publishing is accurate. Obviously there are exceptions: some editors publish fiction. But in general the task of checking material or ensuring its accuracy is at the heart of editorship. If we as journalists and editors are to profit from the electronic media it will be because we have convinced readers that our material is worth paying for because it is true.

Another of the editor's tasks is the organisation of material. Editing is not simply about gathering and checking material: it is also about organising it in a way that makes sense, is accessible and is appealing. We direct people's attention.

Finally, editors are responsible for bringing material into the public arena. That task can be as simple as pressing the button on the photocopier or as difficult as motivating a large staff through the myriad processes involved in producing a weekly magazine. The editor then takes responsibility for that publication and what stems from it.

No-one ever learned to be an editor from a textbook. This book cannot replace experience. But it can offer a modest amount of encouragement and perhaps inspiration, as well as a core of relevant information. You can read it from front to back, you can dip in or you can use the index. This flexibility remains the preserve of the print medium. Make the most of it while it lasts.

Chapter 1

Becoming an editor

I note what you say about your aspiration to edit a magazine. I am sending you by this mail a six-chambered revolver. Load it and fire every one into your head. You will thank me after you get to Hell and learn from other editors how dreadful their job was on earth.

(H.L. Mencken to William Saroyan, 1936)

The American humourist's jaundiced account of the pleasures of editing will strike a chord with some readers. But it is only part of the picture. Many journalists take becoming an editor as the pinnacle of their career, the summit of their ambitions. The irony is, however, that editing is not solely about journalism. Journalism is simply the skill that gets you the job. Once installed in the editor's chair, other tasks take over. Editors need to learn a publishing role, a managerial role and a leadership role.

In practice, if someone offers you the chance to become editor you do not normally refuse. It may be years before you get such an offer again; moreover, your chances of continuing peacefully in your own existing position after refusing such an offer are not high. Managements mistrust people who turn down promotions, suspecting them of lack of commitment, laziness or ulterior motives. New editors mistrust potential editors among their own staff, though those who refuse the offer are less troubling than those who have applied only to be rejected. But the consequences of refusal can be high.

The time to consider your own readiness for the task is before it becomes a realistic prospect. That way you will have time to prepare yourself and consider your own skills and attributes. You may, indeed, realise that your strengths lie elsewhere. There is no shame in wanting to carry on writing and reporting. One of the problems of journalism is that successful and skilful writers and reporters can only gain advancement by moving to supervisory roles where their talents are lost to the readers.

As your career develops, you must assess your own ambitions and abilities. Then, when new prospects are held out to you, you can assess the job that is being offered. Only when the two aspects make a good match will you have found a niche in which you are likely to succeed.

ASSESSING YOURSELF

In the case of a journalist considering a move into editorship, the key question is one of maturity. This is not a matter of age, nor even, ultimately, of professional experience, although both can help. It is about assessing your own skills, attitudes and personal situation and deciding whether you are ready. When you apply for your first editorship, you can be sure this question will be uppermost in the minds of those assessing you.

You will need the confidence that comes from a thorough mastery of the fundamentals of journalism. You will, probably, have achieved most of your ambitions as a reporter, writer, section editor or sub-editor. These may have been private triumphs, for instance producing a substantial number of news 'splashes' or cover features, editing successful supplements or mastering the complexities of production. Or you may have achieved outside recognition in the shape of awards, appropriate compensation and interim promotions. It is not always a good idea to embark upon editorship while there are still stories you are burning to write.

But there is a more important type of maturity. You must ask yourself how you will cope with the responsibilities of leadership. Immediately, you will find yourself removed from your former peers. You will have business you can discuss with no-one. You will have to give instructions and advice to those who are older and sometimes more experienced than you. You will have to praise without patronising and, on occasions, to reprimand. You will have to turn down people's pet ideas, refuse them pay rises, even, on occasion, end their employment. You must be ready to be the person that everyone turns to when there is a crisis, or when, as sometimes happens, no-one has any ideas. The option of passing the buck will no longer be available.

You must be ready to take full legal and moral responsibility for what appears in your magazine, what happens in the editorial office and what happens to the magazine in its market. That may mean appearing before a judge to explain your actions in publishing a particular report, appearing at an industrial tribunal to stand up for your decision to dismiss someone, and standing up to a publisher whose commercial schemes threaten the editorial integrity of the magazine. Success in all these tasks demands strong resolve, supportive domestic circumstances, good health, excellent technical knowledge and skills, but above all, great personal maturity.

The essential journalistic skills

In an ideal world you would already have done every editorial job on a magazine before you were appointed to edit it. Not because you will be required to do every job, but because you will be required to know the language of each department, to know their interests and their drives, and to be able to lead, where necessary, by example. Even if you never write a headline, you will gain a certain confidence from knowing that you always can if you need to.

This is, however, a counsel of perfection. All-round training is less common than it should be, and once in a first job, young journalists tend to move vertically rather than horizontally. A reporter will tend to become a news editor rather than a sub-editor, for instance. A features editor may well have started as an assistant in the features department, and may never have attended a press conference or copy-fitted a story.

Jobs which involve production have often provided the most appropriate route into editing. Increasingly magazines are developing an 'editor class' of section editors and commissioning editors who acquire and edit material as well as writing headlines and standfirsts: at IPC, for instance, these people are called a magazine's 'focus group'. But close textual editing of written material remains the province of the sub-editors. Those working in this capacity should have learned both the skills needed to assemble a magazine and the verbal dexterity needed to sell its ideas to the reader.

There is, too, an important difference between the way reporters and writers look at journalistic material and the way those from an editing and sub-editing background approach it. Reporters want a story to be true to what they have learned from their sources. Sub-editors, on the other hand, approach material from the viewpoint of the reader. They want it to be clear, coherent and internally consistent, and if necessary they are prepared to adjust it to sharpen its appeal to the reader. This is one of the fundamentals of editing.

But beyond that, editors require a number of specialised skills that tend to be acquired in a section-editing and sub-editing context. The first is a command of the 'selling' elements of the magazine. These are the things that 'sell' the publication or its individual stories to the bookstall browser and the reader: the cover-lines, headlines and standfirsts (often called 'sells'); even, sometimes, lines for poster campaigns and promotional material.

It is possible that other people will write these – indeed, a lot of the time they must be allowed to – but as editor you need to have a feel for what is good and what is bad. These things come with practice, but at the same time there is usually an aptitude: a long-standing interest in word-games, puns, even poetry can all help when it comes to finding a pungent phrase to put at the top of a 2,000 word article on pension planning or developments in midwifery.

The second essential skill is that of seeing particular groups of words and pictures as magazine 'shapes'. You will need to learn that so many words turn into so many columns or pages when laid out in various different ways. And, vice versa, that a particular type of layout demands a certain number of words. Accurate 'casting-off', the technique which sub-editors used to assess to the line how much space a particular article would occupy, has now been made redundant by the use of computer page make-up. Nonetheless, you don't want to have to delve into QuarkXPress every time you want to make a decision about how long something should be or how many pages a given feature will occupy.

On the subject of technology, sub-editors (and designers, particularly) often acquire a greater understanding of the editorial computer systems and software than writers, most of whom ask no more than that it produces a blank page for them to write on. This knowledge can be an asset to editors. (See chapter 9: The editor and technology).

The third major area in which sub-editing and production form a good preparation for editing is in the technicalities of the production process. As a writer, you will know almost nothing of flat-planning, scheduling and copy-flow. You may have heard of deadlines, but your relationship with them will be fairly relaxed. A background in sub-editing gives the editor a deeper understanding of the process, and may have allowed you to develop relationships with outside agencies such as colour houses and printers. Again, except on very tiny magazines you personally will not be working out schedules and copy-flow charts, but you will need to assess what is proposed and consider whether it is practical and sensible. You will also need to understand flat-planning, a tedious process that lies somewhere close to the heart of editing. These things can be learnt, but sub-editors have a head start. (See chapter 8: The editor and production).

A fourth skill is that of making decisions on legal and ethical questions. All journalists should have a working understanding of press law, but sub-editors have to spot problems in the first instance. As editor you will have responsibility for this area, including keeping on top of any changes in the law, and this will be easier if you have had experience in assessing run-of-the-mill legal risks before taking up the job.

The final aspect in which a sub-editing background is helpful is in the maintenance of standards. Writers and reporters tend only to read their own stories. They may try to keep to that collection of rules and regulations known as 'house style', but they often fail. In fairness, that's not the most important aspect of their jobs. Sub-editors, on the other hand, have to supervise grammar, accuracy, punctuation and style, watching for inconsistencies within and across different articles, pages and issues.

The quality of attention that sub-editors give to the written material is very much higher than that which is usually expected from writers (except of course where their own articles are concerned, in which case they tend to be quite punctilious). One of the editor's most important tasks is to ensure that the verbal texture of the magazine is as good as it can be: as the architect Mies van der Rohe said, 'God is in the details'. In practice, this is a task that must be delegated to others, but the editor is responsible for establishing unambiguous standards.

On the other hand, writing has certain advantages as a background for editing. Sub-editors, and desk-bound journalists generally, sometimes develop a kind of professional agoraphobia. People may become sub-editors and section editors because they can't face dealing with the public. Desk working allows a bit more control over their working lives, with, usually, regular hours, comfortable or at least familiar surroundings, and a certain amount of routine. This may, in extreme cases, lead to a detachment from the readers, especially since sub-editors often end up dealing with their complaints.

All this is fatal for an editor, who must be the public face of the magazine. The reporter's ability to talk to strangers, and to meet people up and down the social scale, is something that editors would do well to acquire. Second, editors can take from a reporting and writing background a keen nose for what constitutes 'a story'. This is something that applies not solely to the news area, but to everything: it's a matter of knowing what is appropriate for the magazine and its readers. Unfortunately, sub-editing sometimes loses sight of that aspect in its urgent need to process raw material into finished magazine pages.

Third, writers and reporters should have a sense of narrative, which remains an important device for making people read journalistic material. Fourth, writers and reporters learn how things are done. They discover the mechanism whereby stories are unearthed, important interviews arranged and interesting documents secured. They can fix things, or they know people who can. They are used to mastering new subject areas quickly and asking the right questions. All these are important for editors too. The greatest magazine technicians in the world will not achieve anything unless they know the appropriate mechanisms for putting their readers in touch with what they want to read.

The essential visual skills

Sub-editors and section editors will have had considerable contact with the visual aspects of magazine editing. On newspaper-format magazines they may have designed and laid out pages themselves. On most magazines they will have worked alongside designers. Reporters and writers will have had less to do with the design world, other than occasionally working with photographers in the field. None of these is much preparation for the design aspects of becoming an editor, although features editors or section editors on larger publications will have gained more useful experience.

For most new editors, design is an unfamiliar problem. It is hard to overestimate the importance of design as an editorial tool. Few editors will have had any form of design training, but they will be taking responsibility for an enterprise that will stand or fall on the ability of the design to articulate its editorial message.

No-one expects the editor to design the magazine: the task is to know what is possible and to have a clear vision of what is required. The ability to speak in language the magazine's art editor or art director will understand is a definite advantage, but beyond that there is a general requirement to be 'visually literate' and to know the possibilities. The best preparation may well be close study of other magazines, not only in your own field but across the whole range, indeed, the whole world.

It must become second nature to think of any proposed article not simply as a series of words but as a composite built from words, pictures and other design elements. Journalists habitually think of writing an article and finding a few pictures to 'illustrate' it, but that is not the way magazines work.

These questions will take on greater prominence in the future if, as seems likely, magazines become even more visually based. This will be especially critical if magazines are to be read on screen rather than on paper, because on screen text will always lose out to images. Prospective editors who are confident in their verbal skills should do what they can to cultivate their visual awareness, from studying elegant foreign magazines to haunting art galleries. Subscribing to the kind of publications designers read may be another aid to finding common ground in a relationship that can be stimulating but tricky.

The essential management skills

Becoming an editor is always an entry into management, although this is not always recognised either by your staff or by your employer. It's a matter of your individual contractual position, of course. But by most definitions, to organise the activities of staff and to take actions with financial consequences is to be a manager. Both management and editing are about leadership. There are training courses available in all these areas, but sometimes they are only made available to editors after they have struggled alone for months or years. The transition to managing is difficult enough on a personal level: the least you can do to prepare yourself is to take some time to deal with the obvious professional aspects.

The skills required to handle money may well be quite new to you. There is a strong argument for saying that everyone should know how to make some sense of a balance sheet and a company report, if only because the business model is now dominant in all spheres of life. Certainly most news reporters will need to acquire this information early on. Editors specifically need to learn how to handle the documents that tell the financial story of their organisation: the budgets and the cash-flow. At the very least you need to be able to understand a budget that is presented to you. Better, though, to be able to draw it up yourself. (See chapter 4: The editor and money.)

As an editor you will be responsible for considerable sums of money. Decisions about freelance payments, for instance, are obviously in your domain. But other aspects of your practices will have their financial effects, from the amount of paper your department uses to the precise way you deal with outside production facilities.

It is also worth remembering that you are constantly making contracts, all of which are potentially enforceable in law. Journalistic contracts tend towards the informal: valuable commissions may stem from a two-minute telephone conversation. That does not mean they are any less of a contract, however, and you should be aware of the issues involved each time you make such an agreement.

This is particularly important now that the acquisition of the right to reproduce copyright material has become such a complex and contentious matter. The purchase of material for publication is one of the most crucial parts of the editing process and needs to be thoroughly understood and managed with great care. Even the practice of keeping a 'bottom drawer' or 'slushpile' of editorial material for those occasions when inspiration flags or something goes missing has cost implications.

'People skills', too, may be new to you. Managements today make great play of their commitment to their 'people'. Publishing is a classic example of a business in which, as the cliché has it, 'the assets walk out of the door every night'. Editors, however, must go beyond simple slogans. Managing creative people, most of whom feel no need to be managed, is a task that will require all of your knowledge, skills and experience.

Anything you do must be based on a thorough understanding of your legal responsibilities. Not all editors have the power of 'hire and fire' (although purists would insist that if they don't, they're not really doing the job). In some cases this is a task for the personnel department or some other higher authority. Nonetheless, the way you deal with people, as their immediate boss, will have legal implications should later disciplinary action be necessary. You will also be expected to assess people's progress, make recommendations about their level of remuneration, put them forward for training, and so on. Anything you can learn about these areas before you start will pay dividends.

Leadership expresses itself through the way you communicate with your staff, whether in meetings, in writing or in brief conversations in the corridor. There are techniques which can be learned. If you are offered the opportunity to attend any such training, you should take it.

Beyond that, another set of 'people skills' is required for dealing with your peers, your readers and the general public. Those who lack confidence in such settings will find their progress blighted as publishers grow ever more PR-conscious. Anything you can learn to enhance your public confidence will be invaluable.

Personal qualities and attributes

Beyond the skills that you will require, there are also your personal qualities and attributes, your 'character'.

Self-reliance may well be the quality most needed by new editors. It is hard to overestimate the sense of isolation that descends on you when you first take charge. If most of your friends have also been your workmates, you can find the distance which must now exist between you and them extremely difficult to bear. The fact that you now have new colleagues among your peers in management is of little consolation.

You may feel you have nothing in common with them, but everything in common with those whose 'boss' you now have to be. At the same time, everyone immediately expects you to know everything. It is no surprise that so many new editors disappear into their offices and close their doors, communicating only by memo and trusted messenger. Once there, however, it is difficult to emerge. You must get used to the new realities. Throughout your career as an editor you will have to take unpopular decisions and you will not get much sympathy: most journalists are, naturally, convinced that they would be better at your job than you are.

Determination will see you through these things. It is no good being self-reliant if you don't have the necessary determination to take the magazine in the direction you think right. This is a quality that comes from within but you may be able to learn techniques for demonstrating that determination in a way that won't threaten everyone else.

You will need imagination to keep the level of inspiration high, both for yourself and for your staff. The key to leading a successful team is to release the ideas and talents of others. But at first everyone will sit back and wait to see what you can do, and throughout your career there will be times when you have to take an unambiguous leadership role.

You must also have a thorough understanding of the market your magazine is intended to serve. You don't have to know everything about the area before you begin – otherwise no-one would ever change jobs – but you must know at least enough to get you started. It helps if you can form an emotional attachment to the magazine. There are those who insist that management tasks are complicated by the presence of emotional involvement. There are even those who believe that a good editor is a bloodless professional who can move from publication to publication without a care. Well, perhaps, but a successful editor needs a passionate relationship with the magazine and through that with the readers. If you can develop a great affection for your staff (all of them rather than specific individuals), so much the better, but this should be secondary: you are not their mother.

A deep enthusiasm for magazines in general is another necessity. You should not be able to pass a news-stand without taking a look at what's new. When you come back from a foreign holiday your suitcases should be bulging with local publications, even when you haven't a clue about the local language. Your magazine will have a ravenous appetite for ideas, and you never know where you might find them.

Beyond that, of course, you should have real curiosity about the world around you, but that is central to all journalism. As an editor, you will find yourself squeezing much of what the world has to offer through a particular filter: the interest of your readers.

The life of an editor can be physically and emotionally demanding, and you will need to be on solid ground. Your physical and mental health will need to be robust. Ask yourself about your ability to deal with long hours and a sedentary lifestyle, punctuated by unhealthy working lunches and periods of high stress.

Your emotional life will need to be sturdy too. Being an editor is notoriously incompatible with the demands of family life. While you should ensure you take enough rest to keep healthy and mentally alert, you cannot expect fixed hours. There will be crises. It is as well to establish this with your loved ones before your new career begins. There are many people who will take the decision that other people and other interests are more important to them than work. In their case, other paths within journalism may be more appropriate.

ASSESSING THE JOB

An honest assessment of your own skills and character is only half the task you need to undertake when you are contemplating taking up an editorship. The other half is making an objective assessment of the position you are aiming for or are being offered.

No-one ever turns down the offer of a first editorship. More experienced editors turn down jobs all the time, however, not because of doubts about their own capabilities, but because of realistic doubts about the jobs they are being offered.

The process of winning your first editorship may be as simple as a chat in the pub (although usually this only applies to deputies and the like) or it may be as complicated as a long series of interviews and panels. You will be primed to answer all sorts of questions, but you should also be ready to ask them. Most interviewees manage a halting inquiry about terms and conditions, but there is much more that they should know before they make up their minds.

Is it for you?

An editorship may be a perfectly acceptable proposition for someone else without ever coming close to being suitable for you. There needs to be a match between the subject matter and approach of a publication and the person editing it. If you cannot muster up an appropriate level of enthusiasm for the material and those who read it, you must look elsewhere. Other things can be changed: the way the subject is dealt with, the kind of writers used, the design approach. But the fundamentals of subject-matter and readership are usually fixed. A professional can do a good job in almost any circumstances, but as a professional you also need to be honest about where your real inclinations lie.

Your new magazine

Consider the character of your new magazine. Start with the fundamentals, for instance its frequency and format, and then work out towards the intangibles, such as its 'tone of voice' and the way it is perceived in the market.

You may be experienced in monthlies: what changes will you experience when you move to a weekly? If you know weeklies, can you gear yourself to the different rhythm of a monthly? Now look at how the magazine presents itself. Is it authoritative or irreverent? Is it friendly or austere? Informative or entertaining?

Now where does it sit in its market? Does it lead or trail? Is it growing or shrinking? These are matters of fact. But how do its readers feel about it? What do the readers of rival journals think? If it's a professional publication, what does the industry it serves think of it? What do other editors think? These are matters of opinion, but vital in building up a picture of the task you are taking on.

What is the magazine's history? Is it a brash newcomer, an old faithful in need of gentle tidying up, or something struggling to come to terms with a changing world? And what is the magazine's status in publishing terms: is it part of a group or 'portfolio' of magazines with a common strategy, is it simply one title in a roster of scores, or is it someone's pet project?

Not everything about a magazine is apparent on the surface. Its history may be a living presence in your dealings with staff and readers, as those who try to make radical changes sometimes discover. It may have a symbolic significance that is at odds with the reality. It may remind your readers of happier times. It may be its owner's first magazine, or favourite magazine. It may be where your publisher learned to sell classified advertising. Certain apparently minor aspects of the magazine – typefaces, running orders, individual columns – may have a significance to other people that is not apparent to you as a newcomer.

You may, of course, be considering taking on a new launch, in which case there will as yet be no real answers to these questions. You will be providing them. Thorough discussion will help you decide whether you can create what those launching the magazine seem to want.

Your new employer

Taking up a new editorship will often involve joining a new employer. Aside from general questions that any new recruit would need answered, there are specific things that editors need to know. Every publishing company has a culture, but what does that culture mean for editors? To what extent are editors autonomous and to what extent are their activities affected and regulated by a corporate vision? Does the editor deal with staffing matters, or is that a matter for negotiation with a central personnel department? Where does the editor's budgetary responsiblity end? How much power does an editor have?

You may be only one editor among many. You should ascertain whether the company's editors meet on any formal or informal basis to discuss topics of common interest and to represent the editorial point of view within the organisation.

It is important to learn what you can about your new employer. Producing one magazine among hundreds for a giant public company, answerable to anonymous shareholders via the balance sheet, is radically different from working for an entrepreneur with a small stable of publications, where each has the potential to determine the fate of the whole enterprise. Big companies have the disadvantage of anonymity. Editors feel less 'special', less crucial to the enterprise and more like the rest of the staff, which some may find more comfortable. There is also likely to be considerable support, in the form of centralised training, personnel, production and other functions.

Working for an enterpreneur, on the other hand, is likely to be more of a white-knuckle ride. Psychological studies of entrepreneurs have revealed a number of common characteristics which may not make them ideal employers for everyone. They find it difficult to deal dispassionately with issues of dominance and submission; they find structure stifling; they fear placing power in the hands of others; they have low tolerance of independent thinking; they have a tendency towards paranoia, seeing themselves as victims and looking for plots; they are addicted to secrecy; and they need constant reassurance and praise.

On the other hand, entrepreneurs can be exciting to work for. They are tremendously motivated, which can be contagious. They are creative, capable of inspiring sudden innovation without needing lengthy processes to set things in motion. They often have great energy and can be more passionate, even than their editors, about their magazines. When you are in agreement, this is inspiring. When you are not, it can be a problem.

It is particularly important to recognise that emotion can sometimes override reason. Individual proprietors and long-serving managements are prone to sentiment and are willing to tolerate damaging inefficiencies and anachronisms for reasons that are shrouded in the mists of time. They will not always welcome improvements, no matter how well founded and well argued.

Ask about the structure above you. To whom do you report? In most cases you will work with and to a publisher: in some magazine houses, publishers and editors are placed on an 'equal-but-different' footing, both reporting to a publishing director. This may, in practice, be a semantic distinction but it recognises the complementary interests and attitudes of the publishing and editorial functions. Anything you can discover about the personalities of those holding these positions will be valuable.

Sometimes editors, particularly inexperienced editors, find themselves reporting to an 'editorial director' or an 'editor in chief'. Former editors also, on occasions, become publishers. This should be helpful, but may not necessarily be. The problem with having another editor above you is that it breaks the contract between editor and reader. If every decision you make can be overridden, if there is always a higher court of appeal, if your operational decisions about staff, contributors, cover treatments and so on can be overturned, you are no longer the editor. You are the deputy editor.

This is not to say that there is no place for senior editors, particularly in large publishing houses, to make strategic decisions, to look at new launches, and to make their vast stock of knowledge and expertise available to those editors who wish to make use of it. But this is a role which needs to be performed with subtlety if mutual respect, rather than suspicion, is to be achieved. Editors in chief should be available for consultation, advice and support. All editors have times when they need the assistance of someone experienced. This relationship will not work, however, if the editor in chief is also supposed to be sitting in judgement on those who seek his or her help. Again, the role of any such editor in chief is something that should be explored in interview. In short, the buck must stop with you: if it doesn't, you aren't really editing your magazine.

Your new staff

Before accepting a position as editor, consider your new staff. If you are ambitious in your career you will most likely be a regular reader of the editorial pages of the *Press Gazette* rather than just its advertising. That should be enough to alert you to any horrendous problems in staff relations. Industrial disputes and the like can take an extremely long time to fade from the collective memory.

Beyond that, though, you can learn a great deal by intelligent scrutiny of the magazine in question. Sloppiness about spelling, punctuation, and so on, indicates problems in the sub-editing department. Weak headlines and standfirsts and a general lack of sharpness may stem from inadequacies higher up the chain.

If there is a staff box (or 'masthead', if you prefer), see how it relates to the by-lines that you see. Much of the writing, these days, will tend to have been produced by contributors, but the ideas may well have been generated in-house. Ask yourself what you would expect such an issue to cost, in terms of freelance material: when you reach the final stages of the interviewing process, your budgetary constraints should be revealed. Taking that in conjunction with staffing levels, you can begin to make some assessment of what can realistically be achieved.

It is worth asking, too, about training. Your interview is not the most intelligent time to ask about your own career development, but you should know what is available to your staff and what their attitude to it has been. Some managements persist in using training as a punishment or ritual humiliation, to the despair of trainers, and if that has been the case you will find it difficult to promote a more constructive attitude.

It is worth thinking particularly hard about two key jobs: your art editor (or director) and your deputy editor. It is fair to say that without a happy and mutually respectful relationship with both, your attempt to bring your own personality to bear on the new magazine will face great difficulties. It will be one of your first tasks to ensure that these key colleagues are receptive to your direction or to take appropriate action. It is commonplace for new editors to bring their own deputies. This is neither fair nor necessarily sensible, but the culture of magazines is such that it is often expected.

EDITING AND PUBLISHING

Once editors liked to stand aloof from the commercial aspects of their magazines, which were seen as a necessary evil permitting journalists to go about their business without undue financial restraint. Only when crisis loomed would they be expected to take an interest in advertising and marketing.

This has all changed. Reluctantly at first, and then with increasing enthusiasm, editors have learned to become involved in the publishing process, rather than simply offering editorial services to those whose business is producing magazines. Partly this is a reflection of the tough economic conditions of recent times. It is also connected with changing relationships within publishing managements and the new stress on teamwork. It may, though, have most to do with the spirit of our times, in which entrepreneurship, management and financial expertise have achieved a new status.

Editors, and journalists generally, once enjoyed 'gentleman amateur' status, which they felt could be threatened by contact with money. That has gone: editors are under constant pressure to contribute to the commercial well-being of their magazines as well as their editorial success.

This has left editors unclear about what is acceptable. The way through this ethical wilderness is to look at the fundamentals of the editor's relationship with the magazine market and the commercial imperatives of publishing. The most important relationship for an editor should be with the readers. But the relationship between editor and publisher provides the basis on which that more important connection can be established and nurtured. If the relationship between publisher and editor is to run smoothly, it is important to consider underlying drives, goals and attitudes that may never be explicitly stated.

The word 'publisher' is unfortunately ambiguous, in that it means both the person or organisation which owns the magazine, or group of magazines, and the person responsible for the day-to-day management and commercial performance of an individual title.

In some companies, for instance the National Magazine Company, publishers and editors work on a basis of broad equality. The publisher organises the advertising strategy and personnel; the editor handles the editorial strategy and the journalists. Both are answerable to a publishing director or managing director. More often, however, the editor's opposite number is the advertising manager, with both sections answerable to a publisher responsible for everything involving the expenditure or receipt of company money.

Historically, publishers have tended to come from an advertising background, while editors have always been journalists. These days, however, it is not uncommon for publishers to have started their careers in journalism before 'crossing over' or 'joining the other side'. Increasingly, though, the cultural differences between the commercial and journalistic personnel of a magazine are diminishing. Advertising sales people are now likely to have had the same kind of education and to enjoy the same leisure activities and interests as their journalistic peers. Both journalism and advertising sales are increasingly graduate-entry careers.

The new generation of publishers should not, therefore, be as remote from editors as has sometimes been the case in the past. There are tremendous advantages in this, obviously enough, but also dangers. Important distinctions must be made between the imperatives which drive editorial and those which drive publishing. The interests of journalists and advertising departments are not always identical.

It is possible for editors to approach situations in ways which people from an advertising background find inappropriate, and vice versa. This becomes clear when, as is often the case, journalists find themselves writing stories which have an impact on individual advertisers or the wider industries of which they are a part.

A magazine which never has cause to run stories about its own advertisers is in a privileged position. More often, especially in the business press, the activities of advertisers will constitute a great part of the focus of editorial interest. The interests of individual advertisers can sometimes appear threatened by the legitimate editorial activities of the magazine: advertising sales executives are naturally protective of relationships that have built up over years and may not see the necessity for carrying one story rather than another. No journalist will need reminding that the income of advertising staff is intimately connected with those relationships. In cases of conflict, an appeal is always made to 'the interests of the magazine'. But the interests of the magazine as seen by publishers and editors do not always coincide. These issues come into particular focus in cases in which editors have become publishers. Sometimes their enthusiasm for the new commercial role is such that they lose their sense of the value that editorial independence brings to their publications.

The key phrase here is 'editorial integrity', an expression which has been abused by both parties in the publishing relationship. Editors use it to protect activities which may or may not have anything to do with legitimate editorial strategy. Publishers sometimes use it to circumscribe the area in which the editor is permitted to take an interest. An editor who is told that such and such a project will not impinge on his or her 'editorial integrity' should beware.

The central difficulty is the collision between 'hard' values, as represented by columns of figures, and 'soft' values, as represented by discussion of stories, reviews and editorial comments. Editors would do well to recognise that judgements which appear self-evident to them may not be so transparent to those who have not had the benefit of years of journalistic training, experience and lore.

Increasingly, editors are learning to understand and speak the language of money: indeed, this is essential if they are to play a full part in the lives of their magazines. At the same time, however, publishers will need to make a renewed effort to come to grips with the essence of the journalistic task. What is needed is mutual understanding, based upon respect. This is particularly true in the case of the new electronic media, which will only work for publishers if they are based on genuine editorial material, produced with absolute integrity.

The publishing imperative

A journalist who is only interested in making money, either personally or for his or her publication, is not to be trusted. Equally, any publisher who is not interested in making money should be treated with caution.

In the commercial sector, making money is the essence of publishing, and provides the validation for the activity. Profit is a measure of how well you are employing people's talents and your company's resources. A profitable magazine is one which is wanted, valued and has earned its right to exist. This is not something to be scorned.

A publisher who is not interested in making money has some other motive. This may be entirely honourable. The magazine may be an adjunct to another activity: education, commerce, politics, corporate well-being, and so on. In other cases, the publisher may be willing to run a magazine at a loss while it establishes its place in a market that has not yet matured, for the sake of future profits. Alternatively, such a publisher may be running a magazine that was once profitable in the hope or expectation that changed economic circumstances will once again bring it back into the black. Neither situation is ideal, but editors can make their own judgements about the prospects.

There are also publications which are run permanently at a loss because they provide the publisher with rewards that are not financial in nature. They may provide an entrée into a particular social or professional group. They may provide an outlet for the publisher's views, talents and desire to be a patron. Or they may promote a cause. Looked at harshly, these are types of 'vanity publishing'. An editor will be a necessary part of such publishing, but one which the publisher, on some level, would prefer to do without.

In short, editors should welcome the profitability of their magazines as the mark of success and the guarantee of continued independence and quality. There are cases in which long-term financial success makes publishers anxious and produces a culture of conservatism, particularly with market leaders and magazines in monopoly positions, but in general profitability is to be worked for and welcomed. Unending financial stringency, or even uncertainty, is not conducive to editorial achievement.

The best account of the publishing imperative comes in John Wharton's *Managing Magazine Publishing*. He is blunt. 'Without profit, a magazine has no point or purpose and the efforts of those involved are wasted.' He goes on to say that not all profit is financial, and that magazines may achieve other ends for their owners, but generally speaking his emphasis is on the publisher's responsibility for maintaining and enhancing a magazine's commercial success.

Publishers work by finding market 'niches' into which they can introduce new magazines. That means finding a group of likely readers with a common interest that is not being served, or finding advertisers wishing to reach an particular type of customer, or, more usually, some combination of the two. Publishers have to establish that the figures make sense: the number of readers and their spending power must meet the requirements of the likely advertisers, and numerous calculations follow which attempt to establish the viability of the exercise. Once the magazine is in business, the publisher's job, put simply, is to keep income high and costs as low as possible. Naturally, there is room in both these responsiblities for conflict with editors, whose departments are costly and always have the potential to affect income adversely. According to Wharton, 'Editors and journalists must accept that in the tough world of magazine publishing no action should be taken which harms the profit potential of a magazine or a company.' This is a sweeping statement and one which needs clarification. Running an article attacking the Mafia might well harm the 'profit potential' of a magazine, at least in the short term. Reviewing several products, and finding one to be preferable to another, is quite capable of doing the same thing, especially in markets where hypersensitive advertisers have come to expect a supine attitude from both publications and their own customers. That does not mean that neither type of article should be undertaken. The magazine's long-term profitability depends far more on its ability to give its readers what they need than it does on its ability to keep every one of its advertisers happy all the time.

Naturally, as an editor you must strive for fairness and accuracy in your dealings with everyone, advertisers, potential advertisers and non-advertisers alike. Any suggestion of favouritism, bias or self-interest will be much more damaging in the long term than the occasional row with an advertiser, although it is sometimes hard to explain that to people who earn much of their living from commission on advertising sales.

These are areas in which editors must make their own decisions. The potential for adverse reactions from advertisers may be a factor but not a dominant one. Even in the world of controlled circulation, where virtually the entire income of a magazine comes from advertisers, you as an editor need to appreciate that the interest of the readers comes first, followed by that of the advertisers as a group, rather than any individual advertiser. In situations where advertisers are few, and rival publications are many, this may be difficult advice to follow. Nonetheless, editors should never make the mistake of thinking that their publications exist for the benefit of advertisers: even advertising-only publications require readers.

The editorial imperative

The language of profit and loss is admirably clear and straightforward. Those who work within it have the advantage of a set of objectives and goals around which to structure their working lives. But accountancy is no guide to editing a magazine. Editors should not lose heart in the face of the commerciality of the modern publishing world. The industry exists because of editorial, and editors. What is more, the new media (whether on-line or off-line) seem likely to make that more important than ever. Few people will deliberately seek out advertising, especially when they are paying for the privilege on a 'connect-time' basis. Advertising that is genuinely informative will prosper, but normal advertisements seem unlikely to play their current role in the on-line publications of the future. If people are going to pay for information, and to search for what they want rather than accept what they are given, they will continue to seek independent, accurate editorial matter.

What, then, is the editorial imperative? It is tempting to say 'to tell the truth', but this is not a philosophy textbook. We need to find a more immediately approachable definition. The editorial imperative is to seek and create material (information, explanation, entertainment) that a particular group of readers needs, to check its accuracy and to shape it into a useful and approachable form.

Editing is, in the purest sense, a creative task more than an administrative or managerial one, although both those aspects are essential to an editor's success. A magazine is always more than a collection of parts: it is an entity in itself, and the editor has a dominant, although by no means solitary, role in shaping it. In discussions about editors' roles in the commercial lives of their publications, in managing staff and dealing with money, this must never be forgotten.

Beyond the culture clash

The scene would appear set for an epic battle between the representatives of two philosophies. On the one hand, the advertising fraternity, motivated and directed by money. On the other, the editor, writing wrongs, slaying dragons, tilting at windmills and offending advertisers with abandon.

Luckily, these are caricatures. There are lessons the two sides can learn from each other, apart from the obvious one that journalists need to learn about the role money plays in their working lives, and publishers need to appreciate the importance of editorial integrity.

It is often the case, for instance, that those who have come through the sales route have considerably better 'people skills' than those working in editorial areas. They know how to negotiate, how to structure a discussion, how to present themselves, and so on, and it can be good for editors to come into contact with this kind of expertise. At the same time, people from a commercial background are often very good at sorting out the different interests involved in any discussion or negotiation. In particular, they know what their clients require from them, they know the kind of service they have to provide and they know its value.

Editors lack a solid corpus of editorial philosophy. They are often confused about the web of relationships in which they occupy a central position. How are they to balance the different duties they owe to readers, advertisers and those they write about? Increasingly, all industries are becoming concerned with the provision of service. This only becomes feasible if the focus of that service is as clear as possible, and this idea may provide a guide for editors. As new media develop, it is unclear how important it will be to provide a service to advertisers. But providing a service to readers will always be central.

The reader as customer

Management in the industrial world is currently mesmerised by the concept of 'quality' and how to provide it. Vast edifices of management theory have been built upon a premise that has always been known to small shopkeepers:

that the customer is always right. Of course, applying this simple dictum is perfectly straightforward if you are one person selling greengrocery: applying it to a vast manufacturing or retailing organisation is something else again.

Magazine editors need to be clear that their customer is the reader. Nothing should interfere with the centrality of that relationship. The whole editorial effort of the magazine is directed to finding and keeping each reader. It is to the reader that editors owe their deepest duty and loyalty. Too often readers are seen as an irritant, an unnecessary drag on the smooth running of the publishing machine, a group to be steered, persuaded and bullied but never consulted, engaged in discussion or trusted. This is a great mistake.

It will be argued that your loyalty as an editor should be to your publisher, which is certainly true: the act of publishing needs to be a team effort, and the publisher provides the wherewithal to make it happen. But that's not the relationship that stands at the heart of the editorial task. Nor, by some distance, is the relationship between you and your advertisers. They are not your customers. Your obligations to advertisers are met, in full, through your relationship with your readers.

A compelling magazine will win readers and draw them back time and time again: they will enjoy the magazine, value it, trust it. The advertisers pay for the privilege of joining that relationship, between reader and magazine, but at a tangent. They are the advertising department's customers and they are the publisher's customers along with the readers. They are certainly essential to the economics of magazine publishing as we know it, but they are neither your responsibility nor your customers.

Increasingly publishers, especially in large publishing houses, expect their editors to make themselves available to advertisers. If time and workload allows, you may find this useful and valuable: companies which advertise with you may have interesting and useful information and views on the people and the world you are serving. But it is not a sensible use of your skills or time to be paraded around before advertisers as a kind of trophy, a practice to which advertising departments are prone. An editor is employed to produce a magazine that will attract the readers an advertiser may wish to reach. Your strategy for reaching those readers, your proposals to improve the quality, integrity and standing of the magazine may well have some influence on advertisers' intentions and you may well, on occasions, be persuaded that you are the best person to explain to them what you are doing. You may have created special new projects that will appeal to advertisers and may want to talk about them. But you are not, and must not be seen to be, an adjunct to your magazine's advertising team.

THE TASK AHEAD

Perhaps the most important thing you need to discover upon becoming an editor is what is expected of you. This can be more difficult than it might seem. Employers are not usually enthusiastic about confiding their hopes and fears during interviews, particularly not in the early stages, but by the time your appointment is imminent your task should have been made clear.

If you have been employed to produce a new launch, then you will all be learning together. Otherwise, you will inherit a magazine and a market situation and be invited to do what you can from that starting point. If you are told that your task is to increase circulation by a certain percentage you can make a rational decision about whether that is achievable and over what time period. Bear in mind, though, that circulation is increasingly affected by other, non-editorial factors, for instance advertising, promotion, free gifts, subscription offers, and so on, none of which will be within your control. You may also face new competition in your core market.

Usually, however, the task you are set will not be so straightforward. You may be asked specifically to increase frequency of purchase, to stop the drift of established readers or to find new ones. At the same time, you may well be told not to change the 'essence' of the existing product. Alternatively, you may be told to increase the magazine's 'authority', particularly if it is a professional or industry publication, to make it younger (rarely older), or to take it up-market or down-market where better publishing pickings are to be had. You should be on the look-out for what psychologists call 'double-binds', whereby you are asked to do two entirely contradictory things simultaneously. It is not uncommon for editors to be told to give things a new, fresh look without changing any of the typefaces.

That aside, it is perfectly possible to change the character of any magazine in ways that range from the imperceptible to the radical. But the degree to which change is threatening should never be forgotten. Any changes you do make should have been clearly signposted to those who matter far in advance.

It is worth thinking about your predecessor as editor. In some cases, all parties will be mortified at the departure and will require from you nothing more than a steady hand on the tiller. This can be a gentle introduction to editorship, though in the long term vessels steering an unchanging course tend to collide with immovable obstacles. You may find yourself frustrated when you try to point this out and set a new course.

Alternatively, the last editor may not have been appreciated, and anything you do will be applauded, so long as it is different. This is a trap in its own right. Magazines with excitable managements tend to zigzag as each new editor is appointed, which is exhausting for everyone, notably the readers, who may migrate to find a quieter life elsewhere. Discover what you can about your predecessor's experiences, and make your own judgement, bearing in mind that your own personality is different.

There are two contradictory impulses experienced by those taking on a new editorship. The first is to make your mark, quickly, changing enough to alert your staff, your colleagues and your professional peers to the new realities. It is not unknown for newly appointed editors to arrive and immediately remake the next cover, after deadline. This is a costly gesture that may be applauded if performed with sufficient panache. But changes will take longer to register with your readers. When their attitude is revealed, through the sales figures, it may not be exactly what you sought.

The second impulse is to freeze, to keep everything the same while you struggle with the complications of your new life, from mastering the computer system to learning everyone's name. Your first issues may bear no stamp of new management beyond having a different name at the top of the staff box. Those who have appointed you may be a little disappointed.

It may well be sensible, however, to err on the side of caution. Take a little time to discover why things are the way they are, observe the complex interaction of personalities, discover the inner workings of the magazine, and then act. It is better to make slow changes than to make the wrong changes. In any case, the only audience which really matters is the one which hands over its money to the newsagent.

On the other hand, you should be wary of sheer inertia. Most of your colleagues will have a vested interest in leaving things the way they are. They will not, however, be the ones to take the consequences when this course leads to disaster. It is important to show, early on, that you have the will and the authority to make the changes you consider necessary. It is for you to ensure that those changes are the right ones.

In some cases, unfortunately, you may not have the luxury of time. It is not uncommon for magazines to be left directionless for months while the editorship is touted around. You may arrive to find in progress a new issue composed of nothing more than the scrapings from various bottom drawers, cobbled together by a resentful and demoralised workforce not quite sure what they are supposed to be doing. In that case, act – and act quickly.

Your new job may, of course, be on a new launch, in which case different questions apply. Any publishing project starts with a publishing strategy, created by research, mostly quantitative, which shows how many people in a certain bracket might be interested in purchasing a particular type of magazine, how old they are, where they live, how much money they earn and what they do for a living. Without a coherent editorial strategy, however, this will remain nothing more than a collection of inert statistics.

The editorial strategy takes that group of figures and uses it as the basis for the creation of a coherent magazine. It stops talking about groups and begins to consider individuals: what type of person will read this magazine? What is he or she like? And then it builds a magazine around that imaginative vision, deciding what to include and what to exclude, how to approach the subject matter and, crucially, the kind of address that will be made to the reader: the tone of voice.

In the case of an existing magazine, it is the editor's job to discover the editorial strategy, clean away the patina of years and reveal it anew, by tightening, shaping and focusing. There are various methods of research and analysis that can help, but there is also a great deal of 'feel'. It is in this process that editors are made.

FURTHER READING

Wharton, John (1992) *Managing Magazine Publishing*, London: Blueprint.

Chapter 2

The editor and the reader

Some editors spend their careers trying to avoid their readers, either as individuals, when they call to make a complaint, or in the mass, for instance at a 'reader event'. But even those editors will have somewhere, whether in their minds or on a piece of paper, an image of the reader for whom they are creating the magazine.

A detailed understanding of the readership is the central element of the magazine's marketing strategy. As editor you must 'know your readers'. The presence of an identifiable reader, or rather body of readers, in any publishing relationship is the first essential for the creation of genuine editorial material. If the presence or absence of readers is entirely irrelevant to the success or failure of your efforts, you are not really an editor, except in the most narrow technical sense of someone who prepares words and pictures.

If you are editing an existing magazine, you have plenty of opportunity to encounter your readers. Are they, for instance, to be judged by the vociferous minority who contribute to the letters page? Are they the people you see on the bus, reading your magazine? Or are they the people you meet at trade shows?

Actually, they're all those people, but they are many more people besides, whose presence you can only perceive with a combination of hard fact and instinct. On the one hand, you have the statistics of your readership. On the other, you have your own feelings about the magazine's 'character' and appeal.

The figures you need are obvious enough: how many readers (and how many non-readers in the same market segment); their ages, sex and marital status; their social class; their location; their disposable income; their employment status; their domiciliary status, etc. If you are producing a professional magazine, you need details about their working lives: what exactly they do, how long they've been doing it, whom they work for, where they stand on the professional ladder.

This is essential background material, but you also need to know about their activity in the magazine market: which magazines they buy, which they read, and how often. With this information you will be able to make intelligent guesses about why they read one magazine rather than another, but it takes a different type of research, 'qualitative' rather than 'quantitative', to discover their real interests and motivations.

THE EDITORIAL STRATEGY

The editorial strategy is your contribution to the publishing package represented by the magazine. At some stage in its existence, the magazine will have been the subject of a marketing plan which will have explored in great detail the size of the potential market and the essential statistical characteristics of those whom it comprises. The editorial strategy, meanwhile, identifies who your readers are within that potential market and explains how you propose to keep them interested. It may be in your head, or in some written form. Certainly you will be expected to talk about your strategy at short notice and with confidence.

Your editorial strategy, once arrived at, is put to the test with every issue: the sales figures for each issue may not be an entirely reliable indicator of how your strategy is being received (so many other factors can come into play), but over time patterns do emerge. It is not enough, however, to sit and wait for the sales figures to tell you whether you are heading in the right direction: by then, it may well be too late. The editorial strategy needs to be matched to the interests, desires and needs of the readers at frequent intervals, and adjusted as necessary.

Who are the readers and what do they want?

Turning your attention to the readers' interests, desires and needs, and following where they lead, is frequently called 'focus', and is in many ways the most important part of the editor's job. As editor you may be a brilliant manager, an inspiration to staff, a leading prose stylist and a legend within the industry, but if you fail to pay attention to the readers and their needs all that effort will be wasted.

It is tempting to say that what is needed is an 'instinctive' grasp of what the readers want (and, almost as important, what they don't want), translated into an appealing programme of journalistic material. This may be a simple matter for those who edit magazines which cater to their own personal passions or who are lucky enough to be able to produce the magazine they want and hope readers will come to them. Most editors, however, will need to spend time studying their readers and asking them about their needs.

You should be aware that what people say they want is not actually what they buy. As political pollsters have discovered, people do not always tell the truth to researchers. Recently surveys have shown that women, even young women, feel that magazines aimed at them include too many articles about sexual matters. This does not stop them buying those magazines, however.

Another problem is that a simple 'want' expressed in a market research group or in a discussion with an editor is rarely a compelling enough reason to make someone spend his or her own money on buying a magazine.

The designer Jan V. White, in his valuable book *Designing for Magazines*, came up with a useful dictum for editors and art directors working on magazine covers. He said they should 'appeal to the reader's self-interest'. This is an idea that has a wider application than White intended. The reader's self-interest may well be the most useful guide an editor can have to the whole process of selecting and shaping journalistic material.

What can you give your readers that will make them feel they have a clear advantage over people who have not read the same magazine? In the professional publishing field, information can obviously provide a competitive advantage. In the consumer field, readers can gain material benefits from reading your magazine (better health, more intelligent use of their money, career inspiration, and so on) but they also gain the more abstract benefit of being 'in the know', 'ahead of the game', or simply having something new to talk about.

Readers will not continue to support a magazine that fails to offer them anything new or surprising. In matching the product to its customers, you must go beyond merely the expressed wants and needs, into what are called 'latent needs'. You must look at the way they live to discover the things that will give them that advantage. You must find their self-interest, and that of their families, even when they are unable, or unwilling, to express it for themselves.

Sometimes readers buy magazines because they want to read something specific: the whole structure of covers, cover-lines and news-stand display is designed to make that happen. More often however – always in the case of subscription sales – they buy or pick up the magazine in the expectation that it will contain items of interest to them, even though they don't know specifically what they are. This is the basis of the trust that is established between editor and reader: the editor promises to include the kind of things the readers will want and need and to exclude things that the readers will not need or will find insulting, or offensive.

THE ROLE OF RESEARCH

Much is said and written about 'research' in the magazine-publishing context, in a way that can be intimidating to mere editors. It is easy to form a mental picture of teams of white-coated social scientists feeding strings of numbers into powerful workstations and emerging with a detailed prescription for the perfect magazine, specifying everything from subject matter to typefaces.

Some people might like to think they can do things this way: there is an element of it in the way the larger magazine houses plan their launch programmes. But anything learned from formal research needs to be balanced by editorial experience, common sense and judgement.

Formal research for a specific title is also extremely costly, making it a luxury for those not planning new launches or facing some kind of crisis, perhaps the arrival of new competition or a long-term decline in sales. In all those cases, thorough investigation of the attitudes of both readers and non-readers can provide a great deal of useful guidance about the direction and pace of any changes that are to be made to the product. It is to be hoped, however, that you are sufficiently aware of your readers' changing needs to have made such a crisis unlikely.

While hardly justifying the word 'research', an editor's own awareness of the readership is always at hand and often useful, providing it is conscientiously pursued. The fact that there are professional organisations dedicated to 'objective' research should not discourage the editor from making, and then testing, his or her own assessments of the readers and what they want.

The lack of objectivity is the central problem with the kind of research we do ourselves. On the other hand, outside research organisations have a reputation, not always unfounded, for telling publishers precisely what they want to hear. There is a particular problem with research that is intended both as an analytical exercise and as a selling tool. A research organisation which has been hired to prove that a magazine is adored by its readers, so that the publisher can use the figures in an advertising drive, is unlikely to produce research showing precisely the opposite, even if that might be what editor and publisher really need.

In-house research should always be the starting point, both for economic reasons and to ensure that any external research goes beyond the merely obvious. It is a rare magazine, indeed, that has never been the subject of research, and the starting point for any in-house study should always be to dig out previous surveys and see what, if anything, can be gleaned from them.

Factual material, detailing the demographics of your market sector as well as the progress of your circulation and that of your competitors, should be immediately available. If you are serving a particular industry, its professional bodies and associations may well have information that is relevant, detailing those who work in it and its customers. The trade magazines of marketing and advertising will often have carried features analysing your market, and you should have those. Advertising agencies perennially survey groups of readers and potential readers: some of that information may be available. Various publishing industry bodies produce nuts-and-bolts surveys of readers and their activities. The Periodical Publishers Assocation, to which your company is likely to belong to, can supply more details on most of these.

After all that, you may have more idea who your readers are, but you won't necessarily know much more about what they are like. This is an important distinction. Two people may have the same job, the same marital situation, the same housing arrangements, the same disposable income, and so on, but their attitudes may be quite different.

Qualitative research is intended to provide some insight into that aspect, and some of the existing research material you lay your hands on may be in that vein. But you need to take account of the age of any such material, in terms both of the prevailing attitudes of the time and its relation to the magazine as it was then. In that way you may be able to observe the strange dance that takes place when a survey shows that readers want something, a magazine provides it, and then a new survey shows readers want something else. These studies should give you ideas about the areas you should be considering, whether they be as general as 'What the readers like and dislike in my magazine', or as specific as 'Is our news pitched correctly for our particular readers?' or 'Is our body type too small?'

No magazine exists in a vacuum, and the day of what were called 'solus' readers, people who wait all month for your magazine and won't be fobbed off with anything else, is gone, especially in the cities. Subscribers and those who live and work in remote areas may display more 'loyalty', but most readers will be 'repertoire' buyers, who often buy several magazines and do not read every copy of any one title.

You can't, in this type of in-house analysis, ask the readers directly what they want. But you can take their buying preferences as an indicator for their attitudes: people do not buy magazines that don't meet their needs. So by looking at the magazines in your market, and the type of appeal they make, in subject matter, look and tone of voice, you can work back to assess the readers' attitudes. In other words, those who buy your magazine rather than another one are doing so for a reason.

The task is to look at your magazine as if you had never seen it before, with the innocent eye of a new reader, knowing nothing of the reasons things are the way they are or the work that went into various features. Treat it simply as a product that people can buy or not buy, and then ask yourself what, precisely, constitutes its appeal, what attitudes it expresses and what attitudes it invites from its readers and buyers. Now take the same approach to other magazines in your market sector. Why would anyone prefer their magazine to yours?

This only works if you are prepared to be honest. Anyone else invited to take part must also be honest, and must feel secure in being candid. For that reason, this is not an exercise that should be conducted or discussed in the presence of other members of staff or fellow managers. Any findings can be presented to whoever seems appropriate, starting with your publisher, but the actual examination is really a confidential matter.

You should consider everything, from the look and feel of the package as the reader picks it up at the bookstall, through the cover and cover-lines, through the contents page and features, to the way individuals write, to the crossword and the letters page. This examination may, ultimately, have implications for the direction of your magazine, but for now the object is to think about what the readers see in it (and its competitors) as currently produced.

Characterising the reader

Publishers and advertising people, who work in the realm of hard cash and hard 'data', may baulk at the role of imagination in all of this. But imagination, the art of thinking about other people and their lives in a way that is not reducible to facts and figures, is the well-spring of creativity. As an editor, you will be expected to provide the creative spark that makes the publishing engine turn over.

The act of targeting and focusing on the reader is a creative act. In a real sense, you have to invent that reader. You may well meet individual readers. You will certainly hear about the decisions made by readers in the mass. Your job is to take those clues to what is going on and use them to create a 'notional' or 'putative' or 'imaginary' reader that you, and everyone else in the editorial department, can use as a focus for your magazine.

Indeed, it goes beyond that: increasingly editors are conjuring up a reader – and for this purpose, at least, it has to be a single personality – at least as well characterised as the people in films, plays and popular fiction. If your notional reader is sufficiently characterised, he or she becomes someone to think about, to talk about, to argue with and, above all, to speak to. You can give this person a name, a job, a home address and anything else you need for the purposes of characterisation. The notional reader becomes, to all intents and purposes, a real person who may embody the spirit of the magazine through several changes of editor. The classic case is *Cosmopolitan*'s 'Cosmo girl'.

Any imaginative tool which helps you summon up this vision and communicate its reality to your staff should be welcomed. Free and open exchange of thoughts, however strange, is to be encouraged. The object is to come up with an image that is vivid and immediately accessible, and the means used to achieve this are irrelevant.

Slogans are a start. If they work you can always use them on your cover and on publicity material: hence *Company* magazine's 'For the freedom years'; *She*'s 'For women who juggle their lives'; and *Loaded*'s 'For men who should know better'. Less all-embracing slogans are often seen in the business press. *Building Design* calls itself 'The weekly newspaper for the design team'. The *Press Gazette* is 'The weekly for all journalists'.

Another technique is to use a checklist of characteristics. On the most obvious level, this is just a way of forcing you to make a decision. Does my reader have children? Logic will tell you that some do and some don't, but for this purpose you need to decide one way or the other. Say No. Is my reader a home-owner? Yes. It's a way of turning percentages into individuals, and sharpening up your perceptions. You must also ask yourself questions about the readers of rival magazines. Do the readers of this magazine have professional qualifications? No. Do the readers of that magazine expect to rise higher in their careers? Yes. And so on.

This is useful, but not very evocative. More fun can be had by using variants on the old 'in' and 'out' list idea. For instance, you might say 'Our reader drinks tequila, not brown ale'; 'Our reader wears Marks & Spencer, not Dolce & Gabbana'. And so on.

This is more useful in the consumer market, where there is a parallel between the choice of one product rather than another and the choice of one magazine rather than another, than it is in some other fields. But in, for instance, business-to-business and professional markets where all qualified people get several controlled circulation magazines, not all will be equally well read and appreciated. If there are three magazines for family doctors, why do some read one more than another? It might be because they like a particular columnist or page. Or it might equally be because 'Our reader drives a Volvo, not a Vauxhall'.

There are other games you can try. At one time there was a considerable vogue for seeing the reader through analogies drawn from other areas of life. 'If our reader was an animal, what kind of animal would she be?' 'If our reader was a record, what record would he be?' 'If our reader was a drink . . .', and so on. This exercise can be quite stimulating and amusing, particularly in small relaxed groups, but it can be destroyed by the merest hint of cynicism, so it needs to be applied with care.

Your own research

There is, of course, a strong danger that your imagined reader is either not very like the real thing, or that he or she loses step with the real readers over a period. This is why your own in-house characterisations need to be tested against the reality. As an editor, you have some scope for doing this yourself. If you are a magazine with subscriptions, you can ask the subscriptions department for some telephone numbers of subscribers. Or, perhaps more usefully, lapsed subscribers. Ring them and ask them what they think. It's not scientific – you certainly won't have the time to ring enough people to make a statistically valid survey – but you can set someone else the task if your aim is to get a slightly broader sense of what is going on. However you do it, you should try to ask the same questions each time and to listen carefully to the answers. Bear in mind that people contacted by the editor of a magazine are not usually going to tell the unvarnished truth.

An extension of this idea is the reader panel, which professional magazines have sometimes found useful. This is not to be confused with an editorial advisory panel or board, which is often just a way of getting esteemed industry names on to your masthead in exchange for an annual lunch. The reader panel consists of a small group of readers who agree to read the magazine carefully each week or month, perhaps making notes on their perceptions of it, so that you can speak to them at regular intervals and ask them what they thought. Of course, these occasions (or telephone calls) are as much for you to find out about these readers as they are for you to listen to their comments on the magazine, which is why the readers need to be chosen with care and changed frequently. Again, this will cost you a reasonable lunch now and again, but it might be useful and it is certainly much cheaper than true outside research.

The other perennial favourite of editors looking around for some relatively inexpensive way to gauge the feelings of the readers is the in-magazine questionnaire. This is worth doing occasionally, but as always needs to be treated with caution. For a start, the response rate is likely to be low, and the sample produced is 'self-selecting', meaning you will get a high proportion of people glad of the opportunity to supply you with their pronounced views. They will also tend towards the negative, something that applies also to letters pages, since those who are entirely satisfied with something rarely feel the need to express that view.

Some material incentive for taking the trouble to fill in the form is now considered essential. The greater the value of the incentive, the higher response rate you can expect. These 'extra' respondents, beyond the well-motivated few, may however be less likely to complete the form sensibly, honestly and accurately.

Cunning questionnaire design may enable you to sort out those who are really determined not to help, for instance by detecting internal contradictions in their responses. But you will certainly get some bizarre and unexpected results, as indeed you do with most research, which is why what you do with it needs careful consideration. This is particularly true if your questionnaire includes space for written comments. The total response may well represent only a small proportion of your readership and even fewer will offer written observations. If pungently expressed, as they tend to be, these can have a disproportionate influence on your thinking.

It helps to get expert help in the creation of reader questionnaires. Most editors simply repeat last year's, on the grounds that at some stage in the past someone who knew what they were doing must have drawn it up. If you are going to do that, look at last year's results and see if any obvious omissions or absurdities strike you: it is easier to see this when you are looking at answers rather than questions.

In practice, most in-magazine surveys have an overriding commercial purpose. They are there to gather demographic information to help sell advertising, another reason for the readers' general cynicism. Some of this information may be useful to you as an editor, but that isn't why it's there. Usually the advertising department will be paying to have the results analysed. You may be able to persuade them to carry a few questions of specific editorial interest or you may feel it is better to leave the whole exercise to them. Many in-magazine questionnaires are an uneasy compromise, sold to the readers as an editorial exercise ('to help us provide you with what you need') when their overriding purpose is commercial.

Outside research

You should have a strong sense of who your readers are before you get involved with outside research specialists. That means that you must have in mind both the individual reader and the whole range of material you gathered in the process of creating that characterisation. The material gathered by research consultants can be baffling if you look at it in a vacuum. Better to use it to confront, modify, even destroy, an image you have built up than to attempt to create something directly from it.

The research project will probably be part of a larger marketing plan drawn up by your publisher. This will involve both quantitative and qualitative assessments of the situation. The quantitative assessment may then have a critical bearing on the qualitative research that is done. For instance, a quantitative study of your magazine in its market might be done by your advertising agency as they advise you on a future direction. They might advise that the magazine's best course of action would be to concentrate on finding new buyers, rather than trying to get existing buyers to buy more frequently. So your qualitative research might focus on non-buyers and their perceptions of the magazine.

A classic situation is one in which your research organisation does its quantitative sums first and finds that your magazine is selling fewer copies than might reasonably have been expected, given the size and shape of the market and the nature of the competition. Qualitative research then concentrates on readers' and non-readers' perceptions of your magazine's value for money, personality, appeal and editorial focus, even descending to the level of discussing reactions to individual articles, layouts, pictures and even writers.

Media research consultants are specialists with their own methods and tools. As an editor, you will certainly meet the research team, either formally or informally, to discuss the direction of the study. This can be a strange experience. You might well spend a couple of hours telling these people your hopes and aspirations for the magazine and your perceptions of the people who read it, only to find one passing phrase plucked out and projected on a screen at the researchers' final presentation. This can be embarrassing, but you should certainly make good use of your pre-research briefings to impress upon the research organisation anything you particularly need to know. After that, you must stand aside and let them get on with it.

The kind of issues that will emerge in qualitative research concern your magazine's status in the eyes of readers and non-readers: its credibility, its authority, its trustworthiness. Part of this is the magazine's tone of voice, the address it makes to its readers. Part of it is how the readers perceive the magazine's closeness to their interests and point of view. Beyond that there are more technical questions about the way the magazine looks, reads and performs.

The methods of the researchers vary according to what they have been asked to discover, but revolve around personal interviews with individuals. If you are looking for the answers to a fairly broad question, for instance whether people would like your magazine if they gave it a try, you might want a broad but inherently rather superficial survey.

For a consumer magazine this might mean researchers stopping people in the street until they find a group of perhaps 200 with the same age, sex and class profile as your readers and the same broad areas of interest. They might be interviewed at this stage, then sent the magazine over a period and then interviewed again at the end of that period to determine how, if at all, their perceptions had changed.

At the very least this should enable you to tell whether readers aren't buying your magazine because they just don't encounter it, or whether they actively dislike it when they read it. It might go beyond that to ask which parts of your magazine they like and which they dislike, but the results will be numerical rather than anecdotal, because the demands of the process are such that only very basic interviewing, using multiple-choice forms, will have been conducted.

Alternatively, you might want a much more precise and provocative analysis of how your magazine is perceived. Your problem might be the same, that it isn't selling as well as you'd like it to, but your feeling might be that that is due to the product itself rather than the way it is being marketed. The approach in this case is much narrower and more intense. Small groups are created, representing various demographic types, and they may or may not be given the magazine to mull over some time before they are gathered for a group discussion. This will be led by an experienced research professional, and the comments of the group members recorded for later presentation.

As an editor, you may be invited to observe these discussions via a two-way mirror. This can be a slightly bewildering experience, as you see how your perceptions and those of your readers slide gently past one another without ever meeting. Features you found witty and pointed might just seem rude. Matters of vital editorial import might simply pass them by. They might be more concerned about the crossword than they are about your award-winning columnist.

This problem is particularly acute in matters of design. What seems sophisticated and clean to you may appear boring and empty to them. Readers are, of course, not privy to the kind of discussions and considerations that lead to things being the way they are. They judge purely on what they see in front of them. If there is a gap between your intentions and the way something is perceived, then the design is not achieving the effects it should, and needs looking at.

At the end of the research process, it is usual for there to be some kind of presentation of the results, to which, as editor, you would expect to be invited along with the rest of your publishing management. Presentations are not to everyone's taste: they will inevitably be based upon a selective account of the research results. As an editor you should insist on having the root figures and drawing your own conclusions, at least in those types of research which actually produce figures. It is important to see these for what they are: a tiny sample of your readers or potential readers. The problem with figures is that by their very existence they tend to demand attention, often out of all proportion to their significance.

Sometimes what looks like a significant percentage may represent only a tiny number of people. A base survey of 150 people might be used. From that group, those who say they find your magazine difficult to use might be selected. Then percentages of that group might be presented. For instance, 38 per cent might say they find your running order all wrong. This would perhaps alarm you, until you looked back at the figures and discovered that they represented 38 per cent of 30 people, or a total of 11 people out of the original 150. Percentages are absurd with such small numbers, but that doesn't stop research organisations serving them up.

The 'focus-group' type of research produces a very different type of material. Here the findings are simply a series of phrases, picked up by the interviewer or group leader and selected as worthy of attention. Sometimes research organisations will dress this information up in what are called 'typologies'. Some of this can seem slightly fanciful: you may be told that your readers are divided between 'clubbers', 'stay-at-homes' and 'anoraks', or 'home-makers', 'careerists' and 'fantasists'. Be aware that the suggestion that your readership is made up of different, and apparently unrelated, groups can be slightly misleading.

More damaging is the prominence given to the articulate. A single well-expressed thought by a reader in a focus group will have more impact, and may well produce more consequences, than more considered opinions that never crystallise into a pithy phrase. Once again, there is a danger of being mesmerised by detail and missing the broader picture.

Research can act as a mirror to prejudice. All parties will find within research documents the evidence they need to support views they have already formed. That is why it is important for editors to go into research from a position of some confidence: otherwise, you are in danger of the research becoming one more voice telling you in which direction to go.

Because of the status accorded to anything which makes use of statistics, however flimsy, editors should be aware of the need to use the best research possible. Research organisations employed need to have specialised in media work, and should be made to supply a list of clients. Informal contact with other organisations who have used their services can often tell you what to expect. Flimsy research that you know is flimsy, because you did it yourself, is one thing. Flimsy research that you take for the real thing is something much more dangerous. Examine what you are given with a sceptical eye.

Nothing you learn from research will, however, indicate exactly the direction you should take. It is dangerous to expect it to. Publishing history is littered with the corpses of magazines which presumably researched well but failed to sell to real people: consider the teenage title *The Hit*, the women's magazine *Riva*, and the motoring title *Carweek*. All these were the products of major publishing houses known for their caution, and yet all failed.

A magazine designed to follow a set of research findings is in danger of having no centre, no identity and no soul. And a magazine which constantly resorts to research in an attempt to find the identity which has otherwise eluded it is entering on a dangerous path. Angling your magazine to meet the demands of a few people you encounter in research may lead to your ruining the magazine for those whose opinions have not been asked.

APPLYING YOUR FINDINGS

Research should supply you with a mass of material, some useful, some less so. There will be points there that will surprise you, and many of these will be simple faults and absurdities that you hadn't noticed and that can be easily remedied. More fundamental changes have to be thought through, in all their implications. As always you need to be guided by your ultimate aims. For instance, are you seeking new readers, or hanging on to the ones you already have? You will not always be able to do both.

At the very least, most research of this type will supply you with an indication of the subject areas that are most important to your readers. Your ideal 'menu' of features should approximate to that, if not in every issue, at least over a period. But there are other considerations. A magazine constructed to comply with criteria established by research may not have the required balance, or light and shade. And readers want to be surprised. An editorial strategy based upon giving them solely what they have asked for is dangerous.

Every magazine carries some items that are not going to appear at the top of any popularity list. They may be there for reasons of tradition, or they may be there out of some kind of obligation (this is particularly the case in house journals and institutional magazines). They may be there because the editor thinks their value will be seen in years to come, or they may be there to make a statement about the kind of magazine this is intended to be.

Matching editorial resources to 'page traffic', the degree to which a page is read, is tricky and potentially dangerous. Some sections will be more expensive to produce than others and may not attract readers, but that doesn't mean you can do without them.

Research can, of course, have consequences. That is why, after absorbing it yourself and discussing it in detail with both those who conducted it and your own fellow managers, you need to think about how it is presented to your fellow staff. You could just hand it over and let everyone have a look, but that may not be appropriate. If serious problems present themselves in individual sections of the magazines, it is obviously better that those problems be discussed with the appropriate individuals. More generally, it is easy for a research document to influence the whole mood of an editorial team in a way that is not always helpful. Neither complacency nor outright despair will enhance a magazine's chances of success in a difficult market. You should produce a formal response to any such research document before you let your colleagues see it.

There is a particular problem with research findings that are not applied. If anything in the research is not considered accurate or helpful, it needs to be discussed and a decision taken to dismiss it. A damning verdict on a particular editorial area needs to be challenged, otherwise everyone will be expecting repercussions. Approach research honestly. It may tell you unpalatable things, but it is better that you find out in the controlled circumstances of a questionnaire and focus group than on the newsagents' shelves.

Instinct and vision

Many editors feel uneasy in the world of research. It certainly does not provide much of a help with everyday decision-making. The fact that 28 per cent of your readers have a degree or that 32 per cent of them prefer blue covers to red ones will rarely help you choose a lead feature or write a headline. For those kinds of decisions, and in matters of approach and taste, you need to have a clear central idea: a vision of what you want to achieve, and an instinct for what your readers want and will accept.

It is one thing for publishers to announce that their magazine is designed for women aged 25–35 in social groups B/C1/C2, with jobs but no children. It is quite another for an editor to create something that an individual feels compelled to buy. This is where vision comes in. Research can be a help in building that vision. It is certainly essential in ensuring that that vision does not lose sight of reality. But it is not a substitute for it.

It is also worth noting that people who take part in research find it very easy to say what they don't like about existing publications, and those which are presented to them in dummy form. They do not, however, find it easy to talk about magazines which are planned but which have as yet no real shape or form.

It is a fact that many of the most significant magazines are those which could never have been arrived at by research: no survey would have given any support for the creation of *Private Eye* or the *Spectator*. Magazines which embody the eras in which they were created will often have been the product of an individual's instinctive understanding of the times, established in defiance of publishing orthodoxy. 'On-line' technology, with its minimal start-up costs, may make this pattern more common. For those involved in producing more mainstream magazines, research will have more relevance, setting the limits within which the editor's own instincts can operate.

FINDING NEW READERS

Research needs to have a purpose if it is not to become an expensive distraction or worse. The most obvious goal for most paid-for publications is an increase in circulation: controlled-circulation publications must aim instead at higher readership and reader satisfaction.

Relatively simple quantitative analysis of a market will suggest whether it is feasible to increase circulation by finding new readers (an increase in 'penetration') or whether it would be more sensible to concentrate on retaining the readers you already have and increasing their frequency of purchase. The annual National Readership Survey figures will indicate the percentage of people in your target age range who buy your product. It will suggest whether increased penetration is feasible. Frequency, on the other hand, is a more difficult nut to crack. It raises questions about how your readers are using your magazine, how often they need to buy it. A new launch is, of course, all about finding new readers.

The anatomy of a launch

Editors can be part of a new launch from the very start. It is not uncommon for editors to take ideas for launches to their publishers and set the process in motion. More often, however, editors join at a slightly later stage, when irrevocable decisions have already been made. This can be extremely difficult. It is likely that the format (paper size and shape) of the magazine will have been decided, the staffing will have been broadly decided, some sort of deal over paper and printing struck (including a schedule that may or may not be workable), office space found, computer equipment acquired, and some sort of budget worked out including estimated income (always overestimated) and costs (always underestimated).

At that stage an editor will be brought in and invited to come up with an editorial strategy that will make the whole package viable. This is not the way to do it, but it is often the way it is done, especially when magazines are put together quickly to meet a perceived market threat or to cash in on a new opportunity.

It is obviously better to start with an idea, and work through the process in a painstaking and methodical way. Most magazine journalists at some time in their careers will have dreamed up a new magazine, starting with a broad idea. A magazine for people who use portable computers, for instance, or send their children to private school, or work in the soft fruit industry. Publishers, on the other hand, come up with ideas based on knowledge of the market, designed to find weaknesses in other publishers' products, to cling on the coat-tails of successful products and sometimes to splinter large readerships to make room for several titles. This idea has been extremely successful in recent years. Generic computer titles have given way to individual machine titles, which have since given way to work-based titles and home-based titles for all the main machines.

The first step with any new magazine is to do the qualitative research to work out exactly who might read it: who they are, how many of them there are, what they are reading now, and so on. As is often said nowadays, you need to work out not only that there is a gap in the market, but that there is a market in the gap: in other words that the people who are not buyers of existing magazines are likely to buy your magazine, and in sufficient numbers to make them attractive to advertisers. This number-crunching is your starting point.

From that you might put together some sort of 'paper dummy', identifying the kind of things that your new magazine would include. It need not even look like a magazine, but would contain a potential title or two, some sort of 'mission statement' or slogan, identifying what the magazine is about, a likely running order and list of regular features. There are ways of expressing what these are about without actually commissioning copy or pictures. You can use the headings or standfirsts for the features you'd like to see. For your imaginary computer magazine they might say:

- '10 ways to get more battery life'
- 'Avoiding the crash'
- 'What's on yours: every month a celebrity portable user tells us what's on his hard disk (Stephen Fry, Douglas Adams, Bill Gates)'
- 'You ain't seen nothing yet: the portable of the future'.

Your magazine for parents with children in private education might list:

- 'Paying for it: easing the pain of private education'
- 'Schools review: what's happening where'
- 'The parents guide to . . .'.

In this way you can put together a magazine that you can see in your mind's eye at almost no cost. You would probably include a running order and a flat-plan. Unfortunately, no-one else, other than an experienced editor, will be able to form much of a view of what you are doing based on that. Given that your idea is likely to go out into the world for further research, you will need to work it up into a more elaborate form.

This used to be an expensive project. Modern technology has made it less so. A first visual dummy can be put together, to show potential readers and advertisers something of the themes to be included and their editorial and design treatment. It can be produced on desktop publishing equipment using existing body copy and photographs laid out in an appropriate style. That can be shown to focus groups, although they will have to be told to make allowances for its rough and ready nature.

They should also be shown various titles and potential 'logos'. This is an exceptionally important area. A logo is not just the name of the magazine set into type. It is an artefact in its own right, with a character all its own. You, as well as the readers, have to like it, of course, since it will be staying with you for a very long time, on stationery and promotional materials as well as on the top of your magazine. It is obviously possible to change a logo, but it is not generally advised.

After all that, changes can be made and further dummies produced, along the same lines, or a decision can be taken to go to a genuine printed dummy on the paper that is likely to be used. This will, of course, be a properly designed product. At that stage, a decision can be taken about whether or not to proceed.

That is not the end of the research process. A launch issue will invariably be closely monitored to see that it is reaching the people it is supposed to reach and that everything that has so carefully been planned into the issue is being perceived in the way that was intended. Adjustments can then be made, and more research done, especially if the magazine represents a major investment and needs to be right straight away. Increasingly magazine houses experiment with 'one-off' or 'occasional' publication before going for continuous monthly publication. Most magazines start big, backed by expensive publicity and marketing, then fall away in subsequent issues before recovering. This is called the 'hockey-stick' curve, because of the shape of the graph of sales against time.

These are, of course, just the obvious editorial aspects of a new launch. Wise editors should ensure that they are kept in touch with every other aspect of the process. There will certainly be a detailed financial appraisal of both advertising revenue and running costs. You should be involved in the whole budgeting process, including staff and freelance costs, and the business of defining job titles, drawing up job descriptions and hiring staff. The publisher will also examine circulation policy, printing and paper and will be giving consideration to marketing the new title. Promotion is a very high cost for new magazines and, except in certain markets, it is difficult to see how a magazine can be successfully launched without it. You, too, need to be involved in this. There is no point in carefully creating a magazine for one reader, only to have it vigorously advertised and sold to someone quite different.

Magazines are still launched without extensive research and the creation of a series of dummies, but they are few and far between. They also tend to fail. Anyone who has had the misfortune to be involved in such a launch will know how dispiriting an experience this can be. So it is no wonder that the research process is taken to almost absurd lengths in an attempt to reduce the element of risk. One major magazine company is, at the time of writing, working on the seventh dummy for a new magazine.

But other companies have another approach, gently easing a magazine into a market. National Magazines has used this method. *Zest*, its women's health and beauty magazine, started life as a one-off supplement to *Cosmopolitan*, before gradually being turned into a magazine in its own right. Here readers were given the opportunity to consider a real magazine, rather than a dummy, and reacted favourably.

Finding new readers for an existing magazine

It is one thing to find readers for a new magazine with no previously existing image. It is quite another to take an existing publication and change its direction in a way that will either bring in new readers without alienating the old ones or bring in new readers in sufficient numbers that no-one will worry too much about the departures.

There are, however, times when titles become dangerously exposed, as their readers start to age and are not replaced by new, younger ones. In other cases, titles need to increase their market share at the expensive of rivals, or to establish dominance in a market in such a way as to discourage new entrants. All this means taking readers from other publications: there are few people who read no magazines but are just waiting for the right one to come along.

Look again at the match between the interests of your readers and the content of your magazine. By way of a double-check, look through all your rival publications and ask yourself whether there is anything there that should have been in your magazine. This is not a case of coveting individual features, more of looking at the subjects covered.

Now consider the balance between subjects, both in individual issues and over a period. Is there sufficient light and shade? Are serious subjects, bad news, gloomy prognostications on the future of the industry, bleak accounts of grim medical procedures, outweighing everything else? What is there that appeals to people's curiosity, their ambitions, their aspirations? How much of this material seems familiar? Are you perhaps telling your readers what they already know? Is there anything there that makes you think 'so what?' Above all, what is there that will justify people in their decision to buy the magazine: what is there that gives them an advantage over non-readers?

Now consider the order in which things appear. Is it logical? Is it easy to find things? Then look at the way individual articles are written, designed and illustrated. Do they speak clearly to your readers? Are the attitudes expressed broadly in keeping with what you believe your readers to feel? Or, perhaps, are they sufficiently provocative to summon up a reaction? Is the tone of voice right? Are you serious enough, or too sober? Are you witty, spiky, irreverent, or just plain facetious? Are you confident, authoritative, convincing? In short, does the material hang together? Is it all identifiably part of the same magazine? This is a question of focus, once again.

Now turn from the big things, the major features, to the more routine stuff, the regular 'furniture' of the magazine. Again, is anything missing? Is there anything your rivals do that you could usefully imitate and improve upon?

There is a strong sense in which the soul of the magazine expresses itself through the attention given to regular items which don't immediately catch the attention. Most editors have had the experience of speaking to readers who buy the magazine not for its features, which they barely notice, but for something essential to their lives, be it a particular cartoon or the gardening column. Columnists are particularly important, whether they are serious industry figures holding forth on the week's issues in engineering, minor celebrities telling you about the vagaries of their family lives, or humorists with no other brief than to be funny. Over a period, these can have enormous effects on the image of a magazine, much more so than one-off features and stories.

Apart from its content, the other issue is how your magazine presents and 'sells' its material. In the first instance there is the matter of editorial design, starting with the cover. A cover may be attractive in its own right, but is it appropriate for the readership? If it shows a person, is it someone your readers will recognise, or if not, someone they will feel some sympathy with? Does it, if this is what's intended, give you some idea of the subject of the story? And is that the right subject to put on the cover?

Similar considerations come into play when you look at the photographic and illustrative treatment inside. Is the balance between pictures and text about right? Are the people in the photographs the right kind of people, in the way they dress and look? Do the pictures have impact? Is there a case for using illustration? Is the balance appropriate between formality and informality, sobriety and fun? Is the type readable, in the most literal sense? It is extraordinary how many magazines use type too small for their readership or in inappropriate colour combinations. And what about the colour palette employed throughout the magazine?

Great improvements can be made to a magazine, with a minimum of difficulty, not by changing the actual content or design, but by improving the way the content is sold to the reader. By 'selling' the content, editors mean the whole hierarchy of cover-lines, contents page entries, headings, standfirsts, opening paragraphs, pull-quotes: all the material that is used to draw the readers into the individual stories. There are fashions and styles in the writing of cover-lines and headlines, for instance, that may have nothing to do with what actually works best or is most appreciated by the readers. Sub-editors often favour something clever or punning over something straightforward, and the editor needs to be vigilant.

Cover-lines, especially, need to be functional. They do one job only, which is to make the reader take the magazine down off the shelf. So they need to excite curiosity and they need to appeal to the reader's self-interest. The reader will ask 'what's in this magazine for me?' and the cover-lines must provide simple, straightforward answers.

This examination of content, tone, treatment, regular material, visuals and the way things are sold should have provided you with a long list of potential for change. This needs to be referred, once again, to your mental picture of your reader. Which of these changes will actually be appreciated?

It might be worth dividing your proposed changes up into groups according to the rate at which you want to introduce them: immediate, medium term, long term. These relate to the resources needed to take the necessary action. The immediate group, you can deal with yourself. The medium term might mean some new commissioning and redesigning. The long term might mean alterations in the way the magazine is put together or even printed, and might involve significant costs.

In your immediate group, to be implemented from the next issue, you might have better cover-lines and headlines; bigger pictures in the news section; more- or less-prominent by-lines. In the medium term you might want a new columnist; regular coverage of a new subject area; and better pictures. In the long term you might plan new typefaces; a new running order; even a new page size.

Your changes will, you hope, be noticed by the readers, and if you are doing anything radical you should prepare yourself for a response. The close identification between readers and their magazines means that you must proceed with caution. Research shows that people cling passionately to the 'furniture' of their magazines – the logo, the ancient standing artwork, the outdated typefaces, the page size if it is unusual – long after they cease to have a passionate relationship to its content. What can seem to you a simple matter of brightening the magazine up, or improving its accessibility, perhaps by providing more items on a spread, can easily be misconstrued as going 'downmarket' or making things 'tacky'. You need to draw a distinction between simple knee-jerk conservatism, which we all share about things we love, and a more serious reaction that will show up in your sales or readership figures.

If you are going to move the furniture, and all editors should, from time to time, you have to ensure that you stay close, or move even closer, to your readers' real values and principles. They have to continue to feel that their interests, and beyond that, their feelings about the world, are still represented in your magazine. If your readers have children and care about their homes, you must not lose sight of that. If they are serious professional people, you must not suddenly start addressing them as if they were teenage pop fans. And as you make changes, monitor the response by whatever means are available to you, ensuring that you see all letters on the subject, for instance, and talking to a proportion of those readers who take the trouble to write or telephone you.

BUILDING FREQUENCY

In some ways building frequency is a much tougher prospect. People may reject some issues of your magazine because they have no need for them. Their purchase of the magazine may be connected with something in their lives that you can have no influence over. They may only buy a film magazine when they're thinking about going to the cinema. They may only buy a car or computer magazine when they're planning a major purchase, or thinking about it.

Obviously, you work to keep the quality of your magazine high from issue to issue. Beyond that, you must strive to ensure that each issue has one or two items in it of the very highest interest, that people will talk about and that your unreliable reader will not want to miss.

The trend in recent years has been to put more and more into a magazine: this is especially notable in design terms, where the 'white space' doctrine of the purists has been radically overturned. Continental arrivals in the women's market, for instance *Best* and *Bella*, have made it their business to fill every available space with useful information. This has now spread to every corner of the magazine market: the principles of the higher design still exist in the most profitable areas, for instance high-fashion magazines and colour supplements, but have elsewhere been replaced by a much more economical approach to paper.

But balance has to be achieved. One of the more shocking findings that sometimes emerges from research is that readers think your magazine has 'too much in it'. This discourages them from buying it more frequently, but can even be more destructive than that. Such is people's ingrained puritanism that they resent buying a magazine and not finding time to read most of it. An overstuffed magazine can make people tired just flicking through it. Providing 'just enough' can prove tricky.

Editorial devices for increasing frequency of purchase are unfashionable. If people like a columnist's voice, and know where that column is to be found, that's a treat they look forward to. Sometimes these columns take on a life of their own, with regular characters, almost a kind of plot, and all to the good.

If you have practical items that can be made to 'build up' into a series, so much the better, whether these are recipes or guides to various professional rules and regulations. But the practice of splitting ordinary long features over more than one issue has little in its favour. It's more of a frustration for those who miss one part than it is an incentive to regular purchase.

One device that you will probably use is the 'boost', the box in which you write about next month's attractions. In some rare circumstances, this may be problematical since it tells your competitors exactly what you are up to. More usually, though, it has the valuable effect of creating a small frisson of expectation in the reader. It is a moot point, however, whether that frisson is recalled a week or a month later when the reader sees the new issue on the stand. At that point readers are much more likely to be influenced by the cover treatment and cover-lines than by anything they read in the previous issue. The boost's value is more to reassure the readers of this month's magazine that, in general, they are part of an enterprise that will continue to come up with exciting things in the future. In other words, it serves more to enhance the experience of reading the magazine in hand than it does to sell the next one.

Non-editorial incentives

Incentives can be conjured up to encourage frequency of purchase. There are competitions that require the collection of coupons from successive issues, for instance. There are vouchers that, once collected as a set, offer some kind of free gift or discount. But that's another field which you should leave to your promotional department. If you are giving things away, you might find it better to do so in conjunction with subscriptions or ordered copies at newsagents. There is a case in some markets for 'adding value' to the subscription version of the magazine. The advertising magazine *Creative Review*, for instance, provides subscribers with a valuable CD-ROM of additional editorial and promotional matter with each issue.

INVOLVING YOUR READERS

It used to be thought that most readers achieved exactly the desired level of involvement with their magazines by the simple act of purchasing them, reading them and throwing them away. Increasingly, though, the relationship is becoming more intense than that, perhaps because of modern management's discovery that it is better to keep a happy customer than to go on a costly search for new ones.

So devices are constantly being invented to ensure that the reader's emotional commitment to the product (which, publishers will maintain, is special to the magazine industry) receives some sort of recognition or pay-off. They need to get something from you, a sense of belonging and a sense of being recognised. At the same time, you have the opportunity to get something invaluable from them, priceless guidance on your present and future direction. On-line magazines, in particular, will need to take a particular interest in developing genuine dialogue with their readers.

Editorial involvement

There are many straightforward editorial devices for reader involvement. It is important to make sure that editorial contact numbers are clearly displayed and promptly, efficiently and politely answered. Modern telephone systems make it perfectly possible to supply individual direct lines and to print these in the magazine. Obviously a small proportion of calls will be from time-wasters and cranks, but most will not. Readers should feel able to ring with story ideas and suggestions and, where necessary, with complaints. Most of their ideas will probably be unsuitable, but all should be dealt with courteously.

It is as well to have some kind of prescribed form for handling reader calls. Any promises that are made should be upheld, which is why there should be a sensible procedure for dealing with complaints, which may range from the trivial to the potentially disastrous. At the very least, calls from readers should be logged and investigated, and a follow-up call made. It is no longer enough to treat the reader as passive consumers of what we, as professionals, see fit to serve them.

Much women's magazine journalism, particularly, is based on the experiences of readers, who are invited to call in with their stories. They are often paid for them, an understandable development in such a competitive market. Editors in other markets should be able to establish the kind of relationship that permits that type of exchange of information and experience without the cash incentive.

Every magazine should find room for the views of readers and of those mentioned in the editorial pages. Certainly there should be a page for letters to the editor, with or without incentives, and as editor you should take a keen interest in it. Contrary to the practice in some magazines, a letters page cannot be left to look after itself. It will wither and die. It needs to be cultivated. The most provocative and interesting letters need to be moved to positions of prominence. Others need to be rewritten to make them clearer. Sub-editors habitually rewrite letters on some magazines, but if this is to happen some warning should be placed on the letters page. In more sophisticated markets it should be kept to a minimum and changes discussed with the letters' authors. Controversies need to be stoked, if necessary by inviting contributions from suitable figures, and quickly brought to a close before they become boring. Letters should have headings, and where they make direct requests or complaints, need to be answered, either on the page or in private correspondence.

It is also worth running an 'Errata' or 'Corrections' box. Honest mistakes cleared up in that way can prevent a great deal of trouble later, although seriously aggrieved readers need to be handled in a different way (see chapter 10: The editor and the public).

Editors should consider longer slots for readers' contributions, either written or 'as told to' a journalist. The idea is to impress upon the readers the approachability and openness of the magazine, as well as creating a new source of material. Usually, this material will need a lot of editing. Readers do not have the professional journalist's expertise in polishing material for publication. They may, however, have interesting thoughts and experiences that can be brought to the surface by a skilled editor.

Competitions

One obvious way in which magazines can involve their readers is through reader competitions. These will not usually be run by the editorial department: companies will be cajoled into providing prizes in return for some kind of write-up on the competition page, plus liberal use of their logo. A simple series of questions, usually immediately obvious to anyone who has read the attached copy, attracts a large volume of entries which are then picked from a hat.

Editors should keep this kind of thing at arm's length: obviously they will need to read the copy to ensure nothing misleading is being said and that the readers are being treated fairly, but beyond that it is probably best to look at such a competition as an advertising page in which the advert is paid for in kind rather than cash, although it will usually count as an editorial page for the purpose of flat-planning and determining the advertising/editorial ratio (see chapter 8: The editor and production).

The size and prominence of the item should be measured against the value of the prize, but that is for other people to worry about. On-page competitions are regulated by the Lotteries and Amusements Act of 1976, which prohibits competitions based on the forecasting of results and requires that competitions depend 'to a substantial degree on the exercise of skill'.

Of course, the initiative can come from the editorial side: it is quite common to have, for instance, writing or short-story competitions, with prizes acquired from a publisher or a fountain pen company on the same kind of basis. But at least here the competition can be made to have some genuine editorial value. Every effort must be made to ensure the judging is reputable. Names and addresses must be detached from entries. Those whose efforts are rejected will often prove implacable and should be given no encouragement in their suspicions by procedural irregularities.

On a much grander scale come awards schemes of various types, which are often seen in the business and professional sectors. These have numerous editorial benefits – not least the opportunity for modest amounts of national publicity when the results are announced – but they are time-consuming.

They can be helpful in establishing links with professional organisations, student groups and others. They can also be helpful for editors pressed by management to produce revenue-generating ideas, by bringing in sponsorship. But there is a danger in this: in some markets advertisers have discovered that they can gain considerable kudos and editorial presence by producing their own awards schemes and then bullying editors into publicising them.

It is much better for editors to be involved from the start, to ensure that any such competition or award scheme is run on acceptable lines. It is crucial that the image of the magazine does not suffer. Nor is this, ultimately, a trick that can be repeated too many times: some editors feel that there is a danger of their paying advertising being largely replaced by awards, competitions and sponsored events. It is better to plan an awards scheme or competition that will have genuine editorial benefits, in association with an appropriate professional body, and then look around for someone else, or preferably a group of companies, to chip in to sponsor it.

Participation

Opportunities to meet the readers in person should not be scorned. Too often reader events are organised as a promotional exercise without the involvement of the editor and editorial staff. This is quite wrong. All modern companies are going to great lengths to get nearer to their customers. There should be no reluctance about meeting readers when the opportunity arises.

Several women's magazines have held very successful readers' evenings at department stores. They organise conferences and lunches with speakers from the magazine and elsewhere. Film magazines can usually arrange reader screenings of new movies with the help of the film distributors. It is a shame, however, to hold such events without using the opportunity to speak to the readers both about the magazine's future plans and about their views of the magazine as it is. Readers expect to meet journalists at such events and are disappointed when they do not.

One final area of involvement with the readers is in campaigning. A campaign needs to be more than a series of articles on the same subject. At its best, it arises from a reader experience, followed by an investigation by the magazine's journalists, surveys, further articles and discussions with public bodies or politicians to make something happen. The important thing to bear in mind at the outset, however, is that the readers will expect a result. At some point there must be an emotional pay-off, otherwise the campaign will change very rapidly from a cause of great excitement to an albatross around editorial necks. A wise editor enters a campaign with an end in sight and a plan for achieving it, even before ordering up the special logos. On the other hand, when it works, the campaign can be a tremendous way of binding readers and magazine together, showing your ability to identify the core interests of your readership and speak up for them.

TRACKING THE RESULTS

Serious research, followed by careful changes to the product and accompanied by a sincere attempt to know and serve the readership, should, sooner or later, pay dividends.

Obviously, where funds allow, futher research will give a detailed picture of how your changes are being received. Informal research of your own, perhaps with the reader panels mentioned earlier, will be a cost-effective alternative. You should probably do it anyway. Ultimately, though, you will be judged on the magazine's sales or readership peformance.

It is worth cultivating the magazine's circulation department to ensure that you get an early look at their figures on an issue's performance. Be warned, however, that their 'instincts' for what will and will not sell, in terms of cover image and subject matter, may be no better than yours. As soon as the issue leaves the presses, they will be able to give you an account of how it has been received by the news trade, but that is no great concern of yours providing you don't actually get yourself banned by a distributor or wholesaler. It is better to wait for the real figures, showing print run, geographical distribution, sales and returns.

Many factors, other than pure editorial quality, affect sales. The weather, for instance, can have a dramatic effect. Promotional spending, either your own or other people's, can also be very significant. You cannot look at your own issue in isolation: consider the competiton's performance. Sales need to be judged over a period, rather than on individual issues, where these factors can present a distorted position. Circulation is normally audited independently by the Audit Burea of Circulations (ABC), every six months. You should be able to predict your audited figure, and can make special efforts at appropriate times of the year. The effect of a single disappointing issue can be made up in subsequent weeks or months. It is, however, difficult to avoid the emotional pall cast by a real flop.

The problem is that no-one has ever been able to identify the factors that make an individual cover sell, despite much propaganda to the contrary (see chapter 7: The editor and the visual). There are usually too many factors at work: colour, subject, cover-lines and so on. Unfortunately, however, it is a subject on which everyone has an opinion and on which people can become fixated. In the end, provided the cover is created with competence and confidence, what goes on inside the magazine will have a much greater long-term effect than anything that appears on the front.

FURTHER READING

White, Jan V. (1982) *Designing for Magazines*, New York: Bowker.
Guidelines for New Magazine Publishers (1995), London: Periodical Publishers Association.

Chapter 3

The editor and the team

In many respects, the most difficult task facing a new editor is to make the transition from being a member of staff – whose work is directed, evaluated and supported – to being a manager. But it has to be done. Except on the smallest publications, an editor can achieve nothing of consequence without the active support and co-operation of the editorial team. Creating that team, bringing out its full potential and managing its development, is something for which most editors are unprepared.

As a new editor you should be aware that, from now on, anything you say, good or bad, will receive twice the attention it did when you were a mere colleague. People will laugh at your jokes, for instance, not because they are funny but because of who you are. A harsh word will mean much more to the person receiving it than it does to you, and the same goes for words of praise.

Those whose work you are now required to direct may be either friends and close colleagues or complete strangers. In the latter case, it is important to meet each member of your new team quickly, and individually. This will give you an opportunity to provide reassurance, even a modicum of flattery, but also to put across your drive and ideas. You must also assess the characters of those you are about to work with, making a note of your impressions. At the end of your first week, and then again after a month, look again at what you wrote and reconsider.

Anyone who is on the brink of becoming an editor will have had plenty of opportunity to watch other editors at work. There has always been a distinction between those editors who spend most of their time out of the office, meeting people, promoting the magazine, and so on, leaving the day-to-day running of the magazine to someone else, and those editors who stay in the office, apparently doing everything.

There has been a tendency in the past for editors to be dictators, albeit sometimes benevolent ones. The analogy is with people working in the arts, film directors and choreographers for instance, whose vision has to be achieved through the work of many hands. There a dictatorial attitude is expected and tolerated, for the greater good. There is, perhaps, some sense in this. Veteran editors will tell you that you cannot edit by committee. A single vision is essential.

But there is a difference between a clear direction, which good editors can communicate to their staff and invite them to share, and simple autocracy. Editors have produced excellent magazines in the past by such means, but increasingly editors, like all line managers in industry, are learning that the key to success lies in mobilising the creativity of those individuals you happen to be managing. You must give other people the opportunity to surprise you with their excellence.

Managers today are supposed to be 'facilitators' or 'team coaches' where-as they used to be policemen. By virtue of your position, your staff will normally accept your authority. But you must demonstrate that it is in their interests to do so – and you must succeed in what you are trying to achieve.

As a leader, you will need to set an example of diligence and enthusiasm, particularly in your dealings with the outside world. Readers, in particular, should be treated with courtesy. You need to impress your vision of the magazine upon your staff, and to project enthusiasm and confidence that it can be achieved. You need to show decisiveness and a willingness to take responsibility for your actions. People need to see you and know that you are interested both in their work and in their lives. When you praise, it should be in public. Criticism must be tough when necessary, but it should be in private.

POWER OR RESPONSIBILITY?

The position is quite clear: editors are legally responsible for every word and image that appears in their magazines, in both editorial and advertising matter. Beyond that, an editor has a moral responsibility for the attitudes and expressions within the magazine, and must be prepared to defend them.

But the editor also has responsibilities as an employer, in terms of the way people are treated and their working conditions. There must be fairness in employment practice and adherence to good standards of health and safety. And editors also have responsibilities as members of management, ensuring the profitability of their magazines.

Some of these things happen in practice, but not all. Editors rarely have a say in advertising matters, although they should not hesitate to interfere if anything illegal or morally suspect is contemplated. In some companies, personnel functions continue to be controlled by a separate department. Increasingly this is seen as a luxury, and even if there is a personnel depart-ment or manager, you as an editor must operate according to the rules. The same goes for health and safety.

On a more general level, you as editor may be held responsible for things you have no power to change. Circulation may decline, not for editorial reasons, but because other publications have higher promotional budgets and more vigorous promotional teams. If you are to be held responsible for such matters, you must be represented in the management forum which determines how such things are organised.

Editorially you can expect to be judged as much on the detail of your magazine as on the overall picture, and for that reason your immersion in it has to be almost limitless. While you are setting your initial standards, you need to be everywhere: reading copy, looking at layouts, looking at pictures, suggesting headlines, encouraging, cajoling, persuading.

You might say that editors should be responsible for 'nothing except everything'. This paradoxical statement simply means that you should free yourself from fixed commitments so that you can become involved in what needs doing, as and when it arises. In that way you can look at a feature early on and suggest a rewrite, you can see pictures when they come in, you can stand at the chief sub-editor's shoulder when headlines are being written and you can reassure the lawyer when a controversial piece raises worries. You can also attend the necessary meetings with publishers and other managers without worrying about what you are not doing while you are there.

Important editing and writing tasks can and should be left to your deputy or other senior members of staff, so that you can take a slightly detached role in proceedings, the better to seize on key details and deal with them. This may be difficult, especially in the early stages. But once you have indicated to all parties your direction and your standards, you must let them get on with it. You will have more important things to do: thinking of the issues and challenges to come.

This is not the only model of editorship, however. Some editors find that most of their managerial functions have been taken by their publisher, leaving them to make day-to-day journalistic decisions but little else. And, in the case of magazines with small staffs, you will undoubtedly be expected to undertake numerous specific tasks in the course of an issue's production. Nonetheless, the 'nothing except everything' model is one ideal to strive for.

THE LEGAL FRAMEWORK

In the background of your mind in your dealings with staff, it is essential to have a firm idea of the requirements of employment law. Unfortunately, the law's requirements are not contained in a neat package, but are drawn from many different sources: common law; British legislation, mostly passed since 1963; and European legislation. On top of that, generations of judges have introduced a mass of case law, modifying and elaborating the written principles.

Most companies will have written employment procedures built on these legal frameworks, but some will not. It is as well to familiarise yourself with any fixed procedures. Trouble can come from many directions: disciplinary procedures; racial and sexual discrimination; maternity rights; safety;

holiday entitlements; hours of work; sick leave; the wording of employment contracts; and so on.

This is not the place for a detailed account of these areas. Continuously updated handbooks of employment law are available from various sources (for instance, *Croner's Reference Book for Employers*) and will probably be held by whichever member of management has the full personnel responsibility. For your purposes, more manageable material can be acquired from the Government's Arbitration, Conciliation and Advisory Service (ACAS) or in popular textbooks intended for small businesses. The main thing is to understand, without having to think about them, the key terms that will be used: the letter of appointment; the contract of employment; sick pay; maternity payments and leave; trade union duties; redundancy; wrongful dismissal; unfair dismissal.

In a small company you may well write your own letters of appointment, so should be aware of their legal significance. The actual 'contract of employment' is made when both sides agree orally, without anything being put on paper, so it is vital not to offer anything at the interview stage that will not actually be forthcoming. New employees must receive the following details within thirteen weeks of starting work: the employer's name and address; their job title; the date their employment began; details of pay, sick pay and pensions; hours and holiday entitlement; notice period; disciplinary rules; and a procedure for raising grievances. Once made, the contract can only be changed by mutual agreement.

There is a legal requirement to pay people who are sick, providing they and their period of illness meet the conditions laid down in the regulations. There are also many requirements concerning pregnant women, laying down both the payments they receive following the birth and their right to return to work afterwards in a position that, while not necessarily identical, has terms or conditions that are no worse. Requests to job-share or work part-time must be fairly considered.

Redundancy is the procedure whereby people are dismissed because the firm no longer requires that type of work. Remember that the job becomes redundant, not the individual. It is emphatically not a way of removing individuals whom you do not want in a particular job, although some employers try to use it in this way. Individuals must be selected for redundancy by a fair and agreed method, given a redundancy payment, plenty of notice and, where possible, the offer of alternative employment. Trade unions, where recognised, must be consulted. Where correct redundancy procedures are breached, the employee will be able to bring a case of 'unfair' dismissal. This should not be confused with 'wrongful' dismissal.

A wrongful dismissal is one where the employer breaches the contract of employment, either by failing to give sufficient notice of dismissal or by failing to comply with the disciplinary procedures detailed in the contract. Where the employer summarily dismisses the employee because the employee's behaviour constitutes a breach of the contact of employment, no case of wrongful dismissal will be found.

The employee can take an action for breach of contract in the county court, or the industrial tribunal system, but damages are usually limited to the wages that would have been paid during the notice period. A payment in lieu of notice will generally prevent a wrongful dismissal action, as will compliance with normal disciplinary procedures. Such actions are rare except in the case of the very highly paid on long notice periods.

An unfair dismissal is a different, and much more contentious, area of the law, dealt with exclusively in the Industrial Tribunal system. A dismissal is automatically unfair if a person is sacked for trade union activities, or is singled out for redundancy from a group of people doing similar work without agreed procedures being followed. Beyond that, a dismissal is only fair if:

- it is for redundancy, and all procedures have been followed
- it is on the grounds of failings in 'skill, aptitude or health', a situation which normally arises at the beginning of an employment
- it is on the grounds of misconduct: incompetence, negligence, violence, drunkenness, immorality
- it is on the grounds that the employee can no longer work legally (for instance if a driver loses his or her licence)
- it is for 'some other substantial reason' which you are prepared to argue before an industrial tribunal.

Staff who have worked for you for longer than two years are entitled to take you to a tribunal to contest their dismissal. So are, without any qualification period, individuals who claim they have been discriminated against on the grounds of race, sex or pregnancy. They can seek reinstatement or compensation.

Even if you manage to prove that the dismissal was for a permissible reason, the tribunal will still require that you acted reasonably. In particular, dismissal must come at the end of a proper disciplinary procedure, including a full investigation of the circumstances. Those dismissed must know the case against them and have been given an opportunity to appeal to some higher authority within the organisation. It is vital that you are aware of what is involved before you even think of dismissing anyone.

DEALING WITH A MAGAZINE'S CULTURE

Every magazine has its own 'culture', a set of attitudes, procedures and ways of working that may go on long beyond the professional spans of the individuals who make up its staff. As an outsider joining an existing magazine you will find yourself under pressure to comply with that way of doing things. Although this might feel like a personal defeat, it may be the only way, initially, of getting the magazine out. Changes can come later, once you have determined, as far as any outsider can, why things are the way they are.

This is particularly a problem with magazines which are self-conscious about their past. Certain individuals may have a symbolic significance beyond their apparent contribution to the title, because of contributions they may have made in earlier times. The overwhelming weight of the past may, however, be one reason for a title's poor performance in the present.

Younger magazines are not immune to problems associated with the passing of time. When titles start they often have tremendous drive, both editorially and commercially. Those who supplied that initial drive can move on, but the impetus survives. Sooner or later, however, the initial purpose of the project has become so diluted by generational change that it is necessary to make a new start.

How you are perceived will depend very much on the attitudes and performance of your predecessor. The assumption will be that you will do everything in the same way, or, contrarily, that you propose to turn everything upside down. There will certainly be a period of adjustment during which your expectations and those of your staff will meet.

There are at least two views of how editors should act during their first days. One school of thought says that immediate decisions must be taken about personnel and appropriate changes made. This can leave you with a reputation for dynamism, but also, possibly, for impetuousness and unreasonableness. The other approach is to bide your time and wait for the underlying realities to present themselves. This, too, has its dangers. You may lose your sense of objectivity about the personalities involved: they may see you as weak.

Many editors refuse to enter a new environment, particularly a hostile one, single-handed, preferring to bring at the very least, their own PA or editorial assistant, and possibly their own deputy. It is only human to want a ready-made ally, but the signals it sends out are unfortunate. Such a course of action has the effect of consigning everyone else to the position of also-ran.

On the other hand, you will not be able to secure total loyalty until you have some members of staff who owe you their present positions, either by promotion or new appointments. These must be your own decisions. Long service before your time and a general sense that certain individuals 'deserve' promotion must not influence your decision, which can only be based upon current and future ability and the good of the magazine.

LEADERSHIP

It has been said that managing creative people is like 'learning to herd cats'. Certainly it cannot be done by barking orders and pretending omniscience. Today's leader – and an editor is nothing else – is required simply to make it possible for others to work to the best of their ability. Individuals must be given the power they need to perform and allowed to make their own judgements. As the management theorist Charles Handy puts it, in his *Beyond Certainty*, 'It is morally wrong to steal people's decisions.'

An editor is still required, however, to provide two things. The first is a vision, and the second is a set of standards. Without a vision for the magazine that can be communicated to everyone involved with it, the editor is merely overseeing its decline. A shared vision makes it possible for individuals to act as a team on an almost instinctual basis. If everyone understands who the reader is supposed to be, commissions will be appropriate, the style of writing will be right, and appropriate headlines and standfirsts will present themselves. Every page in the magazine will be alive with that vision. And every page will be impregnated with the magazine's identity, like a watermark.

You will have found that vision through your examination of the magazine and its market and in your search for the reader, and now you must develop it in discussion with your staff. Your enthusiasm must be plain.

The second half of the editor's task is to provide standards: to lay down precisely what is expected of people and of the finished product. Industrial managers say 'what gets measured gets done'. We are not in a quantitative business: most of what we do is not measurable in that sense. But in a broader sense, people's achievements, even in editorial matters, can be assessed. There can be regular appraisals or less formal chats at which individuals' ambitions and fears can be considered and translated into new opportunities or changes of direction.

You must train yourself to listen. The temptation is always to tell people what to do, usually accompanying the advice with an anecdote from your glorious past. But you need people to talk to you, to tell you their difficulties and their discoveries, especially those with direct contact with the readers. You must take what they say seriously and be seen to be doing something about it, otherwise the opportunity is wasted.

Nonetheless, setting standards comes first. It is only right, as well as more economical, that people should be told what is expected of them before they start.

THE RIGHT TEAM

A successful magazine works as a team. But a team is more than a loose agglomeration of people. It requires both a careful choice of individuals and a defined structure. As a new editor, unless you are being invited to create a new launch, you will have inherited someone else's idea of what a team should be. In time, you can adjust that to something nearer your ideal.

Structure and the key jobs

What is the smallest team necessary to produce a magazine? It can be done by one person, providing the magazine is not too frequent and communicates mainly through text rather than pictures or design work. As the editor of that type of publication, you would commission and process everything you didn't write yourself, as well as handling all the administration, perhaps even selling the odd advertisement. House journals, 'fanzines' and professional newsletters are often produced in exactly this fashion, sometimes by people with other day jobs. They depend for their success on minimal production, a ready supply of material, and willing assistance.

Newsletter production, however, is very often a two-person job: one to handle administrative matters, including getting in and sending back any photographs and contributions, and the other to edit, but with both involved in final production. Few individuals are capable of perfection, however, which is what is required of editors in such a situation.

A typical small monthly will be staffed by an editor, some kind of editorial assistant or administrative assistant, plus an art editor and a sub-editor on either a full- or a part-time basis. In this set-up, the art editor will take responsibility for the acquisition of pictures. Additional freelance sub-editors and designers might well be required during busy parts of the production cycle. The editor, once again, will do all commissioning and any necessary writing, and will share such tasks as headlines with the sub-editor, who must be well versed in production techniques in order to deal with outside production agencies. The administrative assistant will take charge of such tasks as obtaining and returning photographs and issuing payments. Such a lean set-up will work, but makes no allowances for holidays or illness: it would be as well to be on good terms with several competent freelances. It requires unanimity of purpose but that is perhaps easier to achieve in small teams.

As pagination increases, full-time sub-editors and art staff become essential, as does a full-time picture editor. Bigger magazines will also employ more senior editorial staff: a features editor or commissioning editor, for instance. If the magazine has a news content, there must be a news editor and/or reporters. Once your editorial staff get into double figures, you really need to start developing strong and semi-autonomous sections which can make their own decisions.

Editors of large weeklies can confidently expect their staff to deal with the kind of crises that develop from time to time in the production process, but that is not always the case with very small magazines, where the editor will usually be expected to know everything. In particular, a small magazine does not allow the luxury of a deputy editor. Nonetheless, someone must be nominated to take responsibility in the editor's absence if the whole process is not to grind to a halt. Someone with a sub-editing background is best equipped for this, simply because it is production matters that will require the most immediate attention.

Indeed, an editor needs the support of good, fast and accurate sub-editors more, perhaps, than any other members of staff. It is through the sub-editing area that an editor takes control of a magazine, in terms of both its tone of voice and its overall structure, and ensures that it holds its focus over the long term.

Sub-editing, sadly, has undergone something of a decline since the change to on-screen page make-up, which has reduced the time sub-editors can devote to working with words. If cultivated and prized for their skills, however, they are great allies. They know a magazine's strengths and weaknesses from the inside. And their meticulousness makes all the difference between producing an authoritative, respected publication and an industry joke.

Nonetheless, they are probably not the most important appointment an editor has to make. That will be the art editor or art director. It is essential that editor and art editor are of one mind on a design strategy. A good art editor, working to an agreed brief, will have the single greatest influence over the readers' perception of a magazine.

Beyond that, an editor needs to feel confident that the magazine is being efficiently run on a day-to-day level. It is possible to put together a single issue of a magazine swiftly and imaginatively from a standing start. But administrative control has to assert itself soon, otherwise problems associated with missing post, non-returned or lost pictures, lost contributions, unpaid contributors and the rest will bring it to its knees. The importance of a dedicated administrative assistant can hardly be overstated. In appointing such a person, however, the editor needs to tread carefully. The expression 'editorial assistant', as widely used in magazines, can mislead applicants into assuming that theirs will be a writing or editing role. If no such opportunities will be involved you must make that clear in both the advertisement and at the interview.

Hiring staff

Ask yourself first whether you need to hire anyone. A departure should not be taken as an immediate signal to seek a direct replacement. It is an opportunity to think about the way the magazine is developing and to consider whether some change in job functions might not be a better idea. It is also an opportunity to consider whether the job is absolutely necessary on the present full-time basis. There may be a case for splitting the responsibilities of the job between several existing members of staff, or using freelance cover for part of it.

Probably, though, the decision will be taken to replace. Consider promoting someone in the first instance. Some companies take the view that all vacancies should be publicised and that promotion candidates should compete with outside applicants for the post. This may be reassuring, on all sides, letting the promoted person know they were awarded the job on merit and convincing management that the best person was appointed.

It is, however, an expensive way of arriving at a conclusion that would have cost nothing and may, in the interim, cause a certain amount of discontent. The competitive selection process is unlikely to tell you anything about an existing employee that you didn't already know. There must be an interview, however, if only so that both sides can discuss the job. You can make clear what is required. Applicants can indicate how they intend to proceed.

While it is good for staff to know that promotion is always a possibility, those who have been passed over will need to be handled carefully, to be assured that their time will come and perhaps steered in the direction of the extra training or experience that their careers need.

If you decide to make an external appointment, however, several steps need to be taken. A new job description should, perhaps, be drawn up. A job description is not a description of the person currently occupying the position concerned. It should not list what that person does, but what he or she should be doing. As a check, it may be useful to show the new job description to the departing incumbent to ensure that it equates broadly to what he or she has been doing, but remember that the job description relates to the ideal, not the reality.

The job description should indicate what the member of staff is required to do and to whom he or she is responsible. It needs to be drawn up with care, because it will be used in later assessments of the new recruit's work.

Many authorities recommend complementing the formal job description with a 'person specification'. This is a list of the personal attributes that a person would need to bring to the job to be able to carry out the job description. Person specifications usually attempt to assess a person under a set of headings, including physical attributes; qualifications and experience; innate abilities and potential; interests; disposition or personality; and domestic circumstances.

Physical attributes include such matters as age, health, general appearance and demeanour. University degrees are the norm in journalism today, although it should be remembered that for many years graduates were the exception rather than the rule and the profession was none the worse for it.

On the question of experience, you must consider how closely you need the person's past experience to fit the current job. If you are running a specialist professional journal, for instance, how far does general journalistic experience outweigh specialist knowledge? Would you be better off with a less experienced journalist but one whose limited experience has been in precisely your field? Specialist magazines need a team that balances specialist knowledge and journalistic skills, but it is often better to take good journalists and introduce them to a new area of expertise than to take experts in the field and try to introduce them to basic journalistic concepts.

But this depends entirely upon the demands of the subject matter. It would not be an appropriate approach to appointing the technical editor of an engineering magazine, for instance.

In considering innate abilities and potential you should consider both the job now and its future. Will it develop with its new occupant? Or is it likely to prove frustrating? Interests should be relevant to the subject matter of your magazine, obviously enough, but also they should provide evidence of a well-rounded personality beyond that.

Specifying a particular disposition or personality is rather problematical. Who can really say what type of disposition is suitable for any given journalistic job? And how, in the space of the interviewing process, are you going to assess whether your candidate actually complies?

A candidate's domestic circumstances may be an issue if the job involves frequent travel or unpredictable hours. It is for you to decide how flexible you need a candidate to be. Those with no ties may seen superficially attractive for some jobs; but maturity and stability normally bring domestic obligations.

Many people recruit by word of mouth and personal recommendation, which costs nothing but means you are constantly drawing from the same narrow pool of potential recruits. If you are within a large organisation, you can recruit by using the internal advertising process, but again, the same applies: you may well know all the likely candidates.

A step up from this is to use the services of headhunters for recruitment agencies. You will need to use an agency which specialises in journalistic appointments. The best known of these, The Media Network, charges between 15 and 20 per cent of a recruit's first year salary, although if you don't employ any of its candidates you don't normally have to pay.

In most cases, however, you will probably advertise, either in the *Guardian* or in the *Press Gazette*, which seem to have established a duopoly on this kind of advertisement. Advertisements need to be written with care in order both to attract the suitable and to deter the unsuitable. In general, the way to write an advertisement of this sort is to be absolutely specific about what you want. You should say who you are, and what the job is, in some detail. Simply using the job title is not enough, since jobs with similar names ('Production editor' or 'Assistant editor', for instance) differ so widely from company to company. You must include both the appealing and the unappealing parts, since you want to deter those who are not serious. You must also mention the qualifications you consider vital, and include a closing date for applications.

There are varying views on whether you should mention the salary. There can be occasions when this can cause internal friction, but in general it is a clear indicator to people whether they are in the appropriate bracket before they apply. You should also make some attempt to match the written style of the advertisement to that of your publication: if yours is a lively, chatty publication it would be inappropriate to produce an advertisement that sounds as if it is offering a job with the Inland Revenue. Your advertisements and recruitment procedures must not discriminate on sexual or racial grounds even inadvertently. The consequences could be serious.

What should your advertisement ask for? The curriculum vitae is the standard way of ensuring that you have the right information, although if you are expecting a huge number of applications and you want to ensure they are all directly comparable you can devise some sort of form. Consider, however, how you felt as a job applicant. An application form, packed as it is with impertinent requests for semi-relevant information, can be a serious deterrent even to good candidates, especially since hardly anyone uses typewriters any longer and filling in a form means applicants must reveal their handwriting to the world. Some companies specifically ask for handwritten letters of application, but most journalists' handwriting is atrocious, since it is so little used. A curriculum vitae allows candidates to present themselves to the world in the way they think appropriate, something that does not always work to their advantage.

Depending on the job, there may need to be other enclosures. Writers and reporters can legitimately be asked for samples of their writing, or cuttings of their best stories, but a wise editor is aware of the extent to which this kind of work can be improved in the sub-editing stage. Candidates for writing and editing jobs of various sorts can be asked for ideas, but great care should be taken that these ideas do not escape from the interviewing process into the collective consciousness of the magazine. It will enhance no-one's reputation if ideas submitted as part of a job application subsequently appear in the magazine under someone else's by-line. Fair play demands that if you like the ideas, but not the candidate, you either pay for them or leave well alone.

Designers and art directors will, of course, have portfolios of their work. Sub-editors can supply copies of complex editorial spreads they have assembled, or of features where headline, standfirst and so on have been particularly pleasing, but none of this is especially revealing of what a sub-editor is like to work with.

Any enclosures that people supply with their applications must, of course, be kept safe and returned unless you specify that they will not be.

The person specification comes into its own in whittling down applications. By comparing your candidates' own self-descriptions with the specification you have drawn up, you can sort them into three piles: rejections, possibles and probables. Decide how many people you want to interview, and then adjust the probable pile accordingly, if necessary adding the best of the possibles. All applicants should receive an acknowledgement immediately. It is safe to send rejection letters to your immediate rejects now, but you might feel it is better to leave the possibles for a while.

Interviewing is a skill like any other: it needs to be learnt and gets better with practice. It is, however, rather gruelling. Interviews should be scheduled an hour apart, allowing about forty-five or fifty minutes for serious discussion and the rest of the time for a breather in between. On no account should you attempt to interview more than about four people a day: they will begin to merge into one in your mind, even if you take notes.

You must prepare for the interview, and if there are two of you doing it you must discuss how you are going to handle it between you. The interview should attempt to answer all the questions implied by your person specification. At the very least, you need to know what the candidates are doing at the moment, what they did in their previous jobs, why they want this job and what their plans and ambitions are.

If there are obvious holes in their CVs, or strange career moves, this is your opportunity to ask about them. You are perfectly at liberty to push harder until you get the information, but nothing is to be gained by being aggressive. It may be that people with unconventional career paths make better journalists than those who travel as if on rails, but it is for your candidates to convince you of that, rather than being vague or dishonest.

On the whole, you should be listening much more than you are talking. It is, after all, the candidates' opportunity to tell you what they can do rather than what you can do for them. Make notes as the interview proceeds. At the end, let the candidate ask you questions. This is only partly for the candidates' benefit: these questions should help you to guess how interested or committed they are to the job. Most people will take the opportunity to ask about the salary. While there may have been an argument for being coy in your advertisement, there is no excuse now. As you close the interview, you must indicate what happens next.

Between interviews, you should ensure that you have made a note of your impressions. Some companies go to the lengths of having a formal 'assessment form' that you complete for each candidate, grading them on their qualifications, demeanour and outlook. If two of you are interviewing, you should perhaps have a brief chat about your perceptions before you proceed. Three people is too many interviewers; if more than two people really do need to see each candidate they should do it sequentially rather than simultaneously.

If you decide to have a two-stage interviewing process, you must do your homework to ensure that you actually have something to discuss in the second interview. There may be areas that weren't covered in sufficient depth in the first round. Otherwise, you may find it helpful to introduce the candidate to his or her prospective colleagues. Later you can gauge their reactions.

One thing that it might be useful to bear in mind throughout the process is that you should try to compare the candidates with the ideal encompassed in your original person specification rather than with one another.

Interviewing is the standard recruitment method, but in an area such as journalism it is not always the most important. There is a strong case for informal tests of various kinds. Certainly no-one should employ a sub-editor on the basis of interview alone. It is a fairly easy matter to devise a brief sub-editing test, using some pieces of surplus copy. It should be done there and then: letting people take the work away with them risks proving nothing. There is also a case for an informal quiz for news reporters: they should certainly know what the big stories of the day are, for instance, and in a specialist area they should have some idea about the subject matter.

In certain positions it may be sensible to invite the candidate to do some freelance 'shifts' with you before you commit yourself. You could even offer a short-term contract. This offers you the opportunity to see how the person works. You risk, however, losing your applicant to a less painstaking employer.

These things may help you towards a decision. In consultation with senior colleagues, you must review each of the candidates and evaluate them against the specification you have drawn up. This adds a modicum of objectivity to what is inevitably a subjective process. You should be aware, always, that the person you like best, and imagine yourself getting along with best, may not actually be the best qualified. You might do better to choose someone who complements your abilities and those of your existing staff rather than selecting anyone too similar. Having made a decision, it is as well to have a fall-back position of one or two second-best candidates. Then, when your preferred candidate says 'no thank you', you will not have wasted the whole process. Do take up references.

The oral appointment and acceptance must be immediately followed up by a letter of appointment. This forms part of the candidate's contract of employment and must be written carefully, to include the following:

- starting date
- details of any probationary period
- salary
- hours
- holiday entitlement
- any other benefits

A full contract of employment should follow at the end of the probation period and be signed by both sides.

Induction

Appointing a new employee is only the start. A very high number of new employees drop out very shortly after joining a new firm. This can be avoided by making efforts to help the new employee fit in. It is a minimum courtesy to find a desk and a computer and to clear the previous occupant's debris, but it is amazing how rarely this is done. Staff should also be briefed about the new arrival, and someone, usually the recruit's section head, should be nominated to ensure he or she knows the building layout, the whereabouts of facilities and enough to get through the first days without being overwhelmed.

As editor, depending on the size of your magazine and your direct involvement with the person concerned, you should certainly attempt to corner the new recruit after a week to see how things are going, and then again, more seriously, after a month. At the end of three months, the probationary period for the appointment will be up, and you will usually expect to review formally the new recruit's performance during that period. If performance is not satisfactory, it may be time to accept that a mistake has been made and to give the person notice. Otherwise, you might decide that, while not satisfactory, the employee's performance is salvageable, and extend the probationary period.

Firing staff

Difficult though it may be, hiring people is at least a generally happy experience. Dismissal has no such pleasures, though it is sometimes necessary. A dismissal is a failure both for you as a manager and, more obviously, for the employee concerned. People are supposed to be an asset, after all. You have a duty to make sure that people are happy and working to the best of their capacity.

That said, there are those employees who do not fulfil their side of the bargain. In particular, you will need to be ready and able to remove bullies, thieves, frauds, persistent skivers and sexual harassment enthusiasts without losing sleep. People who fundamentally reject your authority should be given an opportunity to see the error of their ways before they are removed too. This is in everyone's interest, although not everyone sees it like that.

There is a myth that dismissing people is something that can be done on a whim. Indeed it can, but at a price. Those companies which are prepared to pay handsome compensation to those they dismiss can do what they like. Everyone else, however, must ensure that the disciplinary process leading to the dismissal can be defended before an industrial tribunal, which is the employee's first recourse. Sacked journalists used not to use tribunals, fearing damage to their prospects. Recent high-profile cases indicate that things have changed.

In practice this makes dismissal a long and tedious process rather than the result of a rush of blood to the head. The one exception is a case of summary dismissal for 'gross misconduct', which is generally confined to the following:

- theft from either company or colleagues
- fraudulent behaviour
- incapacity through drink or drugs
- arrest or conviction on a serious criminal charge affecting the employment
- violence or destruction of property

- obscene language and gross insubordination
- gross negligence or irresponsibility
- possession of an offensive weapon.

Given the time-consuming nature of the normal dismissal process, most busy editors would do well to think of any number of alternatives first. If it is a case of underperformance, perhaps extra training or reassignment to different work would be a better bet. If it is a case of defiant or destructive behaviour, however, these options are not available. Frank discussion of the problem usually brings nothing more than protestations of innocence: 'What, me?' In any case, rewarding a nuisance with a great deal of attention followed by a change of role sends poor signals to the rest of the staff.

Dismissal is not something that can or should be detached from the rest of the disciplinary process. Your disciplinary process needs to be written in stone and designed to comply with the requirements of employment law. You would do as well to seek the help of a specialist book on the subject (or acquire the ACAS *Code of Practice 1: Disciplinary Practice and Procedures in Employment*).

All disciplinary procedures, however, involve the same sequence of events: oral warning, followed by first written warning, followed by second written warning, followed by dismissal. Those receiving the warnings must be given some kind of right of appeal, and every effort must be taken to show that you have acted in a reasonable fashion throughout the process. Since each of these stages needs to take place at least a month apart, you can see that nothing is going to happen very quickly.

The only good thing, from your point of view as an exasperated editor determined to dismiss, is that many people see the writing on the wall once they have received their first written warning and take the opportunity to leave before their record is permanently blighted.

The use of the word 'disciplinary' is slightly inappropriate. While this procedure is used for matters of misconduct, for instance lateness, poor appearance, working for someone else during company time, damaging property and all the rest of it, it can also be used simply for poor work performance.

Poor performance or incapacity can lead to a dismissal which will be upheld by a tribunal, but it is a long and difficult path. Apart from the effects on the individual concerned (and on your own state of mind) you will need to consider the effect on morale amongst your team. Those who are doing no work and taking no responsibility represent no threat to anyone else and have lots of time on their hands to be everyone's friend. Their dismissal will be resented, although in private people will accept it: indeed, some of those who are most vociferous in their protests may well have been quietly urging you to take precisely this action. Such is the editor's lot. On the other hand, if you are acting fairly and after all other options have been explored, you may find what you have had to do will be welcomed. People may recognise that the individual was not really making a contribution.

In the case of new employees, a problem of this sort should really be detected, and a remedy arrived at, during the probationary period. In the case of established employees, there are numerous quetions which need to be asked. It may be that the employee's capabilities have not changed, but the nature of the job has: in this instance, it is your responsibility to provide appropriate retraining and guidance. This was an issue at the time of the introduction of new editorial technology, though less so now.

If you have promoted this person into a position for which he or she is not ready, the problem is yours once again. You will need to provide appropriate support rather than taking any other action. And then there is the case of members of staff whose personal problems are preventing them working to the best of their capacity: again, you will have to find a solution which supports them while they return to peak performance.

If none of these things applies, then dismissal for poor performance is an option. One of the most shocking things about British management, however, is the way individual employees can be seen as a major problem by their employers and supervisors without ever themselves becoming aware of any failing. As a nation, we hate scenes and confrontations. A quiet word at an early stage can bring about the necessary changes and halt the whole process in its tracks, but very often the situation is left so long that either the manager's mind is made up or the member of staff is incapable of changing.

This must not be allowed to happen. At the earliest possible moment, a serious private discussion should take place in which it is made clear to the employee, by reference to his or her job description if necessary, just what is expected. This need not be a threatening occasion, but it should be absolutely clear. It is very common for managers to convince themselves that they have spoken sternly to staff about their failings while staff have no recollection of any such discussion.

If the necessary improvements are not made, the disciplinary process begins. After one or more informal discussions about performance, an oral warning is given, and a note of what was said attached to the individual's personnel file. A time limit for improvements to be seen should be made and an appointment fixed to discuss them.

If there is radical improvement by that date, you can bring the process to an end, even 'wiping the slate' if you feel sufficiently confident that this is a permanent state of affairs. If there is no improvement, however, a first written warning should be given, indicating that a failure to correct things will lead to further consequences. Again, a date should be set for a further appointment. This warning, too, must be added to the employee's file. If there is no suitable improvement by that date, a final warning should be given. This must state explicitly that the contract of employment will be terminated if there is no improvement.

Dismissal follows if no improvement takes place. It will do no good to back down from the ultimate sanction at this point. The employee will feel that he or she has 'got away with it' and other staff will be bemused. And if you subsequently decide to dismiss after all, your carefully planned dismissal process will be in tatters, making that later dismissal look like a case of victimisation rather than a necessary response to a difficult situation.

In dismissing the employee, you must, of course, give notice. In practice, however, payment in lieu of notice will be made and the employee will be asked to leave the premises immediately. A letter giving reasons for the dismissal should be despatched, along with any holiday pay and payment in lieu of notice. At that point, the employee will take legal advice while you wait to see if you are going to be taken to a tribunal. There can, of course, be a settlement between your legal advisers and the dismissed employee before the tribunal takes place.

Be aware that dismissing a person for reasons connected with pregnancy, for a spent conviction or for trade union activities is automatically unfair. The danger of tribunals is not so much in the actual costs of any award they might make, which are not huge (except in the case of racial and sexual discrimination), but in the damage to your company's reputation. It is for this reason that most employers, if they have to dismiss, prefer to pay off the employee. If this is preferred to the lengthy, tedious but cheap process of conducting a fair dismissal, it must be thoroughly discussed between you and your publisher.

INVOLVING PEOPLE

As an editor, you will find that meetings are the bane of your life. There will always be meetings with publishers, different departments of management and various outside organisations. These should not be allowed to distract you from the central task of communicating with your own editorial staff. Obviously, all day every day is a kind of meeting, as people bring you various problems or matters that need a decision and you talk them through and send them on their way. But you need to find various ways of getting away from the immediate pressure of events to allow you to communicate your vision of the magazine to the team and allow them to report on their experiences and ideas.

Meetings

In a small enough magazine, it could be argued that there is no need for meetings, since everyone is constantly on hand and discussion is the natural state of things. Nonetheless, there are strong arguments for getting people to stop work, put down the telephones and turn their attention to the matter at hand. On a weekly with a strong news content it can be a good idea to start each day with a morning look at the diary and the post, and a discussion of anything that is immediately at hand. Some editors like to see all the incoming post and distribute it at this stage, with an indication as to how important they consider it for the magazine. Such meetings will necessarily be short and sharp. More leisured discussion of the magazine in general can take place outside the building and at another time.

On bigger publications it is essential to hold regular meetings to discuss progress. It is often a good idea to do this when the new issue first becomes available, although on a monthly that alone will not be enough. It is important, though, to review the product as it first appears. This should be an opportunity to discuss the way things have been done.

Some offices have what is called a 'whinge copy', where journalists annotate a copy of the issue to indicate where they find mistakes or have points they want to raise. This is a good idea, providing people are prepared to initial their annotations and speak up for them in the meeting. It is hard to overestimate people's reluctance, especially at first, to engage in a regime based on constructive criticism. But it is absolutely essential if the task of producing a quality product is to be properly shared by all parties rather than imposed by you as editor. You must do what you can to promote this idea by being optimistic, enthusiastic and quicker to praise than to attack.

After the meeting has looked at the current issue, there needs to be a brief review of the state of the coming issue, with contributions by those responsible for the various sections or aspects, reporting any progress or hold-ups and permitting any last-minute suggestions or contributions from those not directly involved. Following that, the meeting may wish to move on to future issues and ideas.

There is a view that formal meetings are no place for creativity. We have all experienced the emptying of the mind that takes place when called upon to produce lists of ideas in settings in which we are not comfortable. Nonetheless, this is an appropriate forum, providing it is not so big as to be unworkable. But it needs work and regular practice to ensure that people feel comfortable. You as editor may or may not wish to chair the meeting, but whoever does so should be given the brief of making sure that everyone contributes, by asking them directly if necessary. There should be a general rule that all ideas will be considered seriously and with courtesy.

It is essential if meetings are not to degenerate that they they are seen to lead directly to action. Notes should always be taken, and each meeting should include an outline of what action has been taken as a result of the preceeding discussion. In general, meetings should be kept as brief and as pointed as possible. One trick sometimes recommended is to hold them at the end of the day, when people have an incentive to keep things short. Others hold them in rooms with no chairs, but you may feel that this is extreme.

The question of who should attend meetings is a difficult one. If your staff is small, then the problem doesn't arise, but as the magazine grows larger this may present problems. Large magazines are much more prone to factional disputes than smaller ones, and you have to find a way of navigating through that. Information, who receives it and who doesn't, can be a major weapon in factional disputes. You need to make certain that it is not misused in this way by ensuring that you tell people the truth.

A good and noble policy insists upon there being 'no secrets', but if you are following this policy it has to be in concert with your fellow managers. At the very least, you must tell your staff nothing that is capable of being contradicted by other sources. But it is essential also to consider how your information is being received. In particular, information about your magazine's progress, the rise and fall of circulation and advertising income, can be misinterpreted. An exhortation to general belt-tightening can be construed as an announcement of imminent redundancies. References to pressures from above can sound as if you are no longer running things. As usual, the rule that says that because this material comes from you it has double weight should be borne in mind.

If something concerns a specific group of individuals, it is right and proper to have them there at the same time and tell them together. For routine meetings, the standard solution is to bring the heads of each department together: chief sub-editor, features editor, news editor, art editor, and so on. Those in the meeting must pass on what they learn to those in their departments. You should check that this happens.

The results of meetings need to be transformed into some physical form. After discussions on future issues it is as well to circulate an early running order, showing the state of play on various sections. There are also various wall displays that you can use, usually on purpose-built whiteboards or pinboards. If yours is a very structured type of magazine you can draw up a type of grid, with issue dates or numbers across the top and the various sections, say, 'news feature', 'first feature', 'second feature', 'picture feature', 'consumer feature' and your regular items: health, fashion, new products, and so on, running top to bottom. Under 'June' each square of the grid will be filled. 'July' will be slightly patchier, and as the magazine moves off into the distance, so the pattern becomes less clear. It is also a good idea to leave some space on the board for finished features that are in stock but haven't been allocated to an issue. Better that they sit there as a constant reminder than that they languish in some drawer.

It is also essential to create a physical record of the state of the current magazine. As pages are completed and sent to the typesetters or colour house, reduced proofs should be pinned up in order. It is even better, from time to time, to lay colour photocopies of the finished feature pages down on the floor and walk around them. This can be enormously useful as a way of manipulating shape and pace.

You should leave people, as far as possible, to make their own decisions and organise their own working arrangements within your overall strategy. That will mean encouraging them to have their own meetings, and a well-appointed office should always include a space where this can happen. It makes sense, for instance, for features and art staff to liaise at the very earliest stage on complex stories. As editor, though, you do need to be kept informed of what is going on, and you should insist on being given a brief note of what was discussed and what was decided. You can, if you are bold, practise the technique of 'subsidiarity', as proposed by Charles Handy in *Beyond Certainty*, whereby decisions are made at the lowest possible level.

All editors have to decide where exactly they wish to insert themselves into the process. On a magazine with a small staff, low pagination and a long production cycle, it is perfectly possible for the editor to be involved in every stage of an issue's creation. As the magazine grows, however, that becomes much more difficult.

Start by looking at the minimum involvement you should insist upon and work up from there as time allows. You certainly need to approve the flat-plan, since the running order and relative lengths of feature material are central to the editing process. You need not, however, do all the necessary sums and negotiation yourself, providing you have a sensible relationship with your advertising department and a competent deputy or chief sub-editor. Since you are legally responsible for the entire content of the publication, it would seem essential for you to see every finished page. In the days when magazines went to press as pasted-up boards it was customary for the editor to sign each page, following one senior editorial figure (perhaps a chief sub-editor or section editor) and your art editor. The physical object now no longer exists, although you should insist on seeing a set of proofs identical to the material being sent by disk or modem to your colour house.

As editor, you should not generally be reading pages for typographical errors. Your concern is with the broad picture: are the headlines appropriate? Does the design lead the reader through the material clearly? Are those the correct pictures? It is sometimes a good idea to stamp proofs with a checklist to ensure that all the elements are in place, particularly picture credits, folios, captions, pull quotes.

But looking at everything this late has its limitations. Your production schedule should include sufficient time to enable you to change things that are wrong without incurring extra costs. But this is not the moment for recasting a major feature or taking a new line on a news story. There will be no time for significant rewriting and certainly not for extra research.

That is why you must make it your business to insert yourself into the process early on, and not always in a predictable way. Some editors see all the raw copy before it is edited. That can undermine the authority of your section editors. But you should be able to dip in and read copy at various stages in the process. You may also like to see rough layouts and early picture-edits when they are under construction, rather than wait until a spread is finished before passing comment.

Most editors find that they have regrettably little time to spend on editorial tasks: instead they are trapped into a round of meetings on more managerial and commercial topics. Consequently, you must find ways to make your editorial interventions count, and be seen to be interested in everything that is going on. There is no better way of doing this than wandering around looking at what people are doing: designing pages, sorting out photographs, writing headlines, and so on. This can be infuriating, of course, but people must learn to expect it rather than see it as an imposition.

Apart from the routine meetings needed to keep the magazine going, however, there is a strong case for regular 'strategy' meetings in which more wide-ranging discussions take place about the magazine, its market and its future. These may benefit from the types of analysis much beloved of management experts, notably the SWOT technique, in which attention is given in turn to the Strengths and Weaknesses of the magazine as it stands and the Opportunities and Threats facing it in the future.

Each of the four terms is taken as the starting point for a wide-ranging discussion. In the case of a magazine in, for instance, the pregnancy market, its strengths might include its specialist nature, the quality of experts used and its good reputation for accuracy. Its weaknesses might be the quality of photography used, low recognition in the market arising from its bi-monthly status, and a lack of topicality. The opportunities open to such a title might include the possibility of spin-off products, for instance books and videos, and potential syndication deals. The threats might come from new titles entering an already crowded market and even the falling birth-rate of the country as a whole. To be complete, the SWOT analysis is then turned on your magazine's rivals and competitors.

Motivation

Information is a prime motivator of people. You must keep your staff informed, but you must also make clear to them what you, and the company, require from them. In the past this information has been provided at their initial interview and never discussed again. Today regular appraisal has become part of most people's working lives. If your company operates such a system, you, as editor, will be doing the appraisals, sometimes in conjunction with section editors.

In a small, busy office, there is never an appropriate moment to tell someone how well they are doing, or, alternatively, to point out a few areas of difficulty. A formal appraisal structure makes that much more likely to happen. It will also be very useful when salaries are discussed, when training becomes available and when you are thinking about reorganising the editorial structure of the magazine.

You need to timetable an hour for each journalist, in a private place where you won't be disturbed. There should then be a frank discussion of both the employee's work and prospects and the more general picture. You may wish to go to the lengths of working through a formal assessment structure, in which the various aspects of the staff member's working life are listed and graded. For a reporter, for instance, these might include knowledge of the subject matter and area; number and usefulness of contacts; determination and ingenuity in pursuit of a story; attitude and demeanour in public; writing style; adherence to deadlines; accuracy, and so on. For a sub-editor they would be different, including speed, accuracy, creative flair, meticulousness, and so on. It might be a good idea to issue the journalist with a list of the areas to be discussed in advance of the meeting, so that he or she can feel prepared. You should also make sure you find something to praise so that the journalist leaves the appraisal feeling it has been worthwhile.

You should know what your staff would like to be doing and attempt to help them in that direction. Unfortunately, however, their ambitions may not accord either with their aptitudes or with what you require from them. In that case, you should refrain from saying 'I'll see what I can do', which will lead only to disappointment. If what they wish to achieve is really impossible it is better that they find out sooner than later.

Training should be treated as a reward, and never as a punishment. Not only is that unfair to everyone else on the course, it sends completely the wrong message to other members of staff. Training is the key to a flexible, enthusiastic workforce and should be wholeheartedly embraced by all parties, including yourself. It is particularly important to let people see that training leads to personal success. The sequence of training followed by promotion is a great motivator.

A sense of mission can itself be a motivator, but there are no short cuts. If people genuinely love the magazine and want to see it triumph over its competitors that will find expression through their work. But it is difficult to motivate people who are either at the top or at the bottom of the market: in the one case, all the battles have been won; in the other, they seem unwinnable. Motivation depends upon the conduct of the company towards its employees. It will not work if people feel frightened, cowed or put-upon. There are times when every editor has to play the heavy, but absolute fairness needs to be maintained.

Most people work better with clearly defined goals. People need to be given investment in their work. The by-line is the obvious motivating factor here, especially for newcomers. Designs which seek to bury by-lines in the gutter do no favours to either writers or readers, who like to know whose words they are reading. Sub-editors cannot be motivated in the same way, but editors can do what they can by singling out people's headlines and standfirsts for public praise. On the other side of the coin, however, problems and complaints arising from copy should be recorded and referred back to those handling the material for explanation. This is particularly the case with inaccuracies, spelling mistakes and proof-reading failures.

It is as well to share your own goals with your staff. The circulation figures are the obvious focus of editorial attention (except on controlled-circulation magazines) and need to be discussed on a regular basis. The improvement of circulation needs to be made everyone's concern, and real-istic targets and deadlines need to be established. Where a bonus scheme exists, the obvious thing to tie it to is circulation. This may cause distor-tions at times, when, for instance, advertising income rises but circulation stays the same, but it is the only area in which journalists have a direct influence.

Increasingly, journalists' wages are negotiated on an individual basis rather than collectively, which makes it possible for you to motivate in the most direct way. Here your painstakingly collected assessments can be a help. But mostly your freedom of action in this respect will be influenced by two factors: the going rate for the job, and the cash limit imposed upon you by your budget. Gross inequities between people doing approximately the same jobs are wrong and can be dangerous if there is a sex discrimination aspect. Often there will come a situation in which your only option is to explain to your staff member that his or her aspirations are not realistic. You can point out that improvements can be made by training and promo-tion, but you must accept that there is the possibility of losing the person if your rates are not broadly on a level with those of other employers.

Delegation

It is in everybody's interest that you delegate. Your staff need to take re-sponsibility for their own areas: to study other people's magazines to see what needs doing and to set about it, to deal intelligently with readers and freelances, and so on. Your staff will benefit by taking an active part in the whole process, and showing initiative, rather than simply waiting for you to dish them out work. You will be able to manage the magazine properly. The one exception to this general principle is complaints from those written about. It is as well to insist that these are dealt with at the highest level early on, for legal reasons. You need a well-oiled machine to ensure that anything that could be legally tricky is immediately referred up. *Ad hoc* solutions designed to mollify angry interviewees and story subjects can often prove unexpectedly costly.

Again, it is the editor's job to be responsible for everything rather than anything specific: you need to make sure that the whole production process can carry on without you. You must be absolutely involved in it, but in an intelligent way. In a larger magazine you should ensure that you have a deputy capable of making serious editorial decisions. In order for that to work you must give that person the authority to do the job, so it is essential that you have the right person in the post and that you share a vision of the magazine and its readers.

Delegating in this way gives you time to take a more strategic role, but it is also important in motivating the individuals you have chosen, giving them the experience they need in handling responsibility. The crux comes when you realise that the person to whom you have delegated is actually better than you are at the task in question. Accepting that marks your maturity as a manager. Delegation is the only way to deal with an ever-increasing spread of responsibilities. It does not represent a dilution of your power: the people to whom you delegate must be answerable to you.

There are things which cannot and must not be delegated. You must not delegate anything confidential, especially anything personal which has been disclosed to you in confidence. You must handle disciplinary matters yourself. And it is not done to delegate those tasks you don't like doing: that will immediately be spotted and will do nothing for your reputation. You must also ensure that you hand over only those tasks you know can be handled by the person to whom you have delegated them. If he or she gets into difficulties, that will represent a failure for both of you, but ultimately it is your responsibility for delegating unwisely.

Negotiation

All management is a series of negotiations, and editing a magazine is no exception. You will constantly want people to do things. It seems obvious, but the best way of achieving that is to know exactly what you want and to ask them, clearly and directly. The words 'please' and 'thank you' come to mind. It is important, bearing in mind our 'team coach' model of editorship, to make requests rather than give orders.

You must ensure that you make a good case. At the very least, what you want must make sense. Sometimes you will have to offer some kind of bargain: if you do this, I will do that. In negotiations with outside parties, particularly freelances, it is important that both sides come away feeling that they have gained something. One other tactic is simple persistence. Ask often enough if the task has been done and it will usually get done. You should act on the assumption that it has been: this will put the onus of explanation or excuse on the person to whom the task has been handed.

In the case of more formal negotiations, there are other matters you have to think about. You need to demonstrate to the other party that you have the power to make the decision, and you need to consider for yourself what are the best and worst positions you can achieve or settle for. It is wise to consider whether you have any concessions you can offer, as well as thinking through what the other party is likely to want. Remember that at the end both parties should come away feeling that something has been achieved: compromise is the essence of negotiation.

TRAINING

It used to be the case that training was something you did at the start of your career, if at all. Now, though, it is generally accepted that magazine journalists will need training at intervals throughout their careers. The Government's National Vocational Qualifications system is designed in recognition of that. That NVQs are measures of competence in different aspects of magazine journalism that can be achieved at any age and at any stage in a journalist's career. They operate across the industry.

There are five NVQs, covering news reporting, feature writing, subbing, subbing with layout and magazine design. Journalists aiming to acquire any one of these qualifications must, however, receive basic training across the whole range of journalistic skills. Most of the training and assessment is designed to be done in-house, with overall standards set by the Periodicals Training Council and the whole scheme administered by the Royal Society for Arts and Sciences. Candidates produce written evidence of their competence in particular skills, and this is supervised by the assessor. As each unit in the scheme is completed, candidates receive a certificate: they receive the full award on completion of all the units.

It remains to be seen how this scheme fares. A requirement for NVQs has yet to become common in job advertisements, which was one of the scheme's intentions. Nonetheless, any training initiative drawn up by you should bear in mind the NVQ system.

Training can be a significant cost. In the case of external training you have both to pay for the training itself and to make up for the loss of the staff member concerned while the training is going on. This is especially difficult for small magazines, which are less able to cope with the temporary loss of members of the editorial team.

Before embarking on any kind of staff training, it is important to assess what it is intended to achieve. Training is important both for the magazine and for the individual journalists. You need to know, for instance, that all the essential skills are contained within your team, so that a sudden absence doesn't leave you in the lurch. But training should only go to those who are willing and able to benefit from it, something that should become clear in appraisals if it is not apparent all the time.

In practice, most training, especially for junior staff, takes the form it always has. It is called 'sitting by Nellie', or 'learning by doing'. The correct name for this is 'supervised practice', and it is popular because it costs nothing, while allowing the trainee still to be productive. It does, however, require a lot from the trainee's colleagues, who may be excellent at their jobs but less so at explaining how they are done. They may not be open to question and may be more interested in correcting the trainee's work to make use of it than in explaining why it is wrong. It also tends only to inculcate the habits, good and bad, of a particular magazine.

In a larger organisation these problems can be somewhat reduced by moving trainees around between publications. This may, indeed, be the only way of allowing them to acquire the necessary range of skills. Such a system may need considerable negotiation between editors. Fairness demands that staff who are exchanged in this way are properly briefed and equipped, and arrangements need to be made to ensure that the trainees are properly appraised during the attachment.

More formal in-house training, in which work stops for the duration of the course rather than being combined with it, can also be beneficial. As an editor, you should expect to take some role in the training of your own staff, whether in a formal session or in individual supervision and coaching. But you should also extend this coaching ethos down through your team. It should be natural for people to expect to share their skills and insights with those working with them. But this kind of training needs planning if it is not to be merely a cut-price substitute for the real thing.

External training can be expensive, but it has several advantages. For a start, an atmosphere of learning is created and there are no interruptions and distractions. Professional training organisations will have suitable premises and equipment. They can introduce a wider range of ideas and techniques than are often found in-house, where inspiration tends to be drawn from the same pool. In an outside training setting, beginners especially will be freer to experiment and make mistakes. At the same time, outside trainers can say what they really think about a trainee's work without having to worry about the effects of the discussion on normal working life.

On the other hand, you must ensure that there is a good match between the training offered and what you feel is required. In particular, you should examine the qualifications and track record of the trainer. After any such training has taken place, the trainee should be asked to evaluate what he or she has been taught.

The single most important thing you can do as an editor is to promote an atmosphere in which everyone expects both to learn new skills and to pass on what they already know to others. This you can do by example, attending specialist courses when possible and sharing your knowledge with less experienced members of staff.

Companies which take a particular interest in training can apply for certification under the Government's Investors in People programme. In return for a demonstrable commitment to training throughout your organisation, monitored by your local Training and Enterprise Council (Local Enterprise Company in Scotland), you can display the scheme's logo on your job advertising as a kind of guarantee of your progressive attitudes.

HEALTH AND SAFETY

There is one further side to your role as a manager of people, and that is your responsibility in matters of health and safety at work. You are directly responsible for the well-being of those who work under you while they are at work, as well as any visitors and freelances working in your offices. Under the 1974 Health and Safety at Work Act, any firm with more than five employees must have a formal, written health and safety policy, which may allocate you certain duties. You should know who is your department's first aider, where the first-aid box is kept, and procedures in the event of fires and accidents.

As the supervisor of people working on screen you need to pay particular attention to the equipment they are using and the way they are using it. There is a detailed government directive, under the Health and Safety at Work Act, on what is quaintly called 'display screen equipment', but adherence to that alone is not enough to stop people falling prey to pains in the arms, hands and neck associated with working on computers.

Usually called 'Repetitive Strain Injury' or 'Upper Limb Disorder', this can have a variety of causes and outcomes: in serious cases it can be crippling. The condition seems to be directly related to stress. Staff should be regularly reminded about posture and the need to take frequent breaks, getting up from the keyboard at least once every thirty minutes. These seem to be the best ways yet devised of preventing RSI from becoming a problem. The approved posture requires the person typing to sit with feet flat on the ground and thighs and forearms parallel to the floor. Chairs should be fully adjustable to make this possible.

Anyone complaining of pains of this sort should be advised to seek medical advice at the earliest opportunity. They should certainly not be ignored or ridiculed. Ensuring they seek early treatment is the company's best policy to avoid more serious and expensive problems later on. Appropriately, the Internet is a particularly rich source of information on the subject of RSI and other upper-limb disorders. Try http://www.demon.co.uk/rsi/ to start.

BEING A MANAGER

If you are to manage your team with any degree of efficiency, you must get to grips quickly with the parts of the job that will cause you the most problems. These are unlikely to be the editorial aspects. You have been given the job, after all, because of your editorial abilities.

Decision-making is one problem area, but it needs to be approached systematically until it becomes second nature. One of the worst things about starting as an editor is that people expect decisions on everything, all the time. Later, once you have established a proper delegated structure, at least on a big magazine, the pressure will ease, but until then you have to be prepared to make decisions quickly, some of which will be wrong. Once you've admitted that, to yourself and others, things get easier. Occupying the editor's chair is not a short cut to omniscience.

It can help to take things logically: to ensure that you are only dealing with one problem at a time, rather than several. Having narrowed things down, ask yourself what extra information you might need to take an informed decision. Once you have that information, you can consider a handful of alternatives and speculate on the likely outcome of each. Then make your choice. There can be few editors who have not, in their time, resorted to the time-honoured device of a list of pros and cons, not to make the decision for them, but to clarify it.

Of course, one factor that makes decision-making very much harder is a lack of time. There are some schools of thought which say, boldly, that 'time management' *is* management. Unfortunately, that doesn't help you much on a practical level. What you must do is cut through the thickets of obligation and demand placed upon you and find room to think, since that, ultimately, is what you are paid to do. Various things will eat into your time. Worrying is one, and procrastination is another. Procrastination is often caused by the fear of making a wrong decision, and you must fight it by setting yourself firm deadlines for action and sticking to them.

You must set aside thinking time and guard yourself against interruptions. While it is a noble ideal to say that 'my door is always open' you will have only yourself to blame if people take that as an open invitation to drop in and pass the time of day. A simple system should be devised to indicate when you are available for discussion and when not, as simple as leaving your door open when you are available and keeping it shut otherwise. There is a temptation here to keep your door shut longer than is absolutely necessary, but it should be resisted.

A better solution is to set aside a time each day specifically for brief discussion on subjects close to people's hearts. Obviously this doesn't preclude people calling on you when something flares up, but it may have the effect of discouraging random interruptions. With luck, people will adapt to your routine. You want to be approachable, but you also want to be able to do your job, and ultimately you will not be judged by how approachable you are.

If you are in the position of having an assistant or secretary, even one you share, you should make the most of the privilege. Your secretary must be entrusted with the bulk of your routine post after the first few weeks, distributing it around the office, filing it or binning it according to a pattern you agree. Your assistant can also help you by keeping a diary for you, but you must ensure that your own pocket diary is synchronised with the main diary every day. Remember that your diary is not only a record of appointments and meetings: it can also be a device for jogging your memory about ideas and schemes to consider at various dates in the future.

An efficient system for taking messages must be organised. The best, but most costly, system is to use a special book which combines a permanent record with a sticky note that can be attached to desk or telephone. You may be able to improvise your own system, of course, but you must not let messages be stored on bits of paper and lost: it is grossly discourteous to those trying to speak to you. At the very least, there should be some kind of log book to record incoming calls.

Time management itself is much discussed but most systems seem to come down in the end to the keeping of lists. If your first impression is that all your time is used up before you start, try to keep a log of how you are spending your days and work back from that to find where the time goes. Beyond that, draw up a list of tasks and, with the help of a diary and calendar, see how you can allocate time to them.

Another well-known scheme is the 'to do' list. This involves starting the day with a list of tasks and allocating them an order of priority, starting with 1 and working down to 10. As one job is done, the priority of the others can be changed. If you persuade someone else to take on one of your jobs, so much the better. At the end of the day, anything left has to be carried over to tomorrow's list. This is such a simple system that it hardly merits further explanation, but if you are a computer enthusiast you can get various computer programs that will do the reordering for you as well as fitting in regular appointments and producing a schedule. Some may feel this is using a sledgehammer to crack a nut, but unlike paper lists, computer lists don't get thrown away or lost under piles of junk-mail.

Paperwork is another problem area. As everyone knows, the paperless office never materialised. Again, there are systems galore, but most people will manage with some variant on the traditional system of three trays: in, out and pending. Of course, this usually breaks down within days. Things move from the in tray to the pending tray and stay there indefinitely. It is important that this doesn't happen. Anything that is not being used today should not be on your desk at all. Store it somewhere else. You will need a flat surface on which to examine proofs, do flat-plans and all the rest. You should endeavour to keep it clear.

These matters are, of course, not what being an editor is all about, but they are germane to the task of management. New managers need all the systems they can establish if they are not to fall into difficulties. You will, in any case, have your work cut out trying to avoid the usual mistakes of new managers: trying to be popular with those you are supposed to be managing, having favourites, opening up and discussing your personal problems with your staff, telling everyone exactly how their jobs should be done by reference to your own glorious past, and attacking those above you in the pecking order in an attempt to curry favour with those below you. All of these are mistakes, but you will be lucky is you don't fall prey to at least one of them, if only initially. Be aware, however, that patterns established at the beginning of your editorship can be difficult to displace later.

PRODUCING A BLUEPRINT FOR SUCCESS

Sometimes an editor can lead a magazine by sheer force of personality, disregarding all procedures and rules and scorning the idea of putting anything on paper. In extreme cases, this charisma is enough to keep the magazine on track even when the editor is absent, or once the editor has departed.

Most editors, though, would do well to give a modicum of attention to the question of what happens when they are not there or what would happen if they fell under a bus.

In the first instance, there should be, if not a deputy, someone who is sufficiently involved in future planning to ensure that the first few issues can be put together as normal. At the same time, systems need to be in place to ensure that the normal routine progress of the magazine continues: freelances must still be paid, deadlines met, planning meetings held, and so on. More than that, though, it is a good idea for the central focus and direction of the magazine to survive intact until someone makes a sensible, logical and well-researched decision to change it.

For these reasons, it is as well to consider drawing up an editorial blueprint. This should not be a strait-jacket inhibiting creativity, but a guide to the magazine's established identity.

Such a blueprint document should start with a statement of what the magazine is intended to be and whom it is intended to reach, backed up by the highlights of your research. It can go on from that to include something about staffing and areas of responsibility and the usual editorial procedures and timetable. Details of essential outside contractors, for instance your colour house and/or typesetters, should be included.

You might also include some indication of a typical running order and a list of regular features, with some guidelines as to how material should be written. Your blueprint could also incorporate a brief style sheet and some sort of design manual, which will even include details of the colour palette that has been found to work with your readers. Round off the package with a couple of finished issues with which you feel particularly happy.

This blueprint should, theoretically, be so comprehensive as to allow a set of complete strangers to reconstruct a magazine that is recognisably yours in your absence. It should not inhibit anyone's creativity, but it should focus it. At the same time, the document must not be allowed to linger on indefinitely. Every couple of years it needs to be compared to the realities of the market and remodelled accordingly.

FURTHER READING

ACAS (1977) *Code of Practice 1: Disciplinary Practice and Procedures in Employment*, London: HMSO.
Croner's Reference Book for Employers, New Malden, UK: Croner.

Display Screen Equipment Work (1992) Health and Safety Executive Guidance Notes L26, London: HMSO.

Garratt, Sally (1994) *Manage Your Time*, London: Harper Collins.

Goodworth, Clive T. (1987) *The Secrets of Successful Hiring and Firing*, London: Heinemann.

Handy, Charles (1995) *Beyond Certainty*, London: Hutchinson.

Hicks, Winford (ed.) (1992) *Training for Periodical Journalism*, London: Periodicals Training Council.

Lanz, Karen (1988) *Employing and Managing People*, London: Pitman.

Thornely, Nick and Lees, Dan (1994) *Moving up to Management*, London: Arrow.

Waud, Christopher (1993) *The Daily Mail Guide to Employment Law*, London: Michael O'Mara Books.

Chapter 4

The editor and money

BUSINESS AND THE EDITORIAL TEAM

The language of management has always been money. When you become an editor you will be expected, probably for the first time in your career, to give detailed attention to the financial implications of your work. It is easy to be overwhelmed by this, especially given that most of your new colleagues in management will have more experience in such matters.

You should appreciate, however, as should everyone else, that you are not employed for your financial expertise. No editor ever gained a reader or won an award by keeping to a budget. Money is just the tool you use to achieve your editorial ends: it is not, for you, an end in itself.

Of course, financial control is symbolic of general editorial order. You should extend your new-found budgetary consciousness to your editorial colleagues. Until they become aware of costs, they will be at the mercy of those who already are. And the delegation of responsibility includes the delegation of financial responsibilities. Allowing individual sections and section editors to help draw up and manage their own budgets is a necessary part of the process of freeing them to use their own initiative.

Companies vary in the way they approach the question of budgeting. In some instances, editors will be brought into the annual budgeting process and invited to estimate their costs for the coming year. In others they will simply be given a series of cash figures and told not to exceed them. In some cases, the whole financial responsibility will be handled by someone else, leaving the editor in the dark. This might have superficial attractions to a busy editor but can be very dangerous.

PUBLICATION BUDGETS

The editorial budget forms only a small part of the whole budgeting arrangements of the magazine, and editors should make an effort to understand all the budgets they are allowed to see, asking for advice from the management's accountant where necessary.

Technically, a 'budget' is a statement of *allocated* income and expenditure for any given period. A statement of *projected* income and expenditure is properly known as a 'budget forecast'. In practice, people use the word budget for both.

A budget forecast will include *revenue*, which means income earned, and 'expenses', which means costs incurred. In both cases, these are recorded at the point at which the purchase or sale is made, rather than at the point at which the money changes hands.

A 'cash-flow' forecast, on the other hand, is built around income received, which means cash coming in, and costs paid, which means cash going out. A cash-flow forecast includes the bank balance. Superficially, however, a cash-flow forecast and a budget forecast will look the same. There will be a series of columns side by side across the page, one for each month. And there will be a series of rows, down the page, detailing each significant item of expenditure or income.

A budget forecast is used for establishing and subsequently monitoring spending limits; planning spending and income; establishing the level of sales that will cover overheads; making an estimate of profitability; analysing the relationship between revenue and expenditure; identifying areas for cost reduction, and so on.

A cash-flow forecast is used for more immediate purposes, for instance ensuring that cash covers expenditure, and planning any necessary borrowing.

If yours is a department which does not generate income, which is the case with editorial departments, you will have what is called a 'costs only' departmental budget, which will show how much you will be spending and when during the year ahead. Its purpose is simply to allow you to compare your actual spending with that predicted and to ensure that you do not exceed the sums allocated to your department in the company's overall budget.

The overall company budgets are drawn up early, on the basis of projected sales, both of copies and advertising, and an assessment of the strength of the market. Individual departments submit their budget forecasts, based on an assessment of what they expect to spend in each month, and these are then consolidated into the overall budget, with some adjustments. Eventually each department is be awarded a final budget with definite targets for each month's expenditure, or, in the case of an income-generating department, revenue. Throughout the year, any 'variance' from those targets will be recorded.

It is as well for editors to appreciate in broad terms how the full-scale budgets work before grappling with the minutiae of their own costs. The process starts with the publication's original marketing plan, which dictates such matters as frequency, quality of paper, binding method, staffing, likely income and editorial costs. Drawing up a budget usually starts with revenue.

Calculating advertising revenue is complicated by such matters as series discounts, but eventually an average yield per page of display or classified advertising is arrived at, and this is multiplied by the number of such advertising pages in each issue. If the magazine is weekly, this information has to be considered in conjunction with a calendar, since some months will include five issues and others only four.

From this, the crucial advertising/editorial ratio is drawn up. The object is to find the optimum ratio to provide maximum profit for the publisher without destroying the magazine's value to readers. The ratio can either be left as a ratio (for instance 60:40, meaning that a 100-page issue will contain sixty advertising pages and forty editorial pages) or turned into a percentage: 60 per cent in this case. When these calculations give rise to actual issue sizes they must take account of the fact that the number of pages in an issue must always be divisible by four, because of the binding process. There must also be an indication of minimum permissible pagination. The ratio need not be observed in every issue, but over the year it should average out. As an editor, you will need to know the projected advertising/editorial ratio and your total number of editorial pages in a year in order to calculate staffing and freelance costs.

The budget forecast's assessment of revenue will also include an estimate of circulation, which will be multiplied by income per copy to produce a figure for circulation revenue: obviously projected unsold returns and free copies must be deducted from that.

Then there are costs. 'Overhead' costs (or 'indirect' costs) are those which are not directly related to the magazine's actual production. They include rent, rates, heating, lighting, water, equipment maintenance and the wages of any staff not directly on the magazine's payroll. Traditionally these have not appeared in detail on an individual magazine's accounts and are not under the control of the individual publisher. They are not taken into account when the magazine's profitability is being assessed. Increasingly, however, the vogue for 'internal accounting' has seen these costs being allocated to individual magazines and appearing on accounts, usually as a single line to be deducted from the gross profit figure.

More relevant, in most cases, are the 'fixed' direct costs: these are incurred in the magazine production process but are not intimately related to the number of issues produced. They include salaries, national insurance and employer's pension contributions; travel and entertaining; motor car costs; recruitment and training; and all the costs of administration, including stationery, telephones, computer costs and the purchase of newspapers and magazines.

'Variable' direct costs are those which are the direct result of producing the magazine: they vary with the circulation and with the pagination of individual issues. They include production costs: colour-house origination, any typesetting, printing, binding and finishing. Distribution costs, especially for subscription copies, are included here. The relevant editorial costs are contributors' payments and photographs and illustrations.

Once revenue and costs are assessed, the calculations begin. The 'gross margin' is the difference between revenue and variable costs in a given period. When fixed costs are subtracted, a figure called 'gross publication profit' is determined, and it is that which usually determines the health or otherwise of the magazine. If overheads are subtracted, some kind of net profit figure becomes available, but here the figures are often only notional because of the arbitrary way in which overheads are divided among a group of magazines.

THE EDITORIAL BUDGET

If no previous budget exists, the task of drawing up an editorial budget from scratch is a rather daunting one, particularly for editors with no previous financial or business experience. Even if someone else has done the task before, however, it can sometimes be worth taking a blank sheet of paper (a computer spreadsheet, in practice) and going through the process from scratch.

Your starting point needs to be staff, and the disposition of staff, since this is where most of your spending will take place. A look at the calendar for the year ahead is a start: is yours a seasonal magazine, shrinking back to nothing in the summer? Are there major events that have to be covered in detail? The question is whether these variations are best accommodated by the hire of temporary freelance help or whether they can be built into your staffing arrangements.

Increasingly the tendency is for magazines to be run on the bare minimum of staffing, with the great bulk of editorial matter provided by freelances. The reason for this is that freelances can be taken on and dropped at will, with no complications. But there are disadvantages. Freelances are often skilful and enthusiastic, but they are not really part of your team. It is wrong to expect them to have a deep loyalty to a magazine. They will do their work, probably very well, but cannot make a contribution beyond that. It is wrong to expect them to play a part in your long-term planning.

They can also be costly, especially if you are hoping to make use of their work in ways beyond the immediately obvious, for instance in the electronic media. Staff receive all manner of benefits over and above simple security, and in return they forfeit their copyright in material produced as part of their normal work. Freelances retain their copyright unless you actually buy out that right, and if you do you should expect to pay for it: this is currently an area of great controversy.

Assessing the staffing of a magazine is not simple. The output of creative individuals cannot be measured like that of machinery. Nonetheless, you can start by working out the total number of pages required and working back from that. A look at other magazines in your market will give you an idea how many staff they use and how many pages they process between them. Divide the number of editorial pages by the number of journalists and you get a crude idea of their output per person. Do the same with your projected number of editorial pages and you can get an idea of overall staffing.

Bear in mind, however, that you must compare like with like. Your publication may be intended to be more serious and authoritative, led by news and investigations. These things demand experienced and expensive staff. On the other hand, the crude page-per-journalist ratio can be useful in assessing your magazine's cost-effectiveness over a period. Magazine staffs have a tendency to grow over time, and looking at that ratio is one way of keeping track.

You must make allowances, also, for staff absence. Your magazine may run perfectly on the minimal staffing you first consider, but remember that each member of staff will take holidays, have time for training and can expect a period of illness. Individuals can be replaced by freelances, but it might be better to have an extra person at first.

In drawing up your ideal staffing plan you need to set wage levels appropriately, by keeping track of what similar staff in other companies are paid: you must expect to pay no more than the going rate. After a period, annual increases and merit awards to individuals may push your salaries out of alignment with what is paid in the wider world: but the market should always be your guide.

Bear in mind, also, that simple wages are not your only staff cost. Pension contributions to staff will also have to be included in your budget document, as well as any bonuses. Expenses incurred by your staff will be your responsibility and will need to be examined to ensure that they are both genuine and reasonable. Under this broad heading also come their travel expenses. Bear in mind that at particular times of the year these may become much more significant: there may be a conference season which you will expect to cover.

Still in the area of fixed costs, you may be expected to make an assessment of likely training and recruitment costs. Training organisations will supply you with their prices and it is simply a case of working out how much outside training per member of staff, and at what level, you are likely to permit.

After fixed costs come variable costs. At the top of the list here are contributors' payments. An assessment of the rates paid by rival publishers will indicate in broad terms what you will have to pay per 1,000 words, but it is worth talking to your ideal freelances to see that this is broadly in line with their expectations. Your designer should be able to give you exact word-counts for various types of feature, enabling you to draw up an estimated word count per issue and hence per page. The final result should be a cost per page for words, which can be multiplied back up to give you costs per issue, per month and per year.

The same process can be undertaken with photography and illustration. Picture libraries will quote you prices for using stock material, depending on your projected circulation and the size at which you are using it. If you plan to use commissioned photography, and you probably will, you need to discuss prices with the type of photographers you are likely to be using. Then you can work out the likely balance of commissioned and stock photography in an average issue and arrive, once again, at a cost per page for visual material.

If you are taking charge of an established magazine, of course, all this material should be at hand. There may be priced issues, with the costs of individual features and photographs marked in. There may be breakdowns of spending on freelance material arranged by issue. At the very least, there will be the individual writers' and photographers' invoices, but it is to be hoped that more accessible financial records have been kept. If not, you must institute them, starting with an issue-by-issue breakdown of what was spent and where it went.

Some magazines will place variable costs associated with production on the editor's budget, which can make sense; in general, you should only be accountable for those figures which you can definitely influence. Certain production costs clearly come into that category, however. Making economical and sensible use of your colour house or typesetters is one example. The advent of sophisticated on-screen colour manipulation technology means it is always possible to 'improve' a cover photograph. This can be extremely expensive, so it is important that any such costs are budgeted for and recorded. Other editorial initiatives may have production-cost implications: the use of additional ink colours in cover printing, for instance, or the inclusion of inserts or extra supplements. Any such actions must be budgeted for, including all the costs of their creation and production.

Once you have established with your publisher or your management accountant precisely which items you will be responsible for, it is simply a question of drawing up a simple budget grid. The months of the year run across the page, your individual cost items run down. As stated above, if your magazine is a weekly, some months will include more issues than others, so it will not be good enough simply to include the same figure for each month. Remember you are predicting when costs will be incurred, not when the bills will be paid. Any seasonal differences must be accounted for: for instance, if you always produce a summer special at the start of the holiday season, the costs for that must be included in the appropriate month. If you will need to employ extra freelance sub-editors to produce your Christmas double issue, that must be included too. If you expect an across-the-board pay settlement in April, subsequent salary figures will need to be increased, and the same goes for contributors' payments.

You submit your budget forecast to a higher authority, and it returns, usually with some amendments, as an actual budget with allotted spending limits. From now on, you need to keep a tally of your expenditure as you proceed and compare it with the budget you have been allocated. You might also think it is a good idea to keep your original budget forecast if there is a wild disparity between what you asked for and what you were given.

EDITORIAL AS A COST

Wages/bonuses/expenses

The arrival of a new editor is often seen as a signal for members of staff to ask for more money. You must resist this initial onslaught, since you are in no position to establish the value of the contribution made by these individuals until you have had a chance to see how things work in practice. But they will probably persist, and then you will have to make a real assessment of the situation.

When setting salary levels, there are several factors to take into account. The first, and most important, is what the company can afford. If you are given responsibility for setting your journalists' pay levels you will also be given guidance on the economic constraints within which such awards can be made. The wage bill will be included within the year's budget. In most magazines, it is second in magnitude only to the cost of printing and paper.

You should also consider the going rate for the job in the outside world. This may well be the most important factor in your decision. It is foolish to pay much below the market rate unless you are sure that the opportunities outside are strictly limited or unless you want to provoke the existing staff into leaving. It is also foolish to pay too much. Many employers place themselves in this position by becoming convinced that a certain member of the journalistic staff is irreplaceable. You can find what other people are paying by studying advertisements, consulting employment agencies or headhunters, or simply by asking other editors you know.

You should bear in mind the future shape of the job market. If a new publication is threatened in precisely your area, you must ensure you pay enough to discourage anyone from making a move for the money: they may still want to move, for the challenge, but there is nothing much you can do about that. Particular skills are also in demand at times: this is especially the case in times of technological change. The first people to master desktop publishing were able to cash in on their skills, and the same is true of those who write World Wide Web pages and develop CD-ROM material.

Pay is a factor in motivation, of course. As well as the effect on the individual concerned, who may be demoralised by being paid below the market rate, there is the effect on colleagues to consider. If you choose to pay one person more than others with the same apparent skills and responsibilities, you should have a good reason and be prepared for a great deal of resentment on the part of the others.

In general, pay increases should be used to recognise initiative and the taking of greater responsibility. Increases for simply staying in the same place as another year passes are no longer considered a good thing in most management circles, although your company may have a long-standing policy on this matter. It can be argued that the traditional annual increment rewards loyalty, but it also rewards inertia. An exception might be made, however, for the long-serving news editor or chief sub-editor whose experience is directly to the benefit of the magazine. But even then that experience should really be translated into action, perhaps through taking responsibility for training or the production of some kind of supplement.

In this context, it is worth considering bonus schemes. There is no obvious way of creating an incentive scheme linked to individual production, since magazine journalism is such a collaborative process, but there are ways of linking rewards to output of pages or rises in circulation.

A good bonus scheme counts as a fringe benefit. There are a whole range of others, from the provision of free tea and coffee to share options, pension contributions and private medicine. It is naive to assume, however, that the presence of a range of fringe benefits will ever compensate for a poor basic salary. Journalists tend to measure themselves by their salaries: fringe benefits are not really considered, especially by those changing jobs.

When you join a new organisation, one aspect you must quickly get to grips with is the expenses culture. In some organisations, claims are checked with a high degree of rigour. In others, a certain laxness is traditional, and your efforts to ensure that certain lunches did indeed take place will be much resented. The real answer is to ensure from the start that your expectations are clear and consistently applied. All expenses claims should be correctly detailed, on the right form, and accompanied by appropriate receipts. Point out to your staff that the Inland Revenue is likely to consider that anything not correctly detailed and verified is taxable.

Buying copyright material

The purchase of copyright material, whether written, photographic or illustrative, has recently become a much more contentious issue. In the past, negotiation between editors and freelance writers, particularly, has rarely involved more than a brief chat about the price and the delivery date. Increasingly publishers are interested in buying much more extensive rights than has previously been considered necessary. The standard right acquired, by default, when no discussion takes place, is First British Serial Right. This allows the publisher the first use of that item in magazine form within Britain (including Northern Ireland). If you are publishing in Eire, as is common, that should be made clear.

Publishers are increasingly trying to acquire further rights, to reuse the material in printed or electronic form, if possible without further payment.

The result is that everything now has to be negotiated. You must explicitly point out, in writing, that you wish to purchase *all rights* in the material. Many freelances will baulk at this, before raising their price or declining to do business at all.

Some editors omit to discuss this question at the commissioning stage, letting the writer find out about it when the commissioning form arrives or, more reprehensibly, once the work has been done. In this latter case, writers receive a cheque with a wording on the back which they are expected to sign before payment is issued. The signature assigns their copyright. They don't have to sign, of course, but since they have already done the work most will choose to. This is a shoddy practice and you may not wish to go along with it.

Aside from considering the copyright issues, editors should ensure that they have an infallible system for ensuring that freelances are paid on time. There should be a commissioning form, with copies going to the writer and the magazine's accounts department as well as staying with the commissioning editor.

Buying copyright material is a negotiating skill like any other. Your ability to acquire material may be severely limited by budgetary constraints, but you can sometimes find ways around that. The fee you propose for a single piece or picture may be too low, but you can sometimes assist matters by commissioning several additional pieces or pictures at the same time. The writer or photographer may take the view that it is better to get a lot of work at a lower rate than a small amount at a high rate. Various sweeteners can be offered, in the same spirit: an interesting trip, an invitation to lunch, the use of your research facilities, and so on.

Other costs

Many of the decisions you make as an editor will have cost implications. This is particularly true in the case of new launches, where a great deal of money can be saved by careful choice of magazine format and arranging your press schedules to use your printers' slow periods. Once the magazine is up and running, efficient production at the editorial end is the best way of keeping costs to a minimum. Late pages, missing page elements, wrongly configured disks, font problems, mislaid transparencies and inaccurate flat-planning can all cause serious production delays and costs.

Beyond that, your attitude to costs needs to be the same as that of any modern manager: you must always be looking for ways to keep them to a minimum, whether through a regime of sensible telephone use, the frugal use of stationery or the most minute scrutiny of expenses claims. You should try to spend money on the things that the readers will appreciate: better photography and writing.

EDITORIAL AND INCOME GENERATION

Editorial is usually seen as simply a cost to the publisher: your budget is a 'cost-only' budget, for instance. But as editor you have the potential to play a role in the generation of income in various ways.

News-stand and subscription initiatives

The most obvious way you can play a part in this process is by doing what you can to assist in circulation-building and subscription-building exercises. No editor willingly produces unpopular covers, but there are times when creating an attention-grabbing cover package, with an appealing picture and straightforward coverlines, gets pushed down your list of priorities. This must not happen. Strong bookstall sales will guarantee you the respect and independence you need to achieve your other aims. If you are in the habit of producing posters and press advertisements to promote your issues, you should oversee their production: in too many magazine houses this is a task of such low status that it is deputed to a junior designer to dash off.

Subscriptions are not always central to the British way of selling magazines, unlike in the United States for example. But they can be encouraged by special offers. These should be bold, and in keeping with the magazine's image. A price reduction is the most obvious approach, but other magazines offer free gifts of various sorts. It is essential that any gifts are in keeping with your view of who the readers are, both for the sake of effectiveness and for their effect on the magazine's image. Subscriptions have not been a strong area in British magazines, but in future, because of the direct access they offer to the readers, they may become more important. That will certainly be the case if you are trying to market new forms of editorial product, for instance electronic magazines.

The editor and the advertising department

There is no more vexed issue than the relationship between the editor and the advertising department. A certain distance is desirable if the independence and integrity of the editorial department is to be maintained. As a new editor it is for you to establish the ground rules.

This is not, usually, a moral or ethical question. It is more a matter of using your skills to their best advantage. You should be concentrating on producing the best possible magazine for people to advertise in rather than going round trying to persuade people to advertise in the magazine as it exists. There are exceptions to this, in the case of special new supplements or other products with a strong editorial component, when you should be involved from the start. But you should not be a part of the routine process of selling advertising.

To advertisers spending large sums of money with an organisation it can seem terribly harsh when this is not reciprocated in terms of editorial coverage, or when such editorial coverage as they receive seems unfavourable. Your own advertising colleagues may mistakenly foster the belief in advertisers that they have some influence over the magazine's editorial content. They should not be given any encouragement in this. On the other hand, your advertising sales people may often have closer contact with the industry, day to day, than your staff do. They sometimes come up with stories. But it is for you and your editorial staff to assess the merits of what they have to say, differentiating simple 'puff' from genuine story.

As an editor you should watch for excessive closeness between your staff and those of the advertising department if it starts to manifest itself in favours being done. When commercial organisations receive repeated mentions in editorial matter – or, conversely, are missing when perhaps they ought to appear – you should ask yourself whether this is for clear, justifiable reasons.

It should be said that few editors will pass through their careers without at some point or other receiving a threat of the removal of advertising for some slight, whether real or imagined. The only way to deal with this is to treat the advertiser in exactly the same way as you would treat anyone who is written about and is aggrieved. Ensure, in the first instance, that there is no dishonesty or malice in your journalists' work, that the advertiser is indeed being treated fairly. The story concerned must be fair and honest, and it must have been published for good reasons. If an advertiser is criticised it should, of course, be given the opportunity to state its case within the story.

If there is a complaint following publication, the normal means for dealing with such problems should be employed: publication of a letter, factual corrections, and so on. Beyond that, however, the advertiser must be left to think it over and your advertising department to come up with such persuasion as it can muster. Momentary pique aside, companies' advertising strategies are based on hard calculation of your usefulness to them. If nothing has changed in that respect, the advertising will eventually be restored. This may not, however, mollify your own advertising colleagues: it is always as well to remember that they have a personal stake in relationships that are peripheral to you and your editorial staff. Expect a bumpy ride until normal service is resumed.

Besides, sophisticated advertisers, because of their powerful place in their industries, have many more means of influencing the press than crude threat: they will, at various times, offer you all manner of self-serving 'exclusives'. Again, you should judge these on their own merits. Their source does not make them unusable, but neither does it make them as essential as the advertiser or, more likely, its PR company, might think.

'Special features', 'focus features' and 'supplements'

The one area in which editors have been expected to be directly useful to advertising departments is the provision of 'special features', usually labelled 'focus', 'monitor', 'survey' or suchlike. In-house these are known as 'ad-get' features, since that is exactly their purpose.

The process is this. A list of potentially lucrative subject areas is discussed between editor and advertising director. Details of subjects and dates are then distributed to advertisers and suitable feature material commissioned. The material is true editorial matter: the 'ad-get' feature must not be confused with 'advertorial' features. Nonetheless, it is hard to avoid the impression in many cases that this material would not have made it into the magazine on its own merits. That is a failure of editorship: the section or feature may have been designed for the purpose of generating revenue, but that doesn't mean it can be weak. Used properly, this type of feature can be a useful way of giving new writers experience and building up contacts in industry.

In recent years, however, the trend has been for advertisers, especially in the trade press, to seek ways of 'partnership' with magazines that give them more prominence and hence better value than simple advertising. These may take the form of additional sponsored 'supplements', sometimes of dubious editorial merit, or competitions and awards schemes.

It is absolutely essential that the editor take a lead role in these. Far better to find a subject that you would like to cover in supplement form and then seek an advertiser, or advertisers, to back it or sponsor it, than vice versa. This can be a creative area: the connection between the supplement's subject matter and the advertisers need not be close. The advertisers hope to gain a certain kudos by association with the material the supplement includes.

The same considerations operate when an advertiser seeks to sponsor a competition or award scheme. But there are degrees of quality here. A properly organised competition or award scheme is an expensive and diffi-cult proposition. There are several dangers for an editor becoming involved in such a scheme. A farcical outcome can be disastrous to a magazine's reputation for excellence. The advertiser may simply expect endless edit-orial support for a scheme that the editor has had little or nothing to do with organising. And the proliferation of such events, competitions, exhibitions, and so on, may damage the supply of paid-for advertising. Consequently, such propositions from advertising agencies need to be treated with caution.

The Periodical Publishers Association (PPA) has laid down guidelines on the use of 'sponsored editorial' and 'sponsored competitions' in magazines. Broadly, they state that material and events of this kind should be clearly identified as sponsored, and that the editor should retain control over them.

Advertorial

Advertorials are simply advertisements designed to look broadly like the editorial matter of the publications within which they appear. Exactly how closely they should mimic a magazine's editorial style is currently the subject of lively debate.

Many editors take the view that they should look nothing like genuine editorial matter. Others object to the damage that inappropriately designed and written advertorials can do to the magazine within which they are placed. Some publishing houses, including BBC magazines, have a policy of preparing advertorials in-house, using a separate design and writing team. But the problem of producing advertorial material that is of high quality and 'in keeping with' the surrounding editorial without its actually resembling that editorial has not been resolved.

Advertorials are extremely popular with advertisers, however, particularly in the consumer press, because research has shown that they are very well read. They can be written by the advertisers themselves or by either the advertising or the editorial staff of the magazine, but this must not form part of a normal journalist's workload: such a task must be undertaken by private arrangement.

The PPA guidelines also cover advertorials. In particular, advertorials must not make any claims that would not be allowed in ordinary advertising. Advertorials must be clearly labelled so that readers are in no doubt about the provenance of what they are reading. The words 'advertisement', 'advertisement feature' or 'advertising promotion' are to be used, rather than 'advertorial', which is ambiguous for people outside the industry. Staff writers' by-lines may not appear in advertorials. Finally, the size and number of advertorial features should not be such as to compromise the credibility of the titles within which they appear. It is for others to say how well that particular requirement is being observed in some areas of the British magazine industry. Advertorial and advertising features must comply with the Trades Descriptions Act, whereas editorial features need not.

Colour separations

A kind of creeping advertorial has become common in the business press. The 'product books' (magazines based on promoting new products and services) have increasingly asked those supplying press releases to pay for their inclusion. This straightforward demand has been disguised as a request that companies pay the cost of making the colour separations required to reproduce their transparencies. Theoretically, those who do not oblige will have their photographs used but in monochrome. Most oblige.

Again, the PPA has some guidelines, which state that some form of wording should appear near the photograph, indicating that 'suppliers have contributed towards the production costs of some of the editorial photographs on this page'. This ruling, however, seems to be honoured more in the breach than in the observance. If such a practice is repugnant to you, as it might be, you should discuss it when you are interviewed for the editor's job.

Ancillary activities

There are many other commercial activities undertaken by publishing organisations in which editors have been expected to become involved.

They include various types of inquiry telephone lines, usually paid for by callers; books; reader offers; meetings, lunches, holidays and study tours; and conferences, seminars, exhibitions and touring shows. All of these require editorial input or supervision if they are not to damage the standing of the magazine. But there are only so many hours in the day, and editors should always consider the magazine itself as their priority.

The biggest area of all may yet turn out to be electronic publication in one form or another. No editor should relinquish responsibility for this, however tempting that might seem. The electronic media, whether on- or off-line, are simply another way of delivering the sort of services you are already producing.

The nature of advertising in the new electronic media is still being worked out. There are those who believe that the ease with which advertisers can set up their own 'sites' in the World Wide Web will preclude their taking space in editorial areas, throwing the financial equation of the whole thing into some doubt.

Pure advertising, relying on a simple slogan or visual conceit to get across a single idea, seems unlikely to be appropriate in the new electronic media. People will not want to pay to download something so self-serving. Readers will only take an interest in advertising if it gives them some new value, in terms of information or entertainment, that they can not get elsewhere. It is likely that advertising pages will become more 'editorial' in tone. This may mean more job opportunities for journalists and editors, but it will also place into sharper relief questions of editorial integrity.

There is, and will increasingly be, so much material in the Internet, for instance, that only 'sites' constructed with the most care, and with the most focus on a particular group of readers, are likely to succeed. The Internet removes many of the non-journalistic factors that bedevil magazine publishing. Questions of distribution, bookstall prominence and sheer weight and bulk have great influence at the point of purchase. These are likely to be replaced by a renewed concentration on the material, its presentation, its usefulness, its integrity and how accessible it can be made. These are the traditional areas of editorial expertise.

FURTHER READING

Best Practice Guidelines for Special Advertising Opportunities within Magazines (1993) London: Periodical Publishers Association.

Hargreaves, R.L. and Smith, R.H. (1981) *Managing Your Company's Finances*, London: Heinemann.

Secrett, Malcolm (1993) *Successful Budgeting in a Week*, London: BIM/Hodder & Stoughton.

Chapter 5

Content 1

Managerial skills are necessary for every editor, but on their own they are not the basis on which you will be judged. Your success will reflect your ability to create a convincing editorial vision and bring it into being by inspiring and directing a group of staff. The content of your magazine will not always determine its fortunes on the news-stands, but in the long term it is fundamental to the success or failure of the whole publishing enterprise. As an editor your aim should be to release the creativity and ingenuity of your staff, while ensuring that everyone involved with the magazine understands its essential identity.

BALANCE

The efforts that you have made to understand your readers should give you a strong idea of the subject matter that interests them. You may even have arrived at a set of 'musts' to be included in each individual issue, or distributed across a series of them. The degree to which each issue has to be comprehensive is linked to frequency of publication. Weeklies can maintain a balance of subject matter across several issues, whereas monthlies or quarterlies need to ensure that the most significant topics for their readership are included in each issue.

Your research may have told you which subjects people say they have an interest in. But the real art lies in assessing how far that 'interest' goes towards being an actual 'need'. You may feel that the facts of people's lives, in the case of consumer magazines, or their professional status, in the case of business publishing, may be more important.

Once again, you should look to the reader's self-interest as a guide: what am I, as a reader, going to find in this magazine that will give me and my family (or my firm, or my department) a definite advantage over those who have not read it? This means telling people things that are new and useful: what they don't need to hear are things they already know. The 'so what?' factor can be enormously destructive, whether you are editing a professional journal reporting stories a week or a month late, or a women's magazine providing your readers with fashion or dietary advice they have already read elsewhere.

Every significant article in your magazine must match your vision of the reader: at best, you should feel that each article, not in subject so much as in tone and attitude, could only appear in your magazine. This is asking a great deal, and in practice you must satisfy yourself that what you are presenting is the best possible article on the subject. Even if the subject is a well-known one, it should offer some new insight: it should also be accurate, fair, complete and entirely comprehensible. When dealing with ideas and copy in practice, you may like to keep a mental checklist of qualities. Is it new? Is it relevant? Is it accurate? Is it well written? Is it right for this magazine?

Creating a balanced magazine is not simply a question of selecting subjects: it is also a matter of the way subjects are handled, and the tone of voice in which they are written about. You should ensure that your magazine always has a range of different approaches and ways of speaking.

If you are taking over an existing magazine, it can be an interesting exercise simply to analyse the material in each issue by subject and compare that with what you know of the prevailing interests of the readership. This is particularly relevant in the case of business-to-business magazines catering for readers with a wide spectrum of different job functions and working in different areas of the market. Their own specific interests may be extremely specialised, but they may also need a general sense of what is going on across their industry.

Wide-ranging magazines for particular industries have often found it difficult to arrive at a suitable balance. If you are producing a magazine for industrial engineers, how much common ground is there between those working in the motor industry and those working in power generation? If your coverage is skewed towards the former and your readership towards the latter you will be in trouble. The same goes for magazines which attempt to cater for many different types of people within a single industry: say property developers, estate agents and property users. Consider how much of your content is directly relevant to each group, and compare that with what you know of your readership. This is particularly important in the case of controlled-circulation magazines, where information on your readers' level of satisfaction is not so readily available as it is in bookstall magazines, whose sales will rise and fall.

Another way of getting at the underlying interests of your readers is to look at the sources of your advertising and analyse these in the same way. Advertisers generally only put their money where they get results. This can sometimes be quite revealing. If you are producing a magazine for the parents of young children, you may be convinced that most of your readers have toddlers; but your advertising may come largely from the manufacturers of baby-food. Clearly, something is amiss. If you are doing this kind of analysis, however, you must not forget that some areas of your coverage (news, most obviously) have no natural reflection in advertising.

The range of subjects that you need to cover and the balance between them may help you to devise a kind of template for your own use: a recipe for a typical issue. In the case of a men's magazine, for instance, this might translate into an interview with an attractive woman; an interview with an admirable man; a 'yarn' or piece of sustained narrative; a picture feature; an argumentative piece; a humorous piece; something on sport or adventure; and so on. In the case of a professional magazine, it might mean an interview with a significant industrial figure; a case study of some particularly successful enterprise; something on a new technological development; something on a change in the law or professional regulation; and so on.

Readers like to know where they are: they want a magazine to stay identifiably the same from issue to issue. That is not the same as making it predictable, however. Any such 'recipe' must be a rough guide to categories of material, rather than a list of specifics. Nor should you let it assume the status of law.

QUALITY

The task of finding the right balance of subject matter and tone of voice forms one end of the span of editorial tasks. But in some ways it is as important to look at the other end, the detail. One of your most important tasks as an editor is to ensure that the quality of your magazine is right at a basic verbal level. The reason for this is simple: nothing destroys a magazine's claims to authority more swiftly and comprehensively than spelling mistakes – particularly in people's names – grammatical ineptitude and sub-editing errors.

An inescapable part of the policy of encouraging your staff to show their own ingenuity, to use their own resources and to take responsibility is the laying down of unambiguous standards of what is and is not acceptable. This should not be seen as an eccentricity on the editor's part, a regrettable constraint on other people's freedom of action, but as a critical part of the process of producing the right magazine. You must make it clear from the outset, by sending back unacceptable work for correction, that you will not accept compromises in this area. It is the editor's lot to be a stickler, a perfectionist and a pedant.

Accuracy, fairness, clarity

While all journalists should strive for truth, in practice our stock-in-trade is accuracy. Truth is a concept best addressed by philosophers and poets. Accuracy, however, comes down to a simple rule: anything that can be checked should be checked. Many who come new to journalism find this a difficult concept to grasp, while longer-serving practitioners sometimes neglect it. It should, however, be thoroughly drummed into your writers and production staff.

All spellings, figures and other factual statements must be checked against reliable printed sources: you must ensure that a small reference library is established and kept up to date. Beyond that, the necessity for accurate quoting of individuals must be stressed. With new reporters, particularly, it is worth inviting them to show you their notebooks from time to time to ensure that entries are correctly dated and labelled and that the notes within bear a close relationship with the quotes that appear in the magazine. Most interviewing for anything beyond simple news stories will probably be done on tape these days, but it is important that you insist that such tapes are transcribed honestly and stored carefully.

Beyond simple accuracy, you must inculcate in your staff the concept of fairness. Both accuracy and fairness need to operate at a much higher level than they do in normal day-to-day gossip and chit-chat, where it is quite acceptable to say things that are not true and are certainly not fair. This distinction between everyday life and professional duty is something inexperienced journalists sometimes find hard to grasp.

It is important that those your magazine writes about are treated straightforwardly, honestly and even-handedly. In particular, no-one on your staff should be operating with any concealed motive. It is traditional for journalists in the Western world to aim at objectivity, at least in news stories. This means reporters leave themselves out of the story, and do not let their attitudes colour the way it is told. No human being is actually objective, but it is a stance which most of us value in news writing. It means that we strive to be accurate, to include relevant facts even if they threaten the elegant narrative simplicity of the story, and that we don't take sides.

Much ink has been spilled in the past about whether the general obligation towards objectivity requires reporters to be objective between 'right and wrong'. It doesn't. Personal morality is not negotiable. But a story is not a speech for the prosecution. It is closer to the judge's summing up. It is a device for revealing the facts of a situation, fairly, and inviting the readers to make up their own minds.

Those criticised in a story, for instance, should be given the opportunity to state their side of the dispute. This is not simply an ethical matter: it is also self-interest, since most readers will find balanced and objective news writing more involving and more respectful of their intelligence than selective reporting mixed with opinionated rhetoric. Newcomers to professional journalism find this a difficult attitude to grasp, but they should be encouraged to persist. Feature writing, and personal columns, on the other hand, allow much more subjectivity and the expression of opinion. But they should still be based on accurate facts, not least for legal reasons.

It is one of the virtues of journalistic writing that it strives for simplicity and clarity. At the same time, some areas of magazine writing permit greater flair and stylistic experimentation than is necessary in the news pages of a daily paper. There is a balance to be struck, but on the whole the editor should err in the direction of clarity. Writing simply and effectively, so that everything can be understood at first glance, is a great skill and must not be undervalued.

Ethics

The editor must set standards not just on technical matters but on ethical matters. You can do this in your own conduct, for instance, by ensuring that complaints are dealt with swiftly and efficiently and appropriate corrections and apologies made.

But you may need to alert your journalists, especially the less experienced ones, to situations in which an ethical problem arises. It is, for instance, no longer considered acceptable for journalists to go round pretending to be someone else or failing to reveal their identities when conducting interviews. The exceptions occur when a story is 'in the public interest', a phrase capable of any number of interpretations, and there is no other way of researching it.

Journalists are, however, also members of the public. If a story involves a suspicion that ordinary members of the public are being treated badly, it would seem entirely acceptable for your reporters to experience that treatment before revealing their professional status. But subterfuge of any sort must be referred up to you for your decision. You will certainly be the person held to account for it. Any story written as a result must include some explanation of the subterfuge involved.

Another area in which people often act in ignorance of the ethical problems is interviewing. It is essential that both parties understand the basis on which any interview, however informal it might appear, is conducted. Interviewers should announce whom they are working for. It is not necessary, however, for interviewees to be reminded that their comments will be quoted: that is implicit from the point at which the interviewers announce who they are.

Difficulties arise because of those ambiguous expressions 'on the record' and 'off the record'. All interviewees are 'on the record', unless another agreement is reached, meaning that their real names are used in any story alongside their quotes. When people ask to speak 'off the record' complications arise, and a wise editor advises his reporters not to proceed without at least a conversation to ensure that all parties know exactly what is being meant.

This is because in common parlance 'off the record' can have several different meanings. Often it is signifies 'I will tell you something but you are not to use it', while other people take it to mean 'You can use the information to ask questions of others, and if they confirm it, you can then publish.'

Some use it to imply 'I will tell you something, and you can use the information, but you are not to use my words', while still others think that it means 'You can use my words, but you must not identify me as the source.'

The confusion surrounding the term means it is better not used. In particular, advise your staff to be wary of people who want to tell them things but will also try to bind them on their honour not to use them. Why are they speaking to a journalist in the first place? Sometimes this is an attempt to suppress stories that you might well have heard elsewhere.

Often people will want to tell you things without wanting you to use their words, however they are attributed. Some people will even go to the lengths of having a conversation with you on that basis before ringing you back in your official capacity to give you a statement, which may even deny what they have just told you. Such relationships need careful handling.

Sometimes it is better to tell your source that you will use the words but 'not attribute them'. Then you have to agree on a form of words to describe the source without revealing his or her identity. These things are a matter of negotiation and trust, which means that they can only be used with sophisticated sources or those with whom there is an established relationship.

As an editor, however, you should, by and large, insist that stories are backed up by 'on the record' quotes from named interviewees, or by written documentation. Too much reliance on 'unattributed' remarks is fatal for any publication's claims to authority: in general, if unnamed sources are to be used instead of named ones, it is essential that the story should include some sort of explanation as to why that should be the case. The motives of anonymous informants are not always of the highest.

In the case of longer, feature-type interviews, it is becoming increasingly common for interviewees to demand to see the piece before it is printed. To agree to the demand is unethical. It makes the publication an act of collusion between editor and interviewee: the piece itself becomes a kind of advertisement or propaganda. If the interviewee objects to a phrase or a passage, and a new version is agreed, an act of censorship has taken place. And if such a privilege is extended to one interviewee, it ought, in fairness, to be extended to all. You should point out to your journalists, including freelances, that such a practice is not acceptable. Those requesting it should be warned that to permit publication in such circumstances is to damage their legal right to take action on the grounds of libel: they will be deemed to have 'consented' to publication. On the other hand, interviewees do have the right to check that you have quoted them accurately by asking you to read back your notes or from the tape transcript. If they object to a quote, you can either adjust it or stick to your guns: it may be better to have the row before, rather than after, publication.

Another area of ethical concern, particularly to those working in the business press, is that of 'insider dealing' or profiting from information obtained for journalistic purposes before it is published. In the course of their work your journalists may receive information that could fall into this category. In the past it was often considered acceptable for journalists in this position to profit from their inquiries: even the staff of investment magazines were encouraged to trade in shares, perhaps to give them greater insight. This is no longer considered acceptable. Indeed, they are taking a legal, as well as an ethical, risk. Journalists buying, or arranging for others to buy, shares they are about to 'tip' could be prosecuted under the Theft Act for dishonestly obtaining a pecuniary advantage. Dishonest use of inside information from companies to alter share prices by judicious leaking is likely to be a conspiracy to contravene the 1986 Financial Services Act.

Bribes and inducements are hardly the common currency of most magazine journalists, but it pays for all parties to be open about any 'freebies' they may garner in their normal routine duties: straightforward gifts ought to be tactfully refused. There have, however, recently been a number of disturbing cases of journalists being hired to make public endorsements of products, something that does little to enhance either their reputations or the reputations of the publications they work for. A women's magazine's beauty editor has appeared in television commercials for a hair shampoo, for instance. Yachting journalists have appeared in promotional videos for boatbuilding companies.

There is an argument that in both cases the people concerned are being used because of their professional status, and that this will in some way enhance the status of their magazines. But this is not an entirely convincing argument, and similar proposals should, in general, be rejected. Brochure-writing and other freelance work on behalf of advertisers is, on the face of it, incompatible with maintaining a properly objective attitude to those advertisers. If it is done at all it must be done under a pseudonym, and with your permission. You will probably feel, however, that you do not wish to encourage such cosy relationships.

Another area of ethical concern is the handling of the private affairs of individuals. Intrusions into the privacy of those in public office or in positions of power are more likely to be justifiable than those into the affairs of private individuals. But annoying the powerless is likely to be legally safer. As an editor you have a duty to protect the rights of your fellow citizens from the intrusive behaviour of your staff. It is particularly important that sensitivity is maintained in dealing with the bereaved and with children and the emotionally and mentally incompetent. In the case of children, journalistic activities that might seem justifiable in other circumstances may well come into conflict with the law.

In general, editors have a duty to uphold freedom of speech and public access to information. Ours is a secretive society, and every journalist should think hard before colluding in the closure or rationing by price of sources of public information.

Both the National Union of Journalists and the Press Complaints

Commission publish extensive codes of conduct. Your staff will be held to account under the second of these even if they do not voluntarily accept the first. It is as well to make sure that their provisions are widely known and understood.

House style

One obvious distinction between a high-quality publication and a lesser one is consistency. A magazine which refers to 11 January on one page and January 11th on another, or to the BBC on one page and the B.B.C. on another, is hardly likely to build a reputation for authority. Most offices have a style book or style sheet, although in many cases it may only be a few pieces of paper to supplement some agreed work of reference. For instance, the *Oxford Dictionary for Writers and Editors* is often used as a starting point, but all editors have their prejudices and variants. If your magazine covers a particular professional area, you will need to work out your own style rulings on that industry's technical language.

But your style sheet should also include examples of grammatical howlers and solecisms which you would like to see your staff avoid, the favoured terms of address ('Mr Jones' or just 'Jones'?), the correct spellings of regularly used proper names, a list of registered trade marks that must be used properly or not at all, appropriate rulings on units of measurement, a ruling on whether collective nouns (government, for instance) are singular or plural, and so on.

You should also make it your practice to issue a frequent directive on words, headlines and standfirst approaches which have become hackneyed and which you never wish to see appear in print: 'Natch', 'kiddies', 'forty-something', 'But hey!' and so on. This may seem no more than the exercise of prejudice, but it is part of defining the way in which your magazine speaks to its readers.

You should also ensure that the magazine uses only one basic dictionary, supplemented by necessary technical and foreign language dictionaries, and that your sub-editors have access to a range of current reference books. The task of compiling a style book or sheet is one you can delegate to someone else, probably the chief sub-editor, and you should take the opportunity of talking it through with your sub-editors. They will be your 'style police' in this respect, and it is as well to ensure that if they don't share your views on usage and abusage they at least understand and recognise them.

NEWS

Historically, the roots of journalism lie in news. News may not seem relevant to all magazines, but its disciplines are widely applicable. It is an essential technical skill for young writers and sub-editors. The appeal to self-interest often comes down to presenting people with relevant information that they have not heard before. Most publications will try to do that, even if they don't see their product reviews or star interviews (or even their knitting patterns, to pick an extreme example) as news.

But in their way all these are a kind of news, and can often be given greater impact by being shaped and scheduled as news. Not only that, but feature material will often work better if it is subjected to at least some of the news criteria listed below.

As an editor, one of your most difficult tasks will be to teach your own staff how to recognise the factors that make something newsworthy for your publication. Despite various efforts to formalise journalistic training, most people learn their sense of 'news values' by observing how more experienced colleagues react to a 'story' or a 'yarn' or a 'tale', all of which are ways of saying the same thing.

They are helped by the passing down over the generations of various sayings, in many cases dating back to the popular journalism of the American nineteenth century, the era recalled in *Citizen Kane*. Chief among these is the anonymous soundbite: 'When a dog bites man, that is not news. When a man bites a dog, that is news.' William Randolph Hearst, founder of America's Hearst newspaper and magazine empire and the model for Charles Foster Kane, had his own definition: 'News is something somebody somewhere doesn't want you to print. Everything else is advertising.'

A less confrontational definition is attributed to Charles A. Dana, another nineteenth century American: 'News is something which interests a large part of the community and has never been brought to their attention.' Possibly, but such a definition could apply equally well to advertising. As an editor, you should attempt to identify what constitutes a story *for your readership*. At the very least it must be:

- *New:* this doesn't necessarily mean it has to have just happened, rather that it hasn't come to the attention of your readers before.
- *Relevant:* it has to affect your readers, or be close to them. Once again, the appeal must be to their self-interest. If a story doesn't seem, on the face of it, to affect them, it can sometimes be made to, by an assessment of its implications. A problem for one industry or profession can very often suggest difficulties in another.
- *Simple:* or capable of being explained simply. A more complex situation or development can be explained in a longer feature, perhaps. A news story has to be capable of being grasped in a flash.
- *Finite:* a newspaper story, like a joke or a novel, needs a beginning, middle and end. Something that started long ago, and is continuing for the foreseeable future, will be difficult to turn into a good story.
- *Surprising* (or *shocking*, *alarming* or *amusing*). The element of the unexpected is central to a great story, whether it forms a simple news item or a

longer feature. Women's magazine editors used to speak of the 'Hey, Doris!' story, by which they meant the type of story that made their readers want to call 'Hey Doris, have you seen this?' across the garden fence. It's a variant on the old idea of Man Bites Dog. Extremes often produce this kind of story: big numbers, large sums of money, huge crowds, extreme behaviour, extreme emotions.

There are many other elements which can make a story, depending on your readership. Dramatic events involving children and animals will be very useful in some types of women's magazine, but a journal for accountants would be more interested in an unexpected ruling in a tax appeal.

That said, people are usually the source of news. Most publications, however dry, will have a cast of individuals whose prominence within their industry makes their activities and pronouncements newsworthy. The tendency in local papers, particularly, has been to turn every story into a 'people' story. But this is not an approach that can always be followed in magazines. Some business magazines have done well over the years by personalising conflicts and illustrating every story with dramatic-looking pictures of those mentioned in it: this is entirely right for some industries. But other areas would scorn this approach, and it is for you as an editor to make that judgement. Many readers of professional magazines have a morbid fear of anything down-market or sensationalist. In those circumstances, presenting stories in a bright, vivid, dramatic way that would appeal to people outside the particular industry might well be the worst thing you could do.

Of course, the essence of news is topicality. Magazine editors often fret about this. Stories they put to bed on Monday may be out of date by the time the magazine appears on Wednesday or Friday. It is no consolation to know that similar doubts affect the editors of daily newspapers, fated to follow in the wake of television.

The answer is for the printed media to play to their strengths. Even a weekly magazine cannot expect to stay on top of a breaking story of national significance. By the time it has produced its version of events, things will have moved on and its readers will have read more recent material in their daily newspapers. But a professional weekly has assets of its own. Instead of trailing behind newspapers and television, it can provide in-depth analytical coverage based on its trusted relationships within the industry. It can also make sure that its coverage is focused to the special needs of its own readers in a way that wouldn't apply to media serving the general public.

Some editors, usually of weekly magazines, take the view that monthlies shouldn't try to compete in the news area at all. They should simply use the space for something else. On one level, this is true, but there are ways round it. For a start, the greater time available for a monthly to do its work should mean that genuinely exclusive stories can be discovered and worked up, then the monthly will be leading everybody else, which is good for morale and sales. Greater analytical depth should be available. A monthly should have time to cultivate the sources it needs to produce exclusive stories.

The securing of exclusivity is essential for news in a monthly. Those writing the stories must do everything they can to persuade the people they have talked to to keep silent. They do this by promising them better, more serious, more respectful coverage than they would get in any weekly. This is a matter of building authority for your magazine, and can't be done overnight. A classic example was when *Studio Sound*, a British technical monthly for the sound recording industry, secured a world exclusive on the 1995 Beatles reunion, initially by normal journalistic detective work and then by striking a deal with the parties concerned to say nothing to anyone else. Exclusives can and must be secured in this way. Sources often fail to understand that a story which appears in one publication and is then followed up will have greater impact than those which are distributed equally to all at the same time and thus have no value to anyone.

This may lead to you, as editor, rejecting stories which are otherwise right for your readers on the grounds that you cannot have them exclusively. This can be a dangerous policy, however, if it leaves you presenting only a partial and narrow picture of the professional world you are serving. Instead you should use the focusing power of news design to achieve both ends: you can give great prominence and projection to your exclusive stories, but cover the rest in a much reduced way, in a round-up box or column of news 'briefs'.

The new electronic media offer possibilities for magazines to enhance their coverage. A publisher of professional magazines could use an Internet site to complement its normal printed version. Usually people opt to fill the available space with archived articles from back issues. But it only takes a telephone call to replace one Internet page with another, making a daily news update a comparatively simple matter to produce. Obviously, this should be made to complement the printed magazine's in-depth coverage rather than replace it, and publishers will increasingly seek to ensure that such additional benefits are restricted to subscribers to their magazines or those on its controlled circulation list.

The news team

The ethos of news – spotting stories, putting them together quickly, checking their accuracy – is something that can be encouraged throughout your journalistic team. At the same time, however, many types of magazines will have one or more individuals responsible for producing a news section. You will have to guide and encourage them, something that is best done by constantly showing your interest and enthusiasm. In the run of things, you will probably be spending more of your time out in the outside world than many of your staff, and you should make it your policy always to bring something back, whether it is a tip-off picked up over lunch or a potential lead you spotted in a local paper.

You should also do your best to arrive in the office with new ideas culled from the weekend's newspapers and broadcasting. It should, in any case, be policy to start the day with a brisk session of searching the newspapers and cutting out anything relevant. If you have enough staff, the papers can be divided between them; it should be stressed that this is not an opportunity to look at the horoscopes and sports pages but a functional start to the day.

The City and business pages are usually particularly relevant: increasingly, reporters need to understand this area. The average broadsheet newspaper will generally supply several business magazine story ideas, although it is important to use this material to trigger new ideas and thoughts rather than to slavishly reproduce it a week or a month after its original appearance. You will need to ensure that your news editor or news reporters have a meticulous and comprehensive approach to news-gathering. It is not enough simply to open the post or wait for tip-offs. The key tool for news work is the office diary. Naturally this should include the dates of all relevant forthcoming events in your field, including meetings of professional organisations, important court cases, publication of reports, press conferences, the opening and closing dates of inquiries, and so on.

But beyond that there are many things you must track yourself. If people say they can't give you an answer on something for a month, you should make a note to ring them back in three weeks. It is particularly important to keep a note of the appropriate dates for 'follow-ups' arising from your own stories. All stories need to be followed through to the bitter end: there is nothing more frustrating for a reader than to read that there will be an inquiry into some incident, only to find that no-one has bothered to follow things through and record the inquiry's findings. Even promises made by prominent people should be recorded and followed up at some suitable date.

It is important to anticipate how you will cover important events before they arise. The classic case for most professional magazines is the Budget. You know that the Budget will affect your readers: it is foolhardy to wait until the actual provisions are announced before thinking about how to cover their implications. Better to contact your experts beforehand and go through likely possibilities with them some time in advance. This is particularly important when you are dealing with events that fall on or around your press day. In extreme cases, say that of a crucial courtcase where the verdict is due on your press day, you might prepare two stories, one for each verdict, complete with headlines and even layouts, and hold them in readiness so that you can drop the right one in when you discover what happens. Just ensure that you actually use the right version.

A well-kept diary is the starting point for a successful news strategy. Sometimes 'diary' is used as a disparaging term: 'off-diary' stories, those which come to you over a drink or by a telephone tip-off, are much more prized. But 'off-diary' calls only come from the painstaking work of building up contacts, and that is a function of careful attention to the diary. You should ensure that you have a comprehensive list of people you speak to in each important news area. You must go back to them again and again.

It is surprising how quickly people you speak to regularly (and meet face to face whenever possible) change from being mouthpieces of the official line to valuable sources who will offer you extra guidance and information. They must, of course, trust you and your staff, and the importance of keeping the identity of sources confidential needs to be stressed. As an editor, you should, of course, have your own contacts in important areas of the industry you cover so that you can get a feel for the accuracy and general appropriateness of the stories coming out of your news operation.

If you are working with inexperienced reporters, you should encourage them to be rigorous about keeping their contact books up to date and safe. You should also be wary of asking reporters to contact their valued sources for frivolous purposes. At the same time there should be a general office contact book listing the normal straightforward sources of information. Most magazines should acquire the so-called 'White Book', the Central Office of Information's comprehensive listing of government press officers. You will also need the professional directories for the industry you are covering. It is also worthwhile for your reporters to learn the art of monitoring the Internet for news material. The so-called 'news groups' contain a great deal of material that has nothing to do with news, but they can be a useful place to find contacts and story ideas. Industry 'mailing lists' are also an underused resource. Reporters must remember that even 'private' e-mails are written communications, for which they can be held to account.

The relationship between reporters and their sources is often rather intense, accompanied by a certain amount of self-conscious 'cloak and dagger'. This is all part of the excitement of working in news, and reporters should be permitted to indulge in it. They should be given a fairly loose rein, providing that their absences from the office and lunches with mysterious contacts bring results. The relationship can cause problems, however, when you feel that the source is using the reporter rather than vice versa. Beware of strings of self-interested stories tending to support a particular line. In extreme cases, it is sometimes necessary to reassign the news 'patches' or 'beats', the areas that individual reporters cover.

It is important that your reporters get into the habit of reading their rivals very closely, not simply to see any stories they have missed (it will be too late to do anything about it) but to try and discover where those stories come from. Most experienced news editors develop a strong sense of where their contacts are weaker than the opposition's and set about putting that right.

Geographical coverage is sometimes a problem. Increasingly even our national newspapers cover everything by telephone from the capital. But the problem is hearing about stories in the first place. Young reporters should be given every encouragement to get out of the office. It is important to make contacts across the industry but also across the country. Otherwise uninteresting 'ad-get' features of the 'regional survey' variety are invaluable for allowing your reporters to make contacts with sources in the provinces, who will often be surprised and delighted to speak to someone in person. It is possible to order many of the important regional newspapers in London, and this can be a helpful starting point, especially for off-beat material. And local paper reporters and newsdesks can sometimes be persuaded to offer you material that might suit your news agenda as well as theirs.

Inevitably much of your news material will come from printed sources in which the interesting items are deeply buried: press releases, reports by government, companies and industry bodies, transcripts of speeches, and so on. Letters from readers sometimes lead to stories, and even a magazine's own small ads should be monitored, particularly for information on people changing jobs, but also for more human stories.

Often the task of a reporter in the professional press is to 're-angle' a story from other sources to make it relevant to this particular audience. An obvious case is the publication of honours lists, which should be combed to find awards that have gone to members of the profession in question. But the same goes for lists of victims of major accidents.

The main thing, though, is that all your journalistic staff, not just your reporters, need to keep their eyes and ears open. Good stories often originate in things people have seen from the bus, or overheard in the bus queue.

As an editor, you must leave your reporters to do their jobs, but especially with the inexperienced you should be prepared to offer guidance on reporting technique. Often this comes down to developing the skill of interviewing. Interviewing has two aspects: actually conducting the conversation, and recording what is said. To take the easy part first, news reporters should be reminded that it is essential to use a proper notebook with bound-in pages rather than scrappy pieces of paper. The book should carry their name and telephone number, in case it is lost, and each entry should be properly identified and dated. Notes should be clear and comprehensible, and any shorthand should be transcribed as soon as possible after the interview. For complex and contentious stories and long interviews, particularly on the telephone, reporters may prefer to use a tape recorder. Here the simple practicalities must be observed: the batteries must be fresh, there must be room on the tape, and an appropriate microphone or 'bug' must be used. Afterwards, the tapes must be properly identified and stored.

Interviewing is conversation for a purpose, and people's abilities here are related to their personalities and conversational skills: it is about how well you listen, and how you respond to what you are told, as well as what you actually ask. But any story requires you to think about whom you need to interview, and when. Often the order in which you speak to those involved is critical. If you speak to A, will she tip off B and give him time to get his story straight?

It is often a good idea to tell your reporters to go to the top and work down. These days, of course, many organisations have specific people who are charged with the duty of speaking to the press, which is not an unmixed blessing. But if that doesn't apply, people at the top of an organisation generally have the clout to speak freely without asking anyone's permission, as well as having the appropriate information.

Your reporters should be encouraged to think about the time and place for their interviewing. In the case of a news story, it is essential to establish whether people are able to talk freely. If you ring them in the office, it can be better to try and get a home number and talk to them later. Face-to-face interviews are often better still, but you need to be polite when you go to see people at home. Calling absurdly early in the morning or behaving in a threatening manner is not acceptable.

Encourage interviewers to work from a list of questions. This will ensure that they don't miss anything, but also, if carefully constructed, it should help them put their story together later: the quotes should follow the natural order of the story. And encourage them to shut up occasionally: a patch of silence sometimes persuades people to digress revealingly.

Your reporters will also often need to gain experience in covering court cases and tribunals, a specialist area that needs careful study. Meetings, conferences and press conferences, however, are more of a free-for-all. In these cases, encourage them to arrive early and speak to the participants. They should establish whether there will be time for a few private questions later, or collect a telephone number. Asking significant questions during a press conference, when everyone else can hear, is a strategy to be avoided if you are taking competition seriously.

News writing

News style is one of the dialects of journalism, a particular type of writing that should form part of the range available to a fully trained and experienced magazine journalist. There are always arguments about whether people can be taught to write, or whether it is a gift. Certainly the average young entrant can be taught to write well enough to hold the attention of a magazine reader over the length of a news story or feature. Feature writing at the highest level is a slightly tougher proposition but news style should be available to almost everyone.

At its best news can offer both great economy and narrative drive. A rule of thumb is that everything written in the non-technical sections of periodicals should be understandable in the time it takes to read it: in other words, there should be no necessity to go back over phrases or to puzzle over vocabulary. At its worst, however, news writing degenerates into a string of clichés.

Like the design of news pages, news writing has evolved for functional reasons. The object is to grab people's attention early on, to give them the key points as quickly as possible and then to supply the rest of the essential information in order of importance, in such a way that any cuts can be made quickly from the bottom without losing anything vital; this reflects the way readers work, proceeding through a story until they lose interest and then looking at something else.

If you are employing people without specific journalistic training, this a concept they will find difficult to grasp, especially if they have been in the habit of writing college essays that demand an introduction, several discrete points and then a conclusion.

The important thing in a news story is an introduction, or 'intro' as it is invariably known, that grabs the attention, followed by a clear narrative, but this is easier said than done. Even experienced reporters sometimes find themselves taking as long to get the intro right as they do for the rest of the story, only for it to be rewritten by the sub-editors. In this position, it makes much more sense to write the story first, starting with a working intro of some sort, then work on the intro at the end.

The problem is always the same: you have to get the gist of the story into the first paragraph. But if it is a complex story, you are in danger of running out of words before you have said anything at all. Various techniques have, however, been devised to achieve the necessary compression. They include 'the inverted pyramid'; 'five Ws and an H'; 'the telegram' and 'the key word'.

Journalism textbooks, particularly American ones, are particularly keen on the inverted pyramid. But this is no more than a restatement of the obvious, which is that the weight of a story, the important elements, should be at the top, with increasingly less important material as it carries on. This is a helpful point about the general shape of a news story, but does not assist in the creation of an intro.

The five Ws and an H will be familiar to literary types as Kipling's 'six honest serving men' from the *Just So Stories*. They are, obviously, Who? What? When? Where? Why? and How?' The idea is that all these questions need to be answered in a news story. Sometimes you may hear or read that they should all be answered in the intro, but that is simply wrong. Such an intro, apart from stretching well beyond the usual 25–30 word limit, would be terribly confused as well as making the subsequent news story virtually redundant. It can be done, however, and it is certainly good practice for a quite different news task, that of writing 'briefs' or 'Nibs' (from News In Brief): 'Several hundred angry French farmers released herds of sheep into the streets of Boulogne this week in protest at imports of British lamb.'

A more useful way of looking at the five Ws is that they offer you five ways to angle your intro. Who? 'Angry French farmers . . .' What? 'Herds of cows streamed into the streets . . .' Where? 'The centre of Boulogne came to a standstill . . .' When? 'At first light this morning an angry crowd of . . .'

Why? 'Imports of English lamb drove French farmers to . . .' You can see that some of these are more practical than others, but they are all options: this kind of exercise is particularly useful if you simply get stuck.

Harold Evans, in *Newsman's English*, his excellent book on journalistic style, now sadly out of print, has a good suggestion to help cut through the complications in many stories and to get to the key points for writing your intro. He suggests writing it first as a kind of telegram, then fleshing that out to produce something literate. So our French farmers story could be reduced to French Farmers Block Port With Sheep To Protest Against Imports. Fill in the missing words and you are back to something approaching an intro.

Another useful device suggested by Evans is the idea of using a key word or phrase as the core of the intro. Let the story percolate in your mind for a bit and then ask yourself whether there's a word that sums it up. If it is about an old lady who has been afraid to leave her council flat because nasty local youths have been giving her a hard time, you might think that word was 'prisoner'. Hence: 'A Smalltown woman has been made a prisoner in her own home by the activities of . . .' and so on. This approach is particularly recommended because it forces you to make a decision about what is important. Often stories lead you in several directions at once. If you discover that a company is opening a new factory which will create 2,000 jobs to build a product that safety experts are demanding be withdrawn from sale, you have a problem which can only be resolved by deciding which of those is most important to your readers.

Usually your intro should include the detail that will make it relevant to your readers. The *Smalltown Gazette* will often find it relevant that the person comes from Smalltown. To you, as the editor of a professional or hobby magazine, the relevant detail may be the fact that the person in the story is an architect, or a coin collector, or a clergyman. One way of testing an intro is to try writing a heading from it. If this can't be done, something essential has been omitted.

Not all intros give everything away at the start. One of the characteristics of a good story is the element of surprise. Usually this is accommodated by the use of a dash. 'Computer manufacturer Smallbits is to cut 3,000 jobs – despite making record profits.' But you can, on occasions, give that element of surprise a bit of assistance by doing what is called a 'delayed drop' intro, in which the point of the story is held back for as long as you dare. Connoisseurs of journalistic history will cherish examples from the heyday of the broadsheet *Sunday Express*, most of which seemed to begin 'It was a day like any other for Mrs Jones', proceeding to tell you everything about her day over several paragraphs before revealing, deep in the story, that she was struck by lightning or garotted by the handle of her own shopping bag.

A more disciplined version was the trademark of the *Sunday Times*'s Insight team, strictly speaking writers of news features rather than news. Here a massive array of detail was collected so that the story of a plane crash could begin 'Captain Michael Wallace of Smallair looked at his Rolex Oyster as his BAC 1-11 cleared Number One runway at Stansted . . .' and so on. Used sparingly, this technique can make a nice change of pace, but these days it tends to be reserved for lighter stories and news features.

Once you have your intro, the rest of the story should follow. You will need normally to state exactly who did what, when, where, why and how. If it's an account of some event, get the most dramatic or important points across first, concentrating on their human impact, and then tell what's left as a narrative sequence in approximate chronological order. After that comes any useful background, perhaps relating this incident to other similar events, and any assessment of its implications (unless of course the implications are the point of the story, in which case they should be at the top).

Not all stories are about incidents, however. Some are simply based on speeches or reports. Here chronological order is no guide: most speeches save the interesting points until the end. Instead the reporter has to make some judgement about the importance of the speech or report's content. The most important point becomes the intro, and depending upon its strength it may need to be immediately developed and anchored in direct quotation. Any other relevant points follow on. The inverted 'pyramid' is a less helpful guide for this type of story.

Quotes are important in news stories but should be used for a purpose. They are sometimes less than comprehensible, typographically disruptive, and flabby. So for initial explanation of what has happened or been said it may be better to use straight narrative or reported speech. But quotes should be used where they are vivid, or controversial, and where you want to make sure that there is no doubt about precisely what someone said. Quotes are important for giving a story authority: they show that you have spoken to the important people. This is why quotes should be attributed. Remember, too, that you are under a general obligation to get all sides of the story. If someone is mentioned, they ought to be asked to give their side, and their response to an accusation should not necessarily be left to the final paragraph, where it is in danger of being chopped in the sub-editing process.

The most comprehensive account of news writing is in Harold Evans's book, but that will be difficult to find. Richard Keeble's *The Newspapers Handbook* has a useful discussion of the subject. Keith Waterhouse's famous *Daily Mirror* stylebook, most recently published as *Waterhouse on Newspaper Style*, offers some interesting, if slightly eccentric, thoughts about news writing and journalistic style in general.

FEATURES

Features are central to the success of magazines, particularly consumer magazines. The term itself is not particularly useful, however, because it covers such a vast range, from interviews with celebrities or the leaders of giant industrial concerns, to advice and instruction.

Whereas news is about providing discrete chunks of useful information to your readership, features appeal to their wider interests and aspirations. Balance, as always, needs to be borne in mind. You must cater for the full range of your readership and different features must offer different types of appeal: straight information, inspiration, education, amusement, provocation, and so on. It is not appropriate to fill your magazine with identical interviews or instructional features, nor to rely on design to differentiate between them. A classic magazine feature is a single entity, a words/design/pictures package that has to be planned as such from the outset.

The most obvious type of feature to consider is the straight 'news feature'. This must not, however, simply be a news story that has overrun. It needs to be considered from the beginning as a feature that just happens to elucidate some topical issue or point. News features explore their subject matter at much greater length than simple news stories, and this means that they can include much more in the way of analysis, explanation, colour and background. They do not need the simple punchy intro of a news story and can often start with scene-setting, a key detail or an argumentative statement.

Even so, if they are to be considered as news features their news relevance needs to be established early on. News features allow their writers to explore a wider tonal range than simple news stories. Subjectivity, for instance, may be permissible. At the same time, however, they should be seen as part of the normal role of the news reporter.

More elaborate features may take more skill. There is unfortunately no simple pattern to follow. Most people learn to write features by trial and error or simply by emulation. The starting point is an idea, which may be yours, or the writer's, or may arise in a meeting. Opinions vary about the value of ideas, as such, as opposed to their expression: often the best features come from no very promising start. But nothing should be wasted. Your writers should be encouraged to keep lists of ideas, along with the relevant bits of cutting that sometimes give rise to them.

When an idea presents itself, however, it is important to work it up into some kind of brief or proposal, if only for the writer's own benefit. Narrow ideas, which crystallise themselves in a single encounter or incident or place, are often better than those which try to cover some huge and amorphous subject and fall short. It is good to have a discussion about a proposed feature before the planning and research goes very far, if only to weed out the obvious and the over familiar.

As editor, you will brief writers, and it is good practice to do this on paper if only to concentrate your own thoughts. Briefs presented to writers range from the airy 'give us one of your usuals, about 1,500 words by Friday week' to detailed specifications laying down precisely who should be spoken to and what questions they should be asked. The detail of briefing will decrease with the experience of the writer and the confidence you have in him or her. Writers who are not known to you need to be bound hand and foot. Buying a feature that turns out to be unusable is a costly mistake, and the fear of that is one of the reasons why it is so difficult for those without an established reputation to break into feature writing.

Fundamentally, though, what you want from a feature writer cannot be secured by writing it down on a brief. You want to be enthralled. You want to be made to read on, and when you have, made to feel glad you did. Writers who can do this can get away with straying a long way from the brief.

Today there is an assumption that good briefing and commissioning is about sending someone to collect enough material to create a story you as editor or commissioning editor already have in your head. The commissioning letter then becomes a series of questions to which the writer supplies the answers. This may make sense for those dealing with inexperienced writers, but it makes for predictable and clumsy features. Rather than finding their own story, their own narrative and argument, writers responding to such a brief tend to produce a succession of paragraphs without logic or drama.

There is, however, more of an argument for this kind of commissioning in the case of strictly informational articles for the specialist consumer and business press. Here the brief needs to be precise. All briefs, however, must include such details as the delivery date, length, and fee. You may, on occasions, find it useful to ask your writers to supply you with a single-page brief detailing how they propose to cover the subject in question.

Feature writing

Unlike news writing, where there is generally agreed to be one acceptable approach, feature writing offers great scope for creativity and ingenuity. The requirement for distance and objectivity does not always apply. The word 'I' is permitted, and the writer is allowed to be a participant in the story, although this should not be overdone. There is no agreed form for an intro.

This can make feature writing rather bewildering for the inexperienced and difficult for those, like editors, who are required to lead and instruct. It is certainly important not to impose any kind of uniformity: the variety of people's approaches and styles will give you, as an editor, the choice you need to create an appropriate mix and balance of treatment as well as subject matter.

Thorough research will often help feature writers through their material: they will have discovered the key points, the crucial incidents, the most relevant quotes. But they must be persuaded to marshal these facts before they begin.

Construction is extremely important. Some of the most experienced and skilful feature writers still draw up some kind of point-by-point 'essay plan' before they begin. At its crudest, this turns a piece into a series of points, each matched with a quote that illustrates it. But it enables the writer to keep to the argument, and to decide on the correct order for the material.

Any feature needs a shape, whether that is telling a story chronologically, or starting with general principles and moving down to a specific example, or starting with an individual case and drawing a broader lesson from it. By the time the feature is finished and polished this scaffolding should be invisible, but it will have given the feature great underlying strength.

An arresting opening is as important for a feature as it is for a news story. The difference is that a feature will usually be presented in such a way that there is a separate introductory paragraph (a 'standfirst' or 'sell') written by the sub-editors. This will usually explain who is being interviewed and why, or why a particular issue is topical, or what the story is actually about. That leaves the writer free to start with something bold that sets the tone.

One time-honoured practice, particularly in narrative features, is to start in the middle, at a point of great drama: when you fall off the raft and into the churning waters of the Colorado River rather than when you get a call from the travel company asking you if you'd like the trip. The same kind of thing can work in interviews: you start with the question that made your interviewee lose his or her temper, rather than with the one that happens to come first on your tape.

In both these examples, you may need to double back on yourself to tell the story from the beginning. You only want to do that once, returning immediately to a straightforward chronological sequence. But you will have grabbed your readers' attention, and you should have a greater chance of taking your readers with you than if you creep up on the subject by telling them about your difficulties in fixing up the interview or your adventures at Heathrow while you were waiting for your plane.

Some people habitually put their best quote at the beginning, but that is not always a good practice. Starting with a quote creates a number of problems. It is an irritant to readers to hear someone's voice before they know who is speaking. And if your design calls for features to start with a 'drop cap', starting with an open quotation mark is never satisfactory. Besides, it is not advisable to make the rest of your piece an anticlimax.

In the course of a long feature, you may wish to approach your material from several different angles. You may have an interview with someone, an account of an incident on the shopfloor of their factory, a long technical explanation of some manufacturing process. Increasingly, magazines are turning these into separate elements on the page: panels and boxes.

You should always consider whether anything in your piece would work better as a graphic or diagram than as a piece of prose. And individual elements in a story that can be separated out – long digressions, interviews, explanatory passages, definitions of key terms, passages of historical background – should often be presented as separate panels. These must be discussed with your designers, preferably at an early stage in the feature-planning process.

If you do break out of continuous narrative, you must ensure that the reader can still navigate through your feature. There is a particular problem with tenses. You may wish to make use of the 'historic present', for its immediacy: 'I am just finishing my drink as the first bullet hits the verandah of the Hilton Hotel.' But you may then have to wed this to a straightforward narrative. 'The first signs of the coup were . . .' This needs careful handling. You can't keep switching backwards and forwards.

Features, unlike news stories, are not designed to be cut from the bottom. You need to spread your insights throughout the piece, to keep the reader intrigued, rather than throw them all at the reader at the opening. And you need a strong final paragraph: a conclusion, a powerful quote or an image. The sub-editors should recognise this, which makes cutting features a rather skilled craft.

Stylish writing can cover a multitude of sins in the feature area, but it does not exclude features from having to comply with the basics. You should ensure that your feature writers understand the necessity for their stories to make sense, to be fair and accurate, for names to be spelt correctly and facts to be checked.

Learning to write features is often just a case of doing it and reading the efforts of masters in the field. You can help inexperienced feature writers by the quality of your briefing and by talking through with them their response to the brief. Another idea is to ask them write a one-paragraph summary of their feature before they start to write it. Feature writing is one thing that does get better with practice, and there is nothing more rewarding for an editor than to recognise and nurture a new writing talent.

Feature planning

The starting point for planning a magazine's feature coverage is the editorial diary. A high proportion of your features will be 'date-tied' or 'pegged' to some external event, either as specific as a particular company's annual results, or the outcome of a competition, or as general as Christmas or the opening of the football season. The key to features editing is the manipulation of time: there is always a right time for carrying a particular feature, and if you wait until a particular event has happened and then respond you will usually be too late.

In the case of a company profile intended to tie in with someone's annual results, you obviously have to have approached the company and made any necessary visits and conducted any necessary interviews well in advance. You will very often need to carry out any photography at the same time. Your profile can then run at the same time as the results are released: as long as the general tenor of your piece is appropriate they need not even appear in it, taking their rightful place on a news page instead.

Those in competitive markets will sometimes find themselves worrying about being first with a particular feature. In fact, this is not something that much concerns the readers, many of whom are loyal to your title rather than persuaded to buy different magazines according to what they find inside. But you must not become complacent. It is not a good idea to make a cover feature out of something that everyone else has always carried: as you get further away from being first with a story, so its size and prominence should be reduced.

This all causes particular difficulties in the case of celebrity and arts material, where what you do and when you do it is a matter of negotiation. Securing most film or music interviews will usually involve a demand for you to disclose when you propose to publish, which is extremely unwelcome. The PR companies involved have their own agenda. They will be manipulating the coverage to ensure that it appears at the most suitable time for them, and they will also have struck deals with other publications about timing. You can mislead them and publish when it suits you, but you should expect repercussions the next time you deal with the same PR company. This kind of bluff and double-bluff becomes exhausting. In any case, it is not uncommon for editors to be expected to sign undertakings indicating when they will publish. These may or may not be enforceable, but they have a certain moral force.

The celebrity interview area is becoming increasingly problematical: even the highest-profile newspaper supplements are often faced with extraordinary demands by studios, record companies, PR companies and their clients. Often they will attempt to specify the writer, the photographer, the size of the eventual piece and its prominence. Naturally you should resist this, but if celebrities constitute one of the cornerstones of your feature coverage, you will usually have to come to some sort of accommodation.

Unfortunately, this is a kind of creeping disease, now spreading to other areas which have fallen under the thrall of professional PR people. The word 'No' often comes in useful here. Few interviews are so essential that they are worth surrendering your right to make editorial decisions.

Obviously if a freelance writer comes to you with a celebrity interview already arranged, he or she is at liberty to make individual arrangements, but you should ensure that nothing has been agreed that will damage the good name of your magazine. Such writers may also expect to sell their material to several customers. You should ensure that you get the first instalment. If you fix the interview and then choose a writer, you can insist that nothing of that sort happens. Some interviewees are sensitive about where they want interview material to appear, and you must be able to assure them that your writers are working for you alone.

Luckily, much of your feature material will come about through your own ingenuity and that of your writers. All your staff should keep ideas files, and you should constantly be aware of the possibilities for turning simple news items, even one-paragraph briefs, into features. You should also feel no shame about borrowing other people's ideas and adapting them: they will do it to you. Of course, this does not mean copying your rivals, although it is always worth studying their features to see how they came about and how well they have been put together. It is better to take inspiration from different fields and markets and adapt them to your own purposes. In your usual routine course of meetings you should allow room for free-ranging features discussions. In the process of discussion, a hackneyed idea picked up from another magazine can be transformed into something quite original.

This is particularly important when it comes to the great annual landmarks in the world your magazine covers. Some of these will be specific to your particular topic – the start of the season, the beginning of term – but many will be more general. The obvious example is Christmas, which most magazines will feel some obligation to celebrate. There is a terrible tendency to look at what was done last year and reproduce it, but each time you do this some of the original inspiration has ebbed away. Better to start early and come up with some new ideas.

Scheduled features

There is another aspect to features work, and that is the creation of a features schedule designed to be publicised as a lure to advertisers. You will, of course, have your own schedule of features which you are running solely because you think they are editorially important. But in many markets, particularly in professional and business-to-business publishing, it is considered essential to produce a features programme or calendar. An architectural magazine, for instance, will run features on 'bricks', 'roofing', 'cladding', and so on, in successive weeks, to draw in advertising from manufacturers of those products.

Naturally a balance has to be reached here. The schedule should be drawn up in conjunction with the advertising department, since there is no point in programming a series of 'ad-get' features for which there will be no advertising support. But this is not an area in which you can abdicate editorial responsibility. These features may not be of a type calculated to set the pulse racing but they must be planned, commissioned, edited and presented to the best of your ability and must meet the standards of the rest of your magazine. Within the broad headings listed in the features schedule, there is room for considerable ingenuity and editorial flair. These features can also serve as a useful area in which to try out inexperienced staff and new freelances before you give them some more prominent commission. But they must remain true editorial products. You should not, for instance, allow the advertising department to commission and edit them.

Instructional features

Instructional features, whether they be knitting patterns or recipes or advice on reading music or dealing with tax, represent a particular problem. Despite their unglamorous image, they demand the very highest standards of commissioning and editing. The task concerned must be clearly 'do-able' and within a timescale that is meaningful for the magazine: a weekly is ill-advised to carry constructional projects that take a month to put together. Projects that demand a great deal more knowledge than appears on the surface to be the case should be avoided, as should those with hidden costs and dangers. It is essential that writers giving the instructions have actually done what they are attempting to demonstrate and can show that it has worked.

The instructions themselves need to be crystal clear, and all quantities, temperatures and other numbers need to be checked back against original copy and with the author. Simple common sense should provide a further line of defence against the occasional absurdity, especially in cookery. If you are producing large numbers of magazines, and you are trying to establish an atmosphere of genuine communication with your readers, you cannot afford to ruin their dinner parties or Sunday tea.

Other forms of feature

The classic magazine feature consists of a single continuous narrative illustrated by photographs. Increasingly, however, different types of feature are becoming more prominent. Even a straightforward narrative feature will often now be accompanied by boxes and panels.

But beyond that there are other types of feature altogether. The picture feature, in which the main thrust comes from the visual material, is the most common. A picture essay by a single photographer can be a most appealing way of dealing with a hackneyed subject. If an appropriate fee is agreed it need not be more expensive than filling the equivalent space with words.

Graphic-based features are becoming more common, too, but they need careful research and design. Anything that involves grading or testing a large number of subjects is often better dealt with by some kind of graphical grid than it is in words. With the increasingly visual nature of communication in our society, it is worth asking yourself if an idea can be conveyed other than in words, either as an accompaniment to a traditional feature or as a replacement for it. Obviously such ideas demand the immediate assistance of a skilled designer.

INTERVIEWS AND PROFILES

Interviews of various kinds will provide a great deal of the feature material for many magazines. Obviously, all features involve interviews, often to provide evidence on either side of an argument. But that is different from a feature which principally consists of an interview with a person who is inherently interesting to the magazine's readers.

An interview needs as much preparation as any other feature. If you have specific points you feel should be raised, or issues covered, these should be communicated to the interviewer. Your interviewers must do sufficient research to ensure that their questions are intelligent and to the point. Reference books and directories should allow you to establish the basic facts of people's lives and careers so that you don't have to waste precious interview time on those matters. Your writers can also look at cuttings, but they should not incorporate unchecked quotes and anecdotes into their features. If there is any incident that they particularly wish to refer to, it should be brought up and checked in the interview.

Most interviewers will use a tape recorder, and this makes sense, although the inexperienced should be reminded of the necessity to use new batteries and tape and to find a quiet place in which to conduct the conversation: this can make all the difference when it comes to transcribing the tape. Taping an interview allows journalists to have a more natural and intelligent conversation with their interviewees, listening to the answers and responding to them rather than simply writing them down. It also allows them to bring back plenty of material beyond simply the words: the interviewee's appearance, dress, manner, body language, and so on, plus the setting in which the interview took place.

Very often these are what brings the interview alive, giving it a sense of immediacy. You should make it clear to the interviewer at the outset whether you require this kind of approach. If you have only a telephone interview, of course, this material will not be available, but you do not have to expressly declare in the piece that the discussion took place at long distance. The tone of voice still comes across. Some telephone interviewers go to great imaginative lengths to pretend that they were speaking face to face, even to the extent of describing the interviewee's clothes. If you have this information, all well and good, but making things up is an abuse of the reader's trust.

Experienced interviewees, particularly 'celebrities', often become rather predictable in their responses. It is not uncommon to read several interviews with the same person, to promote the same project, and to find the same phrases. Different, more considered questions may help here, although people with something to promote will tend to use any question as an opportunity to repeat their prepared answers. But it also helps to find something to write about other than the straightforward sit-down discussion: you should try to 'eavesdrop' on the person at work, or attend some event, anything to get a sense of how the person reacts to other people.

A *profile* can mean several different things. It can be a simple interview, even of the 'Q & A' or questionnaire variety. More often it means a more elaborate interview, supported by comments from colleagues, family and friends of the interviewee, and including extensive details on his or her family or professional background, domestic circumstances, and so on. This is a major undertaking that should only be undertaken by a skilled journalist who will be given appropriate time and support.

It can also mean an analytical article, or character sketch, of a person written without the benefit of an interview. Such pieces are often disparaged as a 'cuttings job', after the source of much of the material, but this is too negative. A good profile is often more revealing than an interview. It can have more attitude, more of an argument, which means it is not necessarily either quicker or less work than an interview. It should be seen as a different approach rather than an inferior one, part of the palette available to the editor. Nonetheless, readers will always tend to prefer a new and preferably exclusive interview to even the most erudite of profiles. An interview is also a 'property', something you can sell on your cover and in your cover-lines.

It has become increasingly common for magazines, particularly in the women's weekly sector, to pay people to be interviewed if they have startling stories to tell. This is understandable, given the intensity of competition in that market, where magazines are also competing with tabloid newspapers and daytime television. But it is regrettable for the creeping effects it has on other areas of journalism where payment for information is not yet the norm.

If you are paying for stories, however, such payments must be covered by an appropriate contract to secure their exclusivity. A person must agree both to provide you with appropriate interview and photographic opportunities and not to be interviewed or photographed by anyone else until after the appearance of your magazine's article. At least part of the payment should be withheld until publication to encourage compliance. Unfortunately, once you are operating in an area in which people choose to speak for financial reasons, you can always be outbid. The fact that you have signed a contract with someone simply means that their price increases: the rival publisher must build in a sum to pay your compensation for breach of contract.

Even this, however, can only be achieved by the threat of legal action, which is unlikely to prove cost-effective and may prove damaging to your image, especially if you are having to contemplate action against people whose story involves some tragedy. The act of 'buying up' someone's story should not be seen as the end of the matter: you must continue to convince them of the non-financial merits of telling the story to you and no-one else.

FURTHER READING

Davis, Anthony (1988) *Magazine Journalism Today*, Oxford: Heinemann Educational Books.
Evans, Harold (1986) *Editing and Design Book 1: Newsman's English*, London: Heinemann.
Keeble, Richard (1994) *The Newspapers Handbook*, London: Routledge.
Waterhouse, Keith (1993) *Waterhouse on Newspaper Style*, Harmondsworth, UK: Penguin.

Chapter 6

Content 2

WORKING WITH WRITERS

As an editor, you may continue to write the odd feature yourself. Assigning the editor to do an interview can sometimes open doors which might otherwise be closed. It can be flattering for the interviewee, especially if it is a rare event rather than a habitual one caused by understaffing. It is also seen as a mark of respect. You must ensure that your performance is up to scratch and that you are rigorous in clamping down on any self-indulgence.

Otherwise, however, you will be assigning writers to jobs, briefing them and editing their copy once it arrives. These are all tasks which need your full attention.

Staff writers

There are times when it is better to use staff rather than freelances. Many types of feature require a great deal of research to produce a very modest number of words. Freelances are generally paid on the basis of what they produce: usually per 1,000 words. This type of article may not be viable for them to undertake, and it is not fair to ask them to do it. But for a staff journalist, the necessary research can be conducted around other jobs, in spare time, and the feature assembled over a long period. This type of job may also need the resources of the magazine's office.

It is also sensible to use staff for particularly sensitive tasks, those which are meant to surprise readers and competitors. Freelances are loyal to your magazine while they are actually working for it: their commitment cannot be expected to go beyond that. Consequently, it is inappropriate to expect them to be bound by silence about your future plans. Staff, on the other hand, should have only one loyalty.

Experimental features which may or may not work, and those which require the daily involvement of senior staff including yourself, are also better kept in-house. One of the central tasks of the commissioning editor is to avoid paying for things that aren't used. But you are paying your staff anyway, and if they have time available it is better to experiment with that.

Even if writers are on the staff, they still need proper briefing on what is expected. Just as with a freelance, they should be given clear instructions and an appropriate deadline. When they turn in their copy, especially if they are inexperienced, it is only fair to give it the level of attention a freelance's copy would get. Gentle guidance can be given, as well as encouragement.

There is one clear distinction between staff writers and freelance writers. Employees do not hold the copyright of their work. Copyright is, in bald terms, the right to copy a piece of artistic work, to reproduce it: it is unlawful to do so without the permission of the copyright holder. In the case of employed people, the holder of the copyright in their work is their employer. This is absolutely critical if you are planning to sell on people's stories, or to use them in some other medium, perhaps on CD-ROM or the Internet. Such rights can be acquired from freelances, but only after negotiation and sometimes at extra cost.

If you are putting together a particular project, whether it be a book, a CD-ROM or a particular Internet site or page, it may be sensible to hand it over to staff journalists to do. If you are in the habit of selling your staff's features for wider circulation, perhaps in the national newspapers, you have no obligation to share the profit from the exercise with your journalists, but good manners and harmonious staff relations might make it a good idea to work out some kind of payment.

Commissioning freelance writers

Commissioning writers is one of those areas of journalism which is much mystified. In fact, its basics are extremely straightforward, but it benefits from all the experience you can bring to it. Fundamentally it is about negotiating to buy someone's services as a writer, and everything else flows from that. The first essential is that those given the authority to commission, which could be you or a whole tier of your staff, know the constraints under which they are operating. A certain number of pages have to be filled and a certain sum of money is available to pay for the necessary journalistic material. This will have been worked out during the budgeting process. The budget will show a certain sum per month, which needs to be converted back into a sum per issue.

The person with commissioning authority should be given these figures and told to operate within them. Every month, you, as editor, should compare actual spending with the budget figure, allowing for a certain amount of necessary variance month to month. This reflects differences between issues. Some will have more pages than were budgeted for, some fewer. Some will contain a greater proportion of freelance material, perhaps because of staff illness or the nature of the subjects chosen. In some months, excess material will have been commissioned and held over or, on unavoidable occasions, simply discarded.

It is for the commissioning editor to turn those big figures into something to work with. Take an average issue size, determine the average number of freelance pages, and divide that into the allocated budget to determine a cost per page. Then consider some actual layouts and work out the average number of words per page across a series of feature pages. Divide that into the cost per page to produce first a cost per word and then a cost per 1,000 words. This is not, however, the rate that should be paid, since it includes the wastage mentioned above. But it is there as a guide. An actual minimum rate should be determined, considerably less than the cost per 1,000 words, for quoting to freelances; but any commissioning editor must have leeway to increase the rate for more experienced writers and for more difficult, time-consuming tasks. In a way, it pays to have three figures in mind: minimum, average and absolute maximum. Sometimes it may be more logical to pay on a different basis: perhaps a fee per day, although this must still be accounted for against the overall page budget.

This is the background for discussions between commissioning editors and freelance writers. It is not, however, the starting point for those discussions. First you need to give the writer a brief and this should be, as its name suggests, a short but comprehensive explanation of what you want written. It should certainly not extend beyond a single page of A4. It should include an account of the subject, the approach you want taken, specific questions you want answered, people you would like interviewed (or excluded), and details of any extra material – boxes, panels and so on – apart from the main piece. It should also state if the writer is required to collect any pictures or other visual material.

Then you have to set a deadline. This must obviously allow you enough time to edit the material and arrange any illustration. It is not always wise to tell the author the date you expect to publish it, though most will want to know, especially if your company's policy is to pay '30 days after publication' rather than within so many days of receipt of an invoice. Obviously, the less confident of the writer you are, the earlier deadline you should agree. Next you specify a number of words. Bear in mind that some types of layout are very much denser than others. If the piece is to fit a specified slot you can be very precise about the number of words required. Otherwise, you need to work out an average that will enable you to fill the number of pages required. You might find it handy to make yourself a little chart of how various types of layout work in practice. A single page feature might average 1,000 words, but a double-page spread might only work out at about 1,800. It is likely that your writers will over-write. Most do. But the fee is a fixed figure based on the commission. If you ask for 1,000 words and the writer produces 1,500 the fee remains the same. The extra words are free, on one level, but on another they actually cost you money because someone has to reduce them to fit the specified slot. This circumstance can, however, sometimes be used to advantage. If you know your writer will always over-write, you can undercommission appropriately and save money. It is for the writer to note the disparity and renegotiate future commissions accordingly.

You should also specify delivery method if there is likely to be any doubt about it: fax, post, modem or disk. Some magazines also ask writers to spell out that their work is original, not previously published, their own property, factually true and not 'libellous'. The legal status of this last is not entirely clear: as editor you make your own decisions about what is defamatory or not and cannot expect to shift responsibility to anyone else, even the writer.

What remains to be discussed is the crucial question of what 'rights' you wish to purchase. All literary and artistic work is 'copyright', which means that it cannot be reproduced without the permission of the copyright owner. The owner of the copyright in freelance material is the freelance writer or photographer. If an editor wishes to produce such material, the right to do so must be acquired.

In addition, the 1988 Copyright Act provided for the first time certain 'moral rights' for the authors of copyright material. These include the right to be identified as the author of the material and the right not to have the work subjected to 'derogatory treatment', meaning addition, deletion, alteration and adaptation where these have the effect of distorting the work or damaging the reputation of the author. However, it is important to note that the Act specifically excludes work made for the purposes of publication in any 'newspaper, magazine or similar periodical' from these provisions.

You may occasionally encounter freelances who have read far enough into the Act to hear about these 'moral rights' but not far enough to realise that they don't apply to magazine work. They should be gently advised on the subject. The exclusion even applies to book extracts and other pieces of work made for other media: once they are made available to you as an editor of a magazine, with the consent of the author, moral rights no longer apply.

Some editors like to spell out, in their commissioning letters, that they require the unlimited right to cut, amend, add to and generally edit the text. The author is required to sign his or her acceptance of these terms. You may feel, however, that there is no point in spelling out so baldly what is the accepted custom and practice of the trade and creating an air of suspicion where none need exist.

'Moral rights' are, however, a side issue. The real issue is the right to publish, and that has recently become a battleground, at least in Britain. Until very recently, both sides of the question, writers and editors, were happy with what copyright law makes standard when no other agreement is reached. That is to say, the writer sells First British Serial Rights. This means the right of first publication, once only, in a magazine or newspaper circulating in Britain. Any extra rights, for instance to syndicate the article outside Britain or to use it in a book, had to be negotiated separately. There were exceptions: those writing for 'part-work' type reference works would sign 'all rights' contracts and would often be amazed to see their work recycled year after year.

Recently, however, this state of affairs has been shattered by publishers eager to acquire comprehensive rights at the point of initial commissioning, ostensibly to facilitate moves into the new electronic media, CD-ROM and the Internet. Usually the demand has been that the freelance 'assign' copyright, which is to say sell it. Other publishers have preferred to demand an 'unlimited licence' giving them 'all rights', usually accompanied by a list of every conceivable medium, whether yet invented or not. Sometimes this has been accompanied by the demand that all future commissions by that freelance be undertaken on the same basis. Clearly the idea has been to establish once and for all a new contractual basis between magazine publishers and authors that would allow publishers to use journalistic material in new ways without their commercial ingenuity being shackled by the need for endless negotiation each time a project was undertaken.

You can see the point: if the idea is to move existing products wholesale into new media, publishers will naturally not want that process to be dependent on the agreement of every individual involved. A nightmare of tracking down contributors and agreeing terms is in prospect unless some more sensible system is agreed. (An obvious parallel is with the 'repeat fees' system used in television, whereby actors, writers and others are guaranteed extra payments when programmes in which they were involved are repeated. This can be a useful income stream for those concerned, but complicates the decision to repeat, and in some cases failure to reach agreement has kept excellent programmes off the screen for years.)

Unfortunately, when these new contractual terms are written down in the terms used by solicitors, their alarming implications for freelances are made crystal clear. One major British magazine publisher sent out commissioning forms worded thus:

> You assign to us exclusively throughout the universe the entire present and future copyright and all other right, title and interest of any nature (including rental and lending rights, the rights of any communication to the public by satellite and cable re-transmission, and any similar or allied rights which may come into existence in the future) in and to (a) the commissioned work and (b) all other products of your services under this agreement, and we will then own (a) and (b) absolutely for the full period of copyright including any renewals and extensions and (to the extent possible) for all time. This means that we have, in relation to the Work, the exclusive and unrestricted right to use it in all media and all formats, including publications on optical and magnetic disks, cartridges, smartcards, networks, and online, without any further payment to you.

The contract then went on to insist that: 'You waive unconditionally, irrevocably and permanently the benefit of any moral rights to the Work, including similar or equivalent rights in any part of the world, and agree not to take any action over moral rights.' Other publishers used less explicit wording and were less demanding on the question of the exclusivity of future rights, at least leaving the freelances the right to use the material for their own purposes after its initial publication.

This is not a quibble: freelances often hope to sell and reuse their old material in various ways. The advent of the World Wide Web has given them another outlet, either through the production of their own Web sites or through licensing their own material to other sites, many of which are run on a non-profitmaking basis and are grateful for contributions in their own areas of special interest. None of this would be permissible under the contract quoted above.

What has made matters worse is that none of these demands for the comprehensive renegotiation of the traditional basis of publisher-freelance relationships has been accompanied by vastly improved rates of payment. The result is an unfortunate and largely unnecessary stand-off, with editors in the middle.

It has been argued that publishers wanted to acquire these rights simply for convenience, there being no appropriate mechanism for the payment of royalties on electronic media use. The publishers argue, also, that their investment in the electronic media is experimental and has not, as yet, resulted in any sort of increased income. However, the aggressive wording of most of these documents has enraged freelances and their representatives in the National Union of Journalists and thirteen other writers', illustrators' and photographers' organisations.

The reality is that most written journalism is not reused, though pictures may be. Surrendering copyright in the past was distasteful to many writers but did not do them any actual harm. Now, however, writers can see that the potential is there for their material to be reused, and for profit, and they have decided, quite understandably, that they want to benefit from any such publishing activity. The current uneasy stand-off has no clear outcome.

Many companies have produced all-rights clauses in their commissioning letters, and many freelances, at least those who have taken advice, are refusing to sign them. This is one difficulty that busy editors could do without, and it is to be hoped that an equitable solution is found, perhaps along the lines of the agreement established by Time Inc. in New York, which assures freelance contributors of payment for reuse of their material. There are also proposals for some kind of outside agency to take over the job of collecting and distributing copyright payments. Contributors would still be required to give publishers an unlimited licence to publish, but would be assured of a fee each time it was used.

It is worth noting, in this context, that staff writers in Britain have no copyright over their material so the problem does not arise. Unfortunately, the arrival of the electronic delivery systems that have given such an impetus to republishing projects has coincided with a general move by publishers towards running their magazines with tiny numbers of staff and large volumes of freelance material. A failure to resolve the copyright issue could mean some movement back towards the pattern of employment traditionally seen in local newspapers, with large staffs and less freelance input.

In practice, all these matters – brief, terms, deadline and fee – should be embodied in a printed form. At least two copies are required, one to go to the writer and one to be kept by the commissioning editor. If you require the author's written agreement to the terms, which you certainly will if you expect the author to assign you copyright or give you a particular licence to publish, the writer must be sent two forms so that one can be returned, signed, to the office.

This is merely the mechanical part of commissioning. The more creative part comes in matching writers to ideas. Obviously the safest way to handle commissioning is to deal with a tiny number of trusted writers, who can be briefed in a moment and who never quibble about what is done to their copy or what they are paid. However, this can lead to a certain stagnation. A commissioning editor must look for new writers. Most people will be inundated with letters from hopefuls, but it can be better to approach people whose writing you have enjoyed in other fields. The path of commissioning strangers is extremely fraught and there are no short cuts. Every commissioning editor has various freelance directories, but except in the case of needing to find someone in a particular geographical location or with a particular expertise, they are rarely opened. Freelances may speak to you convincingly and with very appealing ideas, but that is no proof of an ability to write. If you are trying someone new, it is common sense to give them something small to do. That way, even if the whole exercise is a complete write-off, the loss is small.

The commissioning editor's task does not end with actually signing the commissioning letter or form and sending it on its way. The piece itself must be shepherded into print. Every editor discovers, before very long, what it is to receive a completely unusable piece of work. First the piece should be compared with the brief. If it is unsalvageable, though still within the range of professional work, some kind of payment should be offered to bring the contract to a close. This is often referred to as a kill fee, although technically that term should be used for a commission which is stopped before it is completed. If the piece is simply hopeless then you may feel justified in refusing to pay for it. This would leave you open to a proceeding in the small claims court, where you should be prepared to defend your action.

In cases where the piece is acceptable, but not right, the author should be contacted, the deficiencies listed and a rewrite asked for. It is reasonable to expect at least one rewrite under the terms of the original commission. However, having asked for a rewrite, you are effectively committed to paying the full price for the piece even if you do not use it. At this stage, your best bet is to rewrite it yourself or ask your sub-editors or commissioning editors to do so, thereby salvaging something from the debacle.

Given the difficulty in securing a commission, some freelances, especially the inexperienced ones, may attempt to sell you material 'on spec'. But the terms of any such arrangements need to be made very clear at the outset. If you agree to 'take a look' at a piece, some freelances, especially those from a local newspaper background, are likely to claim that you have 'ordered' the piece, which is to say commissioned it. Consequently, if you agree to look at a piece submitted speculatively you must spell out, in words of one syllable, that if it is not used there will be no payment.

REGULAR FEATURES

A large proportion of your magazine's content will be designed to be re-assuringly similar from week to week or month to month. These elements are called the 'regular features' or the 'departments', and they are extremely important to the magazine's appeal. Very often they are neglected by new editors, who turn their attention to the more immediately noticeable elements first. But research shows that the regulars are often as well read as the features, with columnists and readers' letters getting a particularly high score. At some early juncture, you should take the time to look at each of these elements and ask yourself if it is doing as much for your readers as perhaps it should.

The editor's letter

Many editors find the 'editor's letter' a tremendous chore. It is however, the one exception to the general rule about making yourself responsible for nothing except everything. You should certainly take care over this slot, since it provides you with a valuable opportunity to communicate directly with your readers. One obvious use is to draw attention to parts of your issue which might otherwise go unnoticed. Some editors go beyond that, using it to draw their readers into a relationship with themselves and their staff; certainly it is a good place to announce any awards that have been won.

But in other markets it plays a quite different role, as a kind of 'leader column' allowing you to comment on the state of the industry, and specifically to point out and uphold the interests of your readers. This is important in establishing an identity of purpose between the magazine and those who read it. And at the very least, the editor's letter should be used to stimulate correspondence for your letters page.

Readers' letters

It is a common belief among journalists that only lunatics write to letters pages. It's not true, of course, but your own letters page may be suffering from excessive contributions from those with axes to grind, those with complaints, and those with nothing to say but a burning desire to see their names in print.

If this is the case, it is your own fault. Readers' letters are copy like any other, and need to be edited. It is not enough to stand aside and let material dribble in. At the very least contributions need to be edited so that they make sense, cut to enhance their impact and placed in some kind of order, with the interesting ones in a position of prominence. You should also give each letter an appealing headline. Letters which demand a direct answer from you or your staff should be answered on the page, but this can go too far. You should not allow letters to be used as a starting point for you or your own staff to exercise their sarcasm.

But beyond all that, it is actually worth soliciting letters on occasions. If you are a professional journal, you really need the leading lights in the profession to use your letters page as a forum for debate. If they are criticised (and you must ensure that any such criticism does not slip over into defamation) they should be told about it and invited to respond. A letters page which regularly plays host to the big names in your field will both attract plenty of letters and enhance the authority of your journal. And if the supply of letters increases, the quality will rise. In particular, you should remove merely informational letters, requests for assistance, form letters, and so on, and find somewhere else for them.

Columns

Columnists are part of the same communication process as a lively letters page. Ideally, you want columnists who will enhance your magazine's reputation. They may be authoritative figures from your industry, or simply good journalists with strong views and a good turn of phrase. Ideally, of course, they would be both. You need them to be reliable and self-sustaining. There is nothing more dispiriting than the columnist who has to be told what to write every week. But at the same time they should not feel as if they are working in a vacuum. A courtesy call to ask what they are writing about, or to praise a previous effort, or to suggest a thought, can be much appreciated.

Specifically humorous columnists are required to meet one criterion only, which is that they be funny. Humour is very subjective, of course, and what amuses you may not have the same effect on all of your colleagues. But this is a case where rank has its privileges, and if you think something is funny you should stick with it. Your humorist should be answerable only to you. No-one can be funny for a committee. Nor is humour amenable to subbing.

If a piece doesn't fit, it can be cut, but only by removing whole chunks and not by delicate trimming. Clipping a word here and a phrase there is liable to destroy the delicate rhythm on which jokes depend. Nor can a humorist's language be adjusted to suit house style or some sub-editor's prejudices. These things are best left alone.

Columnists are not obliged to abide by the general requirement for objectivity, but their material must be read extremely carefully with a view to its legal implications. The law defends strong opinions honestly held, but only if they are based on the accurate statement of facts. Libel juries are perfectly capable of detecting that something is a joke, but this does not mean that they do not think someone should be compensated for having such a thing said about them.

The diary column

All publications need some element of humour, and many, especially in the business press, attempt to achieve it by means of the diary column. This has several functions. Sometimes it is little more than a kind of notice-board of events and causes, mentioning a retirement here and a charity ball there. More often, however, it attempts to become a kind of gossip column. But there are a number of problems with that idea. Suitable gossip is rarely available. When it does become available, it is not usable, principally because your readers do not expect to see their peers written about in that way. If you do run any genuine gossip, you can expect outrage from those written about, leading to all manner of threats from withdrawn advertising to a libel writ. In the end, your hapless diarist will be reduced to looking for amusing misprints.

Nonetheless, a good diary column can serve a number of useful purposes. If it is filled with events it gives a strong sense of the magazine being active within the world it serves. It also makes a good place to store reports of good works, promotions, awards and a lot of good news that doesn't make it into the news section. Local newspapers make it a policy to photograph as many people as possible, especially groups of children, on the grounds that doting relatives will buy copies. Something of the same can be achieved with magazine diary columns.

The gossip element can still be there if you have someone capable of researching it thoroughly and writing it up in a way that stays within the bounds of both good humour and the law. But you should not expect to challenge *Private Eye* or Nigel Dempster.

Contents

A magazine's contents page is as much a design problem as it is a writing problem. It is to be considered principally as a selling device for the content of the magazine, an extension of the billboard or the cover-lines. The object is to present the material inside the magazine in the most appealing light, while at the same time providing solid information for those who actually use the page to find things. Research suggests that they are a relatively small proportion of the total readership, but they must not be positively thwarted.

Most magazines give most of their pages over to regular features of one sort or another, but to use the bulk of the space on the contents page (or pages) simply to list them is a waste of a valuable selling pitch. So your design needs to accommodate some way of dividing off those 'regulars' from everything else, and listing them simply by page title and number. If there is something extraordinary in those pages, there is no reason why it shouldn't be listed twice, in the 'regulars' section and in the main listing of features contents. It may suit you to break your long list of contents into many different sections, but you should be wary of simply using the divisions you have invented for your own purposes, which may have no meaning for the reader. A heading saying 'features', for instance, is meaningless to most people who will read your magazine, whereas 'Hollywood' or 'Health' over a group of features will make perfect sense.

The emphasis should be on the straightforward 'sell'. Where suitably strong pictures are available, they should do most of the talking. Alongside, above or beneath the relevant picture should be the heading from the piece (providing it is not too obscure) and a brief, positive outline of its contents. Using different headings on the contents page and on the actual feature is to be avoided, simply because readers have to know they've arrived at the right place. But if you must, you must: it is absolutely essential for the casual reader of the contents page to know who, exactly, is being interviewed. Above all, keep contents page blurbs to one short sentence and keep the type size high.

People pages

Most magazines will have some sort of 'people' page or section, whether the simple list of people changing jobs that you find in most professional magazines or the selection of small interviews that is common in consumer publications. In the case of the former, the options are limited, but for the latter it is important to ring the changes. There are several ways of writing and illustrating interview material and they should all be exploited to avoid making the material too 'samey'. 'Q & A' format interviews, 'as told to' first-person interviews and questionnaires should alternate with normal feature-type interviews. The same page might usefully accommodate quotes of the week, gossip, and so on. It should not be overlooked, being a useful section for introducing new faces, stories and personalities into your magazine. It can also be a good place to allow new feature writers and editors to practise their skills.

Products

Most magazines will have some sort of 'products page'; some will consist of nothing else. The degree of editorial input required will vary. In some cases, your product page will amount to no more than press releases sub-edited to fit and to remove some of the more outrageous claims. At the other end of the scale, these pages will actually test and rate the objects described.

The common denominator is accuracy. Any information you include must be accurate, and this is particularly the case with telephone numbers and prices, which must be checked as near to publication as is feasible.

Actual comparative testing of things, particularly of technical equipment, is a very expensive and complex process but it may be necessary in your particular market. Computer and hi-fi magazines are constructed around such tests, both objective and subjective, and go to considerable lengths to ensure their credibility. In particular, you as editor should be aware of all the commercial relationships of your testers. It is not unheard of for the reviewers of hi-fi equipment to be involved with manufacturers as design consultants, publicity advisers or simply brochure writers. Those who take this kind of work must be required to declare it to you and, if appropriate, to the readers. Unexpected exposure of such links can be very damaging

More informal comparisons, without pretensions to true objectivity, are appropriate for less technical products, from household appliances to foods, but they still require fairness from the writer and skilled editing. It is essential that like is always compared with like: a simple printed form may be the best way of ensuring that the same points are addressed when each object is examined, and if more than one tester is involved this becomes essential. The results need not be presented as a table, but the use of a printed form ensures that the underlying structure is solid.

If you are simply reporting the availability of a range of new products, then there are two common approaches. The first is pictorial, but this depends upon photographic material of suitable quality being available. For high-quality consumer magazines, the free publicity shots will be unsuitable, so you must expect to do a shoot. In trade and technical magazines this does not necessarily apply, and standard publicity shots can be used in a tight grid.

The other approach is to apply some kind of news filter to the material. Which of these objects is the most interesting and why? This then leads you to a hierarchical approach to writing them up, with the most important products given the most space and prominence and the others reduced to fillers.

Diary/listings

Most magazines will include some sort of weekly diary of events: this is not to be confused with a 'diary column' as discussed above. The object here is simply to list, accurately, a selection of useful and interesting events for your readers. Some magazines, of course, are composed of little else. It is essential that a smooth and fairly foolproof method exists for ensuring that the information comes in in the first place and makes its way into print. Your copy deadlines need to be published prominently, and whoever deals with the post needs to ensure that the material is moved swiftly to the person or persons compiling the section. Especially in the early stages, it is essential that the outside organisations whose events you are publicising understand exactly what you require and when. It is for your diary or listings editors to ensure that the flow of information continues. If something has not arrived, they must be aware of that and seek it out. In the writing, a balance needs to be struck between the simple listing of facts and something more positive: the difference here is between listings and previews, which attempt to make some sort of assessment of the likely value of events. Where that balance is struck will depend entirely upon the nature of the magazine. But the straightforward listing of information is the starting point and must take priority when space is short.

Campaigns

One useful tool in the struggle to develop and maintain a close identification between the magazine and the reader is the campaign. But it needs careful planning if it is not to be either a long anti-climax or, worse, a positive embarrassment.

The cynical would say that there is no point in pursuing a campaign which you cannot win. An obvious example of this was a campaign run by one national newspaper against the price of compact discs. While the newspaper's investigations were followed by other studies, including hearings before a parliamentary committee, they did not actually lead to any great change in the prices charged. People, it emerged, were happy to pay the high prices that shops and record companies were demanding. The invisible hand of the market had set the price and against that the moans of newspaper columnists were irrelevant. Nonetheless, the campaign did succeed on one level, in that it encouraged readers to contribute a flow of information about discount record shops.

On entering a campaign, it is important to have a strong sense of where it is going and how you expect to withdraw from it, with honour, at the end. There must also be a strong sense that the impetus from the magazine will be met by equal or greater enthusiasm from the readers and the outside world. It helps if the campaign is not entirely self-interested: publishers' efforts against VAT on reading material have not always convinced on that level.

The campaign may start with a single news story or feature article, perhaps identifying some injustice that could be removed by an Act of Parliament or, better, some simple governmental order or change of practice. The first article will need to have considerable emotional impact if it is to generate enough response to carry a campaign. Readers' letters should arrive as a result, but if the intention is to make a campaign on this basis, they must be edited and projected for maximum impact. Thereafter, the campaign proper can take off.

Some kind of identifying logo and slogan is usually devised. A journalist is given responsibility for the campaign. An immediate follow-up reports on reaction. Each issue after that must carry more material on the subject. A list of objectives or demands must be drawn up and published. Celebrity or industry support can be solicited, as well as some kind of official backing.

Members of parliament must be targeted and persuaded of your *bona fides*, and you should speak frankly with them about the possibilities. Thereafter can come the whole panoply of questions in the House and the soliciting of government and opposition support. Some campaigns of this sort end in the drafting of a Private Member's Bill, but this can be extremely frustrating, since the simple drafting of a bill is no guarantee that it is to receive any kind of reading. And if a government sets its face against your campaign, you are heading for a defeat and some graceful method of withdrawal needs to be found: you may, for instance, be able to be instrumental in the creation of some sort of new pressure group or charity that will continue the fight once you have moved on to something else.

No magazine campaign will succeed unless it is driven by genuine enthusiasm on the part of both the editor and the appropriate journalists. Campaigns can very quickly become a tedious obligation if no-one is passionate about them. For that reason they need to be chosen with care.

SUB-EDITING

The craft of the sub-editor is absolutely vital to successful magazine journalism, which increasingly relies on the seamless incorporation of copy from many different writers. Sub-editing has three strands: a kind of quality control, ensuring that everything is accurate, well-written and likely to be legally safe; a production function, ensuring that everything fits and that deadlines are kept; and a key role in the projection of material, through the writing of appropriate and attention-grabbing headlines, standfirsts and captions.

Depending on your staffing and structure, some of these tasks may not be done by sub-editors. It is common for editors to write headlines and standfirsts themselves, but it is probably better unless you are on a very small magazine to give your sub-editors a run at these things, which are among the more enjoyable aspects of their job.

Dealing with copy

Writers and sub-editors approach a piece of work from different ends. Writers' loyalties will tend to be to their sources, their interviewees and the facts of the story itself. This can mean a lack of detachment, the inclusion of too much confusing detail and, on occasions, deliberate obfuscation. Sub-editors' loyalty must be to the readers: they are there to represent the readers' interests. This means making sure that everything is as clear and accurate as is possible. Sometimes this leads to the loss of nuance but that is the price that is paid for clarity. It is inevitable that there will on occasions be differences between writers and sub-editors, but editors must draw the line between the two sides, bearing in mind their separate loyalties. Since the editor's loyalty, too, is to the readers, if the sub-editors are making the right decisions they should be able to count on the editor's support.

Clarity of verbal construction is the starting point: everything in a piece of published copy must follow logically, and there should be no internal contradictions. After that, the sub-editor can look at individual sentences and paragraphs to ensure that they are as well-expressed as they might be. The writer's language, too, can be examined for redundancies and padding, for clichés and jargon. Every sub-editor will have a favourite library of linguistic authorities: particularly to be recommended are the *Oxford Writers' Dictionary*, Fowler's *The King's English*, Harold Evans's *Newsman's English* (out of print), and Keith Waterhouse's *Waterhouse on Newspaper Style*, which despite its provenance offers excellent guidance for those striving for a plain style that is not dull. Even sub-editors in the business press should encourage language that is comprehensible to the mass of the public rather than let their pages become clogged with acronyms and technical buzzwords where English synonyms exist. These things can easily become tedious even to those who know what they mean.

The sub-editor must also look out for inaccuracies. While the main thrust of a story will necessarily be taken on trust, it is within the sub-editor's range of responsibilities to check those things which can be verified from printed sources or by a simple, uncontroversial telephone call: names, telephone numbers, dates, registered trade marks, and so on. The sub-editor must have at least as much general knowledge and topical awareness as the average writer, and beyond that should use common sense. It pays to be sceptical. Naturally, spelling should be corrected too: the computer spelling checker can be a help but it must not be relied upon.

Another key part of the sub-editing process is spotting defamatory and potentially actionable statements. Libel cases often come about by accident.

Any statement that is critical of any living person, company, product or organisation needs to be thought about. If necessary, it should be referred to you as editor. Sub-editors should get into the habit of asking 'Would I like this said about me?' If not, there is likely to be a problem.

Beyond mere verbal policing, sub-editors will often be expected to make substantial cuts in submitted articles and to engage in major rewrites. In both cases, if the cuts and changes are more than minor, it can be a good idea to inform the author. In the case of cutting for length, it will often be necessary, and indeed advisable, to remove whole themes, episodes or characters from a feature rather than tinker on a verbal level. Here guidance must be provided to ensure that the essentials emerge unscathed; and of course, it must become standard practice for sub-editors to work on copies of computer files rather than on the originals, since the option of returning to the original form of words must always be available.

The same considerations apply to rewriting, which should only be attempted if it is necessary. On the whole, it is preferable to leave well alone: a properly commissioned article should be publishable on arrival, or at least once the author has provided a second draft. Feature writers especially are prized for their style, which may be considerably more florid and adventurous than would be acceptable on a news page. Sub-editors should restrict themselves to a limited amount of re-angling and reordering. Sometimes this can take the form of pulling passages out and turning them into sidebars, panels and captions, although it is better if such things are discussed at the commissioning stage.

Rewriting is not usually a case of recasting the way in which a piece is written. Any substantial changes must be discussed with an author, if good relations are to be maintained. Often these changes will be necessary to reflect new developments in a story or to match more closely the tastes of your specific readership, which you may understand better than a freelance with many customers. It is unhelpful for such discussions to revolve around matters of linguistic taste. Nonetheless, it is sometimes necessary for otherwise unpublishable pieces to be saved by sub-editors, and in this case you as editor should be ready to defend their work in the event of an adverse reaction from the author.

Sub-editing and production

A magazine's production schedule is designed to allow time for the range of necessary tasks to be carried out, from initial commissioning, through picture research to sub-editing and layout. The actual policing of the schedule, ensuring that copy arrives and leaves on time, lies with the sub-editors. Time overruns can have important cost effects, so it is vital that the sub-editors are given the support that they need in this area.

They are also responsible for keeping control of copy-flow, ensuring that the correct files come in and go out. A logical structure of filenames is important here, as is a system of logs to record traffic between editorial office and outside facilities. Mastery of the editorial computer systems is essential too.

As well as sending material through on its first pass, sub-editors must read proofs, and here it is vital that paper proofs are made available. Studies repeatedly show that a very much higher proportion of errors is detected on paper than on even the best screen. As well as checking for typographical errors and missing lines and words, sub-editors must watch out for wrong fonts, type sizes and styles, all of which have become much more common since the change to on-screen page makeup.

Sub-editing and projection

On some magazines, particularly those professional publications which use newspaper-style layouts, it is common for sub-editors to handle page layout as well as the verbal tasks. They obviously have a key role in the projection of editorial material.

But even those sub-editors who aren't involved in the visual aspects of the magazine will have some responsibility for those verbal aspects which are central to projection: the art of persuading people to read. They will be writing cover-lines, headlines, standfirsts and captions. There are as many approaches to these as there are magazines, or indeed, as there are sub-editors. As editor, you must set the pattern and ensure that it is adhered to, but this does not mean stamping out any element of individual inspiration on the part of your sub-editing team.

Your magazine's cover is its most important selling tool. The picture must make a direct appeal and the cover-lines are there to support it. Most magazines will have fewer than half a dozen cover-lines. Any more than that is counter productive. The main cover-line should be part of a concept with the cover picture: they should have come about at the same time, even if the eventual cover-line represents little more than the name of the person being interviewed and what he or she represents.

The remaining lines represent the five or six most appealing articles inside, rather than the longest, most prominent or most costly. This is another area in which the law of self-interest can usefully be applied: what do you have to offer that will convince the readers that buying this magazine will offer them a distinct advantage? Then it is simply a matter of phrasing that offer in a straightforward and appealing way. Clever puns and allusions are rarely required in cover-lines.

There is still a lot of life in simple concepts such as 'How to' and 'Why x will be doing y'. Negative concepts and expressions, on the other hand, should be shunned. 'How to avoid . . .', 'Don't miss out on . . .' and so on, are better replaced by positive formulations. If you can intrigue, all well and good: 'My secret life by . . . ' Otherwise it may be better just to tell the reader straightforwardly what you are offering.

Headlines inside the magazine can be less commercially-minded. They should have due respect for their function, however. News headlines are the most straightforward: they simply inform readers of the gist of the story and usually have some relation to a story's standfirst. This does not mean using identical words.

Outside the news area, headline style will depend very much on what the magazine design requires the headline to do and the space it provides to do it. A reader looking at a page or spread needs to know exactly what it is about. If your design allows you to incorporate that most basic of information in a strap line or sub-heading you don't need to put it in your main heading, which can therefore be more allusive and clever. For instance, if you have an interview with someone whose name is well known to your readers your strap-line can say 'Interview: Joe Smith'.

Your standfirst can then say what Joe Smith is all about, as well as introducing the interviewer (if your design does not demand a separate by-line): 'The head of Amalgamated Widgets foresees a hard time ahead for industry', etc. Meanwhile your headline attempts to tell readers more about what Joe Smith is like: 'Man of iron' or 'Hammering out a grim message'. The trick is to use the various elements to ensure that between them they provide all the necessary information, without necessarily providing it more than once.

Headlines must, of course, be legally sound. It is disastrous to amend copy to nullify its defamatory undertones only to reinstate them by sloppy choice of a headline.

Consumer magazine sub-editors in particular tend to think that writing a heading is about writing puns. It is not. Other types of wordplay are often more appropriate, including topical or artistic allusion. Readers don't like puns half as much as sub-editors do, and if they are allowed it must only be when they are absolutely appropriate as well as funny. Simply making a play on words based on someone's name is foolish unless the new formulation absolutely captures the mood of the piece. If the pun is particularly appealing then it must be integrated with the standfirst so that it makes sense, but the standfirst is not there to justify a heading that is otherwise unacceptable.

Editors should be aware that there are fashions in headline writing, even within a single sub-editing department. Occasionally it is good to produce an edict, for instance that there must be no more headlines incorporating people's first names, just to try and make inspiration run on less familiar lines.

Standfirsts are another essential element of the feature package. They free the writer from the task of having to explain what a feature is about in the opening paragraph. They can also indicate the tone of what is to follow or set the scene. Brevity, though, is of the essence. Most contemporary standfirsts consist of no more than a single punchy sentence, two if the writer's by-line is to be incorporated.

Crossheads are short headings between paragraphs in the body of a feature or story. They are rarely more than two or three words long and are placed for design purposes, usually, rather than for editorial purposes. They should give some flavour of what is immediately beneath them, but few readers even notice them.

Captions are there to label the elements in a picture, though not to describe them. Those who are writing captions should ensure that they know exactly what the cropped picture will show, and be careful not to state the obvious. The caption should, where possible, add something to the picture which the visuals alone cannot convey, whether that is actual information – 'Minutes before the fatal crash . . .' – or simply atmosphere. There is no need to say 'This picture shows . . .'. Sub-editors must also check that the correct photographs are being used. Confusing two people with similar names can be a costly error if one is a known criminal and the other is a blameless Sunday-school teacher.

All these things are the product of solid basic skills, a high level of education and awareness, and sharp verbal intelligence. Editors should value those who excel at them as highly as they value more visible members of the team.

CONTENT FOR ELECTRONIC PUBLISHING

These are early days in electronic publishing, whether on- or off-line. The design constraints and opportunities are quite different from those of traditional paper publishing. The central problem is that electronic magazines are designed to be read on screen, but not even the most expensive monitors (which most customers will not be using) have managed to make this an appealing process. The designer has to decide whether to allow readers to make their own design decisions, choosing typeface, type size and colour, for instance, to suit their own equipment and eyesight. The alternative is to lock up the design at the publishing end, which is how things are done in paper publishing, but this is a difficult practice in a technology in which the publisher has no control over standards of eventual reproduction.

One thing that has become clear is that with the present generation of computer equipment, reading long articles is a chore. Electronic magazines have concentrated on providing short items which impress on the basis of their immediacy. Reading longer items on screen is not a pleasure but it has some advantages. Chief among these is the ability to be able to find things by searching for words and phrases. On-line or off-line electronic publications function in a different way to their printed equivalents: people use them to search for specific items of information. They tend not to read through them in the way they read printed magazines. Whether better display equipment, which may be a generation away, will remove that distinction remains to be seen.

FURTHER READING

Bryson, Bill (1990) *Mother Tongue: The English Language*, London: Hamish Hamilton.
Chambers Guide to Grammar and Usage (1996) compiled by George Davidson, Edinburgh: Chambers.
Flint, Michael F. (1990) *A User's Guide to Copyright*, London: Butterworths.
Fowler, H.W. and Fowler, F.G. (1993) *The King's English*, London: Wordsworth Editions.
Gowers, Sir Ernest (1987) *The Complete Plain Words*, Harmondsworth, UK: Penguin.
McFarlane, Gavin (1989) *A Practical Introduction to Copyright*, London: Waterlow.
Oxford Writers' Dictionary (1990) Oxford: Oxford University Press.

Chapter 7

The editor and the visual

Magazine editing is not simply about leading people and working with words. The essence of modern magazines is visual appeal. A small number of entirely text-based publications continue to exist, usually for official purposes. Every other magazine editor, from the creator of a church newsletter to the person directing a major consumer magazine, must consider the visual aspects of the task.

Publishing is never a purely verbal matter: printing words always involves design issues, even if it is only the selection of a typeface. Magazine design takes that process and extends it through the incorporation of photographic and illustrative material.

Sadly, there can exist a strong clash of cultures between those members of the magazine team who have come from a journalistic background and those with a design training. Early on, you as editor must learn to conceive of ideas in visual terms, considering the illustrative possibilities at the same time as you think about the material itself. Indeed, the word 'illustrative' itself is an unhelpful one, tending to suggest that the task of the designer is to find visual material to 'accompany' or 'support' the words, to prettify someone else's raw material, when the relationship should be much more organic than that.

At the same time, those who come from a design background need to appreciate that magazine design is not a form of fine art. Magazine designers are, increasingly, visual journalists. The object of their efforts is neither for the designers to express themselves nor, actually, to produce something inherently beautiful. The point is to turn design to the task of expressing the underlying ideas and thoughts that motivate a piece of published material; and the end product should be something unique, an amalgam of words and visuals that is greater than the sum of the separate elements.

This is, of course, an ideal. Much of the routine work of a magazine's art department cannot be expected to approach it, for reasons of time as much as anything else. Nonetheless, it is always important to keep the ideal in mind: page creation as one process, rather than the merger of two.

'EDITING BY DESIGN'

The magazine designer Jan V. White used this expression as the title for his classic work on the subject. The book represented a notable attempt to place design at the heart of the editing process, complete with procedures for doing so in practice. White's plea is for editors to see their magazines as three-dimensional objects, in which the third dimension, depth, is created by the progress *through* the assembled sequence of pages. This dimension is easily neglected, and thoughtful editors need to find ways of ensuring that that sequence is always visible to those working on an issue, by intelligent use of page-proofs or thumbnails (reduced-sized print-outs or photocopies of the finished pages).

Much editing takes place on the 'micro' level, as editors fiddle with bits of copy to ensure their accuracy and to get the tone right. But the other end of the scale is vital too: the way different elements are ordered, massed and emphasised, both on individual pages and across the whole magazine. This is about the creation and manipulation of 'pace', the rate at which a magazine presents its material to its readers. The usual assumption is that it is better to have a number of short elements at the front and back, where they will appeal to the casual reader or the person flicking through in adverse conditions, leaving the centre of the magazine for longer, more time-consuming reads which demand more serious attention.

These questions are resolved in the flat-planning of an individual issue, but these decisions must be based on an original design scheme for the magazine's shape. Such a scheme must include a recognition of the importance of landmarks for the reader, who will expect a high degree of consistency from issue to issue. These fixed elements would normally include the contents page or pages, which will be specified as appearing on, say, the first or second right-hand page, and the openings of separate sections, which might also open on right-handers.

Decisions must also be made about how to handle longer features. You can specify a number of possible page permutations. These might include single pages, simple spreads, spreads followed by several singles, a single right-hand start followed by a spread, and so on. The designers then provide suitable typographical and visual stylings for each option, some of which will become a regular type of 'slot' for a specific purpose: for instance, you might always use a spread for your opening interview, which would always be edited and designed accordingly.

The American technique of giving each new feature a spread at the start of the magazine before continuing the story at the back is intended to give a publication a fast-moving features section in which the browser and casual reader are given lots of starting points. Unfortunately, those who want actually to read the pieces are then led on a paper-chase through a mass of purely functional pages with no pretensions to elegance.

This method has rarely been favoured in Britain, where the tendency is to start with an eye-catching opening spread and assume that the reader will follow: thus the density of the page can actually increase once the reader is hooked. This might mean an opening spread which is all picture, headline and standfirst, then a left-hand page with a reasonable selection of pictures, then another with a single picture, then a final page with almost no decoration, except perhaps a pull quote. This soaks up large numbers of words, bringing the feature to an end and allowing the next one to start. The American method, in contrast, effectively writes off a large proportion of a magazine as a sort of filing cabinet.

There is a danger that the back parts of a magazine will seem the natural place to put all those things that no-one on the staff is very interested in: competitions, readers' letters, regular items. If you are not careful it can become no more than a dustbin. But good magazine design works backwards and forwards, to accommodate those readers who habitually flick from the back. You should anchor the final editorial page, usually the left-hander opposite the inside back cover, by reserving it for a strong column or something equally striking, and then you can build backwards from there.

Simply altering the order in which things appear can have a dramatic effect on a magazine's usefulness and readability, and this is particularly true for magazines with a high information content, for instance listings titles. It is essential to finding a logical structure for this type of material.

Jan V. White's other fundamental idea is to bring design into the initial story-planning process. He proposes a 'story conference' for each significant feature, to include writer and commissioning editor but also designer and picture editor. This is an excellent idea that is rarely practised, simply by reason of the speed and economy with which most magazines are put together. Those who have the staff and the time to do it, however, will find that it pays dividends both for individual stories (which can benefit enormously from the planned integration of verbal and visual approaches) and for the improvement of mutual understanding between those who work with words and those who work with visual material.

Even if time does not permit full-scale story conferencing, the question of how a particular story is to be expressed on the printed page should be foremost in every commissioning editor's mind before the writer is instructed. In particular, the picture editor must be involved at this stage. Picture desks and designers rightly dislike the task of being presented with a feature and told to find some visual material to 'liven it up'. The tasks of commissioning new photography or finding the best agency material need time. A good picture editor can call in material from agencies with surprising speed, but this doesn't mean that it is the best way to operate. Better, and often more economical, results are obtained by a thoughtful personal search of agency resources. Both commissioning and agency searching should stem from a proper discussion with the relevant editorial and design staff to determine exactly what is possible and desirable. Having had the discussion, your picture researchers should then be given the opportunity to use their skills and experience.

THE ROLE OF THE ART EDITOR

If the relationship between editor and publisher is the most fundamental to magazine editing, that between editor and art director or art editor comes a close second. No editor can make much progress without the support and co-operation of a good art editor. A magazine's design can have much greater and much quicker effects on its readership and circulation than anything an editor can do directly, although over the long term things even out. An art editor needs to be a close ally throughout, and responsive to both terms in his or her title: 'art' and 'editor'.

The selection of a new art editor or art director (the latter title is an odd one in this context but has a long history) is an extremely difficult task, especially for those whose experience is largely with words. But there are two aspects to it. Art editors must set their magazines' visual tone, even when they are not designing them from scratch. But at the same time art editors have a managerial role directly comparable to your own.

Prospective art editors will present evidence of their visual skills with a portfolio of work. You should take the opportunity to study this in detail before you meet them. It should include covers, feature spreads, even whole magazines. There should be evidence of both adaptability and an inherent, underlying visual ability. Much of what you are shown will not be directly relevant to you, probably, unless you are poaching from a direct competitor, but you want to see the way a brief has been tackled and built upon. It is important to see how mundane work is handled too: look at simple news pages and product pages. It is vital that all these things express themselves, their own essence, rather than merely reflect passing typographical fashions or even their designers' long-standing affection for certain typefaces.

Since they are vital to any magazine's success, you should pay particular attention to your candidate's collection of covers. It is one thing to find or commission a high-quality portrait photograph and use it for a cover based on an interview. It is quite another to find an appealing visual analogue for a complex issue or subject. If your magazine intends to base cover stories on ideas, rather than people, then you must be confident of your art director's ability to come up with ways of expressing them.

It is true to say that it is in this area that contemporary art direction is weakest, if you compare our current publications with those produced during the heyday of the great British and American magazines, in the 1950s and 1960s. Indeed, some contemporary art director candidates will never have been expected to produce a cover out of anything except a picture of a person, reflecting the narrowing range of approaches found in much contemporary magazine editing. If you intend to move beyond that at all, you must be sure your art editor is prepared and enthusiastic.

In the interview, you should ask searching questions about how various finished pieces of design came about and about the constraints involved, particularly of cost. You need to know how your candidate is used to working, the level of consultation expected with editorial staff, the amount and nature of direction required. You need to be sure that your candidate can interpret a brief, and has the ingenuity to work imaginatively within a budget. You must, naturally, ensure that the candidate is familiar with all the technology you use or intend to use in the future, as well as that used by your colour house and/or typesetters.

The job also has its managerial aspects. Any art director or art editor will be responsible for running a studio, from finding and directing designers to ordering new materials and liaising with the magazine's colour house. This is a job with considerable cost-overrun potential, and you need reassurance that the candidate is entirely confident in handling both people and money. You must assess the candidate's ability as a leader and someone who can keep discipline. Studios, as much as production departments, depend upon the rigorous tracking of incoming and outgoing material, from transparencies and prints to page and picture files, and close adherence to deadlines.

Art directors will also be expected to commission photography and illustration, and to organise and run photographic shoots. Their portfolios should show ample evidence of competence in these areas. In all this you are judging temperament as much as ability. Searching interviewing must be followed up by the use of references.

But which should take preference? Aesthetic flair, or managerial competence? This is not a question that can be answered in general terms. Every individual you are likely to interview will display each quality in varying degrees. It is for you to consider how important each aspect is to you. It is the case that a competent deputy, a production editor or a keen administrative assistant can, with proper systems, take some of the managerial burden away from your art director. But no-one else can provide the necessary flair and inspiration to give your magazine a strong, confident visual identity.

You may feel that a certain vagueness on the managerial level is a reasonable price to pay for aesthetic excellence. At the same time, however it is achieved in practice, your art director or art editor must accept full responsibility for the whole art domain within the magazine, in terms of both aesthetic quality and management. Not all creative people find such responsibility easy.

Working with designers

The process of briefing a designer differs according to the exact circumstances. Naturally, the briefing for a new design or redesign of an existing product is infinitely more detailed than that required for the recasting of a single section or the design of a single feature within design guidelines established by someone else.

In the first case, briefing for a new design or redesign, it is essential that the designer is given access to the same information that you have used during the process of getting to know your readers and producing a magazine with them in mind. But beyond all the normal detail about the readers' social status, sex, professional status, and so on, some factors take on greater prominence. It is important for the designer to know how the magazine is going to be used, for instance. Is it to be a leisure publication to be read at home after being brought home or delivered? Or is it intended to be read by commuters? Is it intended to be delivered to people at work and kept there for reference? Each of these makes different demands on the design.

Home-use publications can rely upon periods of continuous reading in relaxed conditions, permitting longer articles, longer line-lengths and more elegant, static design and photography than is found in those magazines intended for people snatching a read in a crowded bus or at the hairdresser's, where short articles, big type and attention-grabbing design would seem to be essential. A professional publication, intended to be held on file, on the other hand, will have a deeply sober look.

The age of the readers is another critical factor, not just in the specifying of type, which must not fall below a certain minimum size, but in assessing the degree of design excitement that is advisable. These are extremely complex decisions. The range of available typefaces, for instance, is vast. But your role as an editor is not to design the magazine: it is very unlikely that you would have either the aptitude or the expertise required. Indeed, you should be wary of providing too much specific guidance on the design solutions you wish to see. Your role should rather be to set out the problems in as clear a way as possible and let the designer work the process through. There can then be further discussions.

You must, however, be vigilant in ensuring that the information you have provided is taken into account. And any decisions must be tested before they are put into practice. It is not enough to make decisions on the basis of laser proofs, or even on true bromides. The one will look absurdly rough, the other absurdly sharp and elegant. You must see things as they will look after they have been through the whole process. If the budget does not run to having your new design elements printed on short-run presses, you must find ways round it. If you are planning to use a new body typeface, for instance, you must find a corner in your existing magazine, a small advertisement or an announcement, put it into the new face and have it printed. Magazine history is littered with fatal decisions made by designers and editors intoxicated by a vision of elegance that proved unreproducible, or unreadable, in practice. *Event*, a 1970s rival to London's *Time Out*, failed in part because its typeface was too small.

You must follow the logic of particular design solutions to see how they will affect every aspect of the working process. Increasing the leading between lines of type, or introducing more generous gutters, may bring much needed light into your pages but at what cost in terms of loss of space? Do you really want to lose that amount of material? Or is it a worthwhile price to pay for greater elegance and ease of reading? Your readers must be your guide: are they paying for information or for elegance? It is no surprise that in recent years the trend has been towards a more compressed and economical style of magazine design.

Consider the effect of adjusting the hierarchy of headings and standfirsts. It may seem a good idea to give each news story a two- or three-word 'kicker' label above its headline. But how much time will writing it require, and how are you going to ensure that it simply doesn't repeat what's in the headline itself? Those centred standfirsts might look elegant when they are properly filled out to fit, but do you really want your sub-editors tinkering with that when they could be doing something more constructive?

And there may also be cost implications. The most notorious of these is paper format. The reason most magazines are produced in standard formats is that they come off the print web with no wastage. More innovative shapes, which designers tend to favour, can involve horrendous levels of paper wastage as standard paper widths are trimmed to fit.

Interim elements of design, for instance the creation of new sections in existing magazines, should be much simpler to accomplish. It is important that you say precisely what you want the new page or section to achieve and what elements you want it to include. A 'people' spread, for instance, might be expected to accommodate between three and five small interviews of 300–500 words each with a headline, standfirst, photograph and caption, plus a slot for snippets of gossip and quotes of the week. A columnist's page might require 1,000 words of copy, a prominent by-line, a pull quote, a headline and standfirst and a photo or caricature.

It is perfectly acceptable to give your designer sheets torn from other magazines, but only to show the kind of elements or feel you require rather than any typographical specifics. Most designers would rightly feel rather insulted at being invited to imitate someone else's design.

As far as day-to-day involvement with design goes, there should be an agreed sequence of events. There may be a discussion about a particular feature before it is written. This is certainly the case with features that depend on tabular and graphical material that may not be within the normal routine or competence of your own studio. These should be discussed early and material commissioned as appropriate. Illustrations can sometimes be commissioned before anything is written, but only after considerable discussion and at the risk of a mismatch that will have to be corrected by adjustments, most likely to the written material.

There is a danger of Chinese whispers. The commissioning editor may

explain the concept to the designer responsible for commissioning the illustrator or photographer. The designer then discusses it with the illustrator,
while the editor talks to the writer. At no stage do the writer and illustrator
speak, and the distortions introduced in the discussion and briefing process
mean that they may be working entirely at cross purposes. It is not entirely
practical for the writer and illustrator to be brought in for a discussion with
the editor and art director, although that is probably the ideal. If such a
discussion takes place, it is a good idea to put something on paper at the end
of it. If no such meeting takes place, both designer and editor should make
an effort to read one another's briefs before they are sent out to ensure that
they, at least, are clear about what is required.

Certainly designers must read the written material and raise any queries
with the writers or editors concerned. Most editors will have at some point
come across designers who considered it no part of their function to read
the copy around which they were creating pages. The view was sometimes
expressed that reading the material would in some sense 'distract' from the
task of creating pages. This is nonsense, of course, and no editor, indeed no
art editor, should stand for it.

It is for the art editor to supervise individual page and spread designs for
visual elegance, adherence to the established style, appropriate use of type,
appropriate colour palette, and so on. But the editor should not be excluded
from the process, and either the editor or a trusted member of the team
should be responsible for passing finished pages. So that this is not a trau-
matic process, it is advisable for an editor to keep an eye on work in
progress, both informally by wandering around and watching what goes on,
and formally by receiving proofs of pages under construction.

When you look at a page or spread or whole feature you must ensure that
it works. It must lead the eye logically through the material. The page itself
must tell the reader what is the most important thing. News pages, which are
made up of numerous different stories, are designed specifically for that
purpose: to embody a whole hierarchy of suggested importance. The lead
story should stand out from the rest, something that can be achieved in any
number of ways: size of story, position of story, shape of story, size of
headline, shape of headline, typography of story, typography of headline,
size, shape and impact of any accompanying photograph, and so on. Thereafter, immediate visual impact should be reduced, on a sliding scale down to
simple one paragraph 'briefs', which should have almost no impact individually, but should have an appealing and obvious presence as a group.

In feature material, the hierarchy of emphasis is applied not to different
stories but to different elements within a single overall story: headline,
standfirst, body text, panels and boxes, pull quotes, by-lines, and so on. A
magazine needs a clear hierarchy for this kind of material, which should be
laid down in some kind of design manual, indicating acceptable typefaces,
sizes and styles for each job. When you look at an individual piece of layout,

you should ensure that the theoretical ordering of elements has been carried through in practice.

The editor must not be deterred by the mystique of design from asserting his or her authority over the whole editorial domain, which certainly includes the look of the magazine. Any failings in the magazine's visual appeal will result in poor bookstall and circulation performance, and responsibility for that will certainly be laid at the editor's door. At the same time a wise editor recognises his or her own deficiencies in visual matters and allows well-chosen and well-trained design staff to get on with the job.

THE ROLE OF THE PICTURE EDITOR

The picture editor's status is not always as high as it might be within magazines, reflecting perhaps an erroneous editorial perception that the job is largely about housekeeping: ordering messenger bikes, packing photographs and paying bills. These are, of course, necessary parts of the picture-editing role, but most picture editors have an interest in visual material that goes well beyond cataloguing and storing it. As an editor it is your task to find a picture editor who can bring that interest to bear on the very specific problems of producing magazines, which are not so much about aesthetics as about the bringing together of images and words in a unified means of communication.

Aesthetic questions are a matter of taste and experience. You may wish to produce a beautiful magazine, but beauty has a static quality that is not always desirable. *Impact* may be a better criterion for picture selection. Again, this requires a discussion between yourself, your picture editor and your art director, but it is your responsibility to have the last word.

Pictures can draw the readers in or repel them. They can say as much as the accompanying piece, or they can simply sit alongside it: a bad picture, which is to say a dull image or a technically incompetent bit of photography, can destroy an otherwise acceptable page. There are many ways of assessing photographs, but for your purposes you need to ensure firstly that their content is appropriate: is this the right person, the right place, the right object to accompany the copy? Then you need to ask about the timing of the photograph: is this what the person looks like now? Is this the right moment in the story, or could we get closer to it?

Finally, and most elusively, you have to consider the quality of the photograph. On one level, this simply means examining it closely through a magnifying glass as it sits on the light-box. Photographs for publication in conventional magazines need to be sharp, despite the vogue for out-of-focus effects among art photographers. In a portrait the point of focus will usually be the subject's eyes.

Any hint of softness in the image will, of course, be much exaggerated as it is blown up on the page. The same goes for graininess. Colour is also a problem. It is most important that you allow for the vagaries of your printing process. It is a good exercise early on to track the progress of a transparency from light-box via scanning and Cromalin proof to its eventual printed form. The deterioration is sometimes shocking: your designer and picture editor should have enough experience to help you make intelligent judgements about this.

They should also make sure that there are no obvious compositional howlers that only appear on a second or third glance: lamp-standards emerging from people's heads, for instance.

But technical quality is not the only important aspect of a photograph. You are also looking for its inherent qualities as a piece of observation of, usually, human beings. There must be a sense of life about it: this can come from something as simple as a facial expression in the case of a potential cover photograph. For feature photography, you need something that tells a story, that reveals something about the people or situation pictured. And it helps if there is an element of drama in either the material or in its composition.

As an editor, your immersion in the world of visual images may be limited but you should take the time to develop it by looking with new attention at photography and the visual arts whenever you have the opportunity. Picture desks and designers spend hours poring over Continental and American magazines in search of visual inspiration: it would not hurt you to take the occasional look, nor to attend photography exhibitions and graphic and fine art degree shows.

Your picture editor must be invited to rise above the routine aspects of the job (while continuing to handle them efficiently) to become a vital part of the creative process. This means early and continued involvement in that process. A picture editor is part of the editorial team, which is both a privilege and a responsibility needing effort and understanding on both sides.

Editors do not need to involve themselves in the practical side of the picture editor's job, but they do need to be aware of what is possible and what is not. There is a tendency for editors to imagine that because they have seen something, or think they have seen something, it is available for inclusion in their magazine. But that image may have been something they saw on television or in a film that does not exist in still form. It may be something they have imagined. Or it may simply be outside the practical and financial range of the magazine's resources. Of course, it may be possible to create the image, by commissioning photography, but that is a separate issue.

If you are using existing photography, it pays not to approach a feature or cover idea with an image in mind that is too specific. On the other hand, it does not help your picture editor if you say that you have no idea what you want but you'd like to see everything to help you think about it.

Agency and library photographs

It seems possible that there was some kind of golden age when picture editors would spend the bulk of their time seeking out interesting new or forgotten images and contemplating the right way to give stories and features their fullest visual impact. Nowadays, any such efforts have to be fitted in between telephone discussions and negotiations. Time should be made for them, for the benefit of both the magazine and the picture editor, who needs space and encouragement to practise the fundamentals of the craft.

More than anyone else in the editorial team, however, the picture editor has to deal constantly with people and money. This is where experience is invaluable. The picture editor is constantly making deals with agencies, libraries and photographers. In this, such essentials as your magazine's circulation and distribution pattern and the size and prominence with which the picture is to be used form the basis of the discussion. But the eventual deal struck may have as much to do with your picture editor's knowledge of the market and negotiating skills as it has to do with any of these purely factual considerations.

This is true not only of the price paid for the material, but of its quality: a good picture editor knows where to go for particular pictures, which photographers are bringing new material into the market, what other magazines are looking for at any time, and so on. This makes them invaluable people, something that is not always reflected in their salaries, which tend to be at the lower end of the senior editorial scale. An experienced picture editor will inevitably be paid more than a beginner, but that differential will often be made up by the sums you as a magazine save by having a skilled negotiator in this key role. You should also see benefits in terms of the quality of the material brought in and photographers used.

Celebrity pictures are a constant problem. Long-standing efforts by the famous to control the way they are photographed mean that the agency pictures may be extremely familiar and uninteresting. Your picture editor must know ways round that, by going to more obscure sources. But almost all agencies now charge a fee for 'research', even if your picture editors or researchers go and look through the material themselves, so the more trawling you do the more expensive it becomes.

It cannot be stated strongly enough that the picture editor must take responsibility for checking in, storing and returning photographs that are called in from agencies or photographers. Some paper form should probably be devised for this purpose, as well as short- and long-term filing systems. Some editors use a system in which transparencies move around the office rather than staying at a central point, but this needs to be handled with care. Losing a transparency is an expensive mistake and will tend to rebound not on the member of staff who happened to have seen it last but on the picture editor, to the ultimate disrepute of the magazine itself.

Photographers

Original photography, depending on how it is done, is often an appealing idea, especially for familiar subjects and people. It can, however, be an expensive business. Those who are used to dealing only with writers are sometimes surprised by the fees commanded by freelance photographers, not to mention the cost of hiring studios, models, stylists and hair and make-up artists when these are required. The reason advanced by the photographers is that they have to carry high overheads, although very often you will be paying for studio hire, film and processing on top of their fees. Unlike writers, though, photographers tend to operate with one foot in the world of advertising, where extraordinary fees are commonplace. Editorial photography cannot compete on money terms, but most photographers will want to do editorial work for their credibility. Having established their credibility, they will then be able to get more money for their advertising work, which means that their editorial rate will increase again.

A skilled picture editor selects a photographer for a job not merely on technical quality and artistic merit but also on temperament. The very best photographers for magazine purposes are those who combine a high degree of competence with amenable personalities. The photographer needs to be matched to the job. If the picture is to be a portrait, two personalities have to be matched. This doesn't necessarily mean helping the two of them form a lifelong friendship, but creating an interesting relationship that will endure for the length of the picture session. Both sides of the relationship need to be considered.

In the case of celebrity photography, involving film stars and the like, this can be extremely problematical. Contemporary show-business public relations is about the control of imagery. Putting a star on your cover will inevitably involve you in negotiation about access, timing and exclusivity. But it will probably go beyond that. You may find that only certain photographers will be acceptable: many 'stars' now insist on specifying their own favourites. Even after controlling the choice of photographer, the star, or his or her 'people', may expect to choose which individual images are acceptable. You may end up asking them to choose a possible three from perhaps forty or fifty originals.

Beware: it is not unknown for stars offered sheets of transparencies to put a knife through those they dislike. Some photographers might be prepared to let that happen to their originals, but whatever is said, your picture editor must ensure that it does not happen by mistake, usually by making certain that only duplicates are placed in such a hazardous position. All these are areas in which the picture editor's human qualities of judgement and intelligence count for more than either managerial or aesthetic abilities.

Either the art editor or the picture editor must be present at any photo shoot and take responsibility for it. This means ensuring not only that any necessary studio hire, equipment hire, catering and all the rest is competently and economically controlled, but that the actual photographs that emerge are what is required. Again, this is a matter of experience. Some photographers do not need to be told what to do, and don't appreciate any such guidance. Others welcome a clear explanation of what is required. The picture editor or art director must take responsibility for ensuring that appropriate photographs emerge from the session, but how they do that is up to them.

One thing that is essential is that the practical requirements are known to all and observed. A cover photograph must be a particular shape. The composition must allow room for the fixed elements of the cover (the logo, price, barcode, and so on) and also for cover-lines. This needs to be clearly communicated to the photographer, by the use of a mock-up cover if necessary. The same applies if the cover is more than a mere portrait and has to express a particular idea or represent a particular activity. In this instance the photographer's ideas may be welcome, but only once the image envisaged by art director, picture editor and editor has been successfully created.

There is always a certain amount of paperwork involved in a photo session. If you are photographing models rather than identifiable people, your picture editor must be provided with appropriate 'model release' forms for models to sign. These make it clear to the model, who may on occasions be an ordinary member of the public, how few rights she or he actually retains over the way the finished work is used. They can be rather alarming documents: no-one likes to lose 'rights', even those they never actually had. Such forms generally require models to acknowledge that they have no claim to copyright and that the magazine can use the photographs in any way it sees fit. They also state that the photographs and any accompanying copy are deemed to be of an 'imaginary person', rather than of the model herself. This is to permit their use in contexts which would otherwise permit an action for libel.

For instance, you might take a picture of someone looking glamorous in a bar and at some subsequent date use it to illustrate a story about prostitution. This is one of the hazards of professional modelling, particularly at the lower levels, where reputation is preserved by the simple line 'posed by models' accompanying the photographer's by-line.

Ordinary members of the public must not be treated in this way. If they have signed the release form, however, you have some protection against disastrous mistakes, when a photograph taken for one purpose inadvertently ends up being used for something else. Recently, for example, a photograph of a group of sinister-looking motor-cyclists in black leather was used to illustrate an article about terrifying gangs. Unfortunately the group in question was a Christian motor-cycling club run by a clergyman.

The presence of a name on a caption attached to a print or transparency, without any indication that the person in question is a model, should be a warning. People who give their names to photographers do not intend to consent to the photographs being used in any unspecified context: they think the picture is for a specific purpose. They retain the right to protect their reputation in a libel action based on the photograph's appearence in a defamatory context. Those who are photographed but whose names are not known or recorded also retain their rights to take action in the same circumstances. A typical example is to show a picture of some peaceful football supporters walking home after a match with a caption stating that they are members of a notorious hooligan gang feared throughout Europe. If they are identifiable, they can sue.

Pictures of models may well come with no names attached. If models' real names are, however, published alongside their pictures, or attached to any statement about them or by them, they regain their right to have their reputation protected, and your model form should make that clear.

The real problem with commissioned photography is one of perceived value. No-one begrudges paying for a sparkling portrait for a cover or a feature. But high fees are often asked for mundane 'mug-shots' destined to end up on the people page or the news pages, where they will be used small and will do little to enhance the layout beyond simply identifying the person being written about. A simple mug-shot can easily cost you as much as a short feature, and you can expect to pay for it again each time you use it unless you acquire the copyright.

It is no wonder that most small magazines are keen to acquire and store free photographs of the sort dished out as publicity material: technically there is usually an implied obligation that the photograph is used only for the purpose for which it was originally supplied, but that is rarely enforced. Another option, frowned upon by some, including the trade unions, is the use of an office camera for basic mug-shots. Here the results are likely to be poor, but using this kind of cheap or free non-copyright photograph in non-critical places releases money to pay for excellent commissioned photography in places where you will get some value from it, most obviously on the cover.

ILLUSTRATION

Illustration is currently rather unfashionable in magazines, which is a shame because it can provide a welcome change of pace and mood. The problem is that illustration is not neutral: however hard or combative the artist might try to make them, illustrations invariably have a more 'subjective' air than photographs. They label a piece as a feature, as something driven more by opinion and analysis than by hard reportage. They create a slight distancing effect, making things seem slightly unreal. But they have their uses.

They are helpful where the real thing simply cannot be photographed, either for practical reasons (no photographer was available, the situation was too dangerous, it was a physical impossibility) or for legal reasons (it's a court case, or you don't want to identify an individual for some reason). They are also very good for emotional and abstract subjects, where the illustrator finds an image that goes to the heart of the matter in a way no photograph could. They are ideal in instructional material, where photography simply wouldn't be clear enough.

One particular type of illustration that is still fairly widely used is caricature, which is a good way to make a 'character' out of an interviewee or profile subject who may be rather bland. Here the effect can range from the flattering to the grotesque and insulting, so your artist should be chosen with care.

INFORMATION GRAPHICS

The term information graphics is used here to indicate those visuals which are there simply to explain. They range from simple tables and grids, used to compare a number of different objects or services, through various types of maps, flowcharts and graphs to elaborate exploded diagrams.

In each case there are two essential tasks: assembling the information and finding an appropriate way to express it. Sometimes this is obvious: if you are writing about a network of long-distance footpaths, you will need a map. At other times things are more difficult. You need to ask yourself how many variables can safely be incorporated in a single graphic, and, indeed, how many the reader requires. Take a simple line graph showing the rising cost of living on the vertical axis and passing time on the horizontal. You might complicate this by showing falling house prices, which would require a different scale but could be done. But if you attempted to include other countries your graph would become far too complicated.

Presenting information in tabular or graphical form is a very useful technique. Unfortunately, it is more complex than it seems. Computer software has made it relatively easy to produce attractive graphics: it has not, however, made the task of creating appropriate and intelligible charts and grids any simpler. You should turn to a specialist in the field, or perhaps encourage one of your design team to become one. This is not, it should be stressed, any kind of short cut. Collecting the material for a detailed graphic, perhaps showing some piece of technology or the scene of some incident, can easily take as long as producing a feature on the subject. But the graphic should be used when words are not appropriate for the task.

COMMISSIONING

The task of commissioning a photographer, illustrator or graphic artist needs to be approached with the same seriousness as that of commissioning a writer. There must be a briefing, a fee, a delivery date and some statement of the rights to be acquired. Illustrators and graphic artists will also require information on the size their material is eventually to be used, although they may work much larger. A photographer will need to know exactly how many photographs are to be delivered, whether they are to be colour or black and white, and whether prints or transparencies. These things should, of course, be recorded on paper for the benefit of both parties.

The briefing will be handled by your picture editor and art director. But if your feature or cover concept depends entirely upon a particular visual image it is essential that this is clearly discussed in-house before the commissioning process begins. It is often appropriate for your art editor to produce a mock-up or rough of what is required. The illustrator should also produce roughs before proceeding too far, so that you can be sure the message has been passed on accurately.

Copyright

Photographers and illustrators were the major beneficiaries of the 1988 Copyright Act. Copyright law makes it unlawful for anyone to reproduce a person's work without permission. For the first time, photographers and artists were considered to be 'authors' for copyright purposes. But there was a more crucial change.

Previously copyright in visual material had belonged to the person or organisation commissioning the work; since the passing of the 1988 Act it has belonged to the photographer, just as copyright in their work does to writers and artists. This is a logical change and a beneficial one for photographers.

It makes it necessary, of course, that agreement be reached on the kind of rights bought by the magazine. Precisely the same problems have arisen over photographic and illustrative material as have arisen over written material, with publishers attempting to secure full copyright so that they can reproduce visual material in other media without further payment. In practice, however, successful photographers tend to be represented by agents, who are extremely canny about their clients' interests. Consequently, this particular area of dispute has not been resolved to the publishers' satisfaction.

It is worth noting that the 'moral rights' aspect of the 1988 Copyright Act applies no more to photographers and illustrators than it does to writers, assuming all parties have voluntarily made their works available for publication in a magazine. This means that in theory photographs can continue to be cropped, reversed and subjected to various types of electronic or darkroom treatment without fear of legal consequences.

Such techniques should not, however, be employed in a cavalier fashion. Photographers, especially those with artistic ambitions, are increasingly demanding the respect traditionally accorded to illustrators, whose work is rarely cropped or amended. The more successful exponents of the art will have agents who will expect you to sign contracts agreeing to do nothing of the sort. So although you have nothing to fear from statute law you may be in danger of a breach of contract action if you do not comply. Even if no such contract is required, it is good manners to ascertain early on the degree of delicacy with which your photographers' works are to be handled.

PHOTOGRAPHIC ETHICS

Ethics are the unwritten rules regulating the conduct of a particular professional group. They run alongside personal morality as a guide to behaviour. As an editor, you will need to preserve your own moral centre and sense of values, and you must ensure that those working for you understand your standards and are prepared to comply with them. This is particularly important when you are dealing with photographers, whose potential for causing offence and distress is huge.

The professional ethics of photography are especially important when matters of privacy are concerned. There is, as yet, no privacy law in Britain, although legislation on the subject is widespread on the Continent and in various American states. Within the confines of the law of trespass, photographers can go anywhere and take pictures of anything. Of course, you as an editor do not have to publish them, nor indeed to encourage this sort of photography in the first instance.

Such questions are regulated, for the time being, not by law but by the Press Complaints Commission's Code of Practice and the Code of Conduct produced by the National Union of Journalists, to which many news photographers, particularly, belong.

The NUJ Code of Conduct (see appendix 1) begins by stating that journalists have a duty to 'maintain the highest professional and ethical standards', although these are undefined. It states also that information, photographs and illustrations shall be obtained 'only by straightforward means. The use of other means can be justified only by over-riding considerations of the public interest.'

This clause implies that photographers should identify themselves if asked to and specifically rules out the age-old tabloid tradition of 'acquiring' family pictures of those in the news. But it does not deal specifically with invasions of privacy. The only mention of the concept comes in clause 6: 'Subject to justification by over-riding considerations of the public interest, a journalist shall do nothing which entails intrusion into private grief and distress.' Nothing there, however, about moments of private happiness, the depiction of which has so often been the cause of public outrage.

The Press Complaints Commission's approach is rather different. Rather than the sweeping statements favoured by the NUJ, it deals with specifics, leading to some suggestions that it is designed to allow unscrupulous editors and proprietors to hide behind the letter of the 'law'. The text of the Code of Practice (see appendix 2) needs to be interpreted in the light of a growing body of precedent. In broad terms, the PCC outlaws invasions of privacy, misrepresentation and subterfuge, intrusions into grief, the photography of children in many cases, and the photography of individuals on their own property without their consent.

Most of these prohibitions, however, are overruled by what is called 'public interest', here defined as the detection of 'crime or a serious misdemeanour', the protection of 'public health and safety' and 'preventing the public from being misled by some statement or action of an individual or organisation'.

Nothing here is straightforward: each of these exceptions is a knot of semantics and interpretation, apparently designed to provide hours of quasi-legalistic debate rather than to make it clear to those with a mind to pursue such activities what they can and cannot do.

The PCC Code was designed to discourage Parliament from taking a greater interest in the affairs of the press, and as such is to be supported. But a you as editor will be wise to keep well clear of the whole area by making it clear to your staff and contributors, including photographers, that they must do nothing that you would have any reason to apologise for or feel ashamed about. And if your own conscience does not guide you, consider the feelings of your readers.

One area in which ethical standards have yet to be established is the manipulation of photographic images to make them show things that have never actually existed. Photographic historians and scholars will point out that the camera has always lied. But between early photography, which consciously imitated painting, and contemporary electronic photomontage and manipulation, there was a long period in which most people were encouraged to feel confident that the pictures printed in their magazines and newspapers represented an actual existing reality, albeit heightened, dramatised and generally distorted by the effects of the photographic process.

Crude photomontages, in which one person's head is placed on another person's body, or two people at opposite ends of the frame are moved closer together, have been with us since the photographic process was invented. They have usually been sufficiently inept to make detection a relatively simple matter, even by ordinary readers. They have not usually been used to mislead, but for the purpose of amusement or to make some kind of point. They have not professed to be something they were not.

Electronic picture manipulation has changed all that. Once the image enters the electronic domain (indeed, with electronic cameras it may never have been anything else) it can be distorted, adjusted and merged with other images in a way that is effectively undetectable. There may, indeed, be no originals at all: the printout of the computer-assembled montage may be the first time the image and its constituent parts take a physical form.

This manipulation need not be extreme. Many magazine editors, particularly those whose covers feature photographic models rather than known public figures, routinely retouch their cover photographs. In some cases this is simply a matter of removing blemishes caused in the photographic/ scanning/reproduction process. In others it is done to correct actual human blemishes caused by Mother Nature.

Sometimes the hapless model becomes merely the raw material for an exercise in creating a perfect man or woman, using a Scitex machine rather than a scalpel. Some editors and art directors stop just short of the point at which their model ceases to look human, perhaps recognising that their readers have to identify with a person rather than a Stepford Wife or an Action Man.

This may seem a trivial example, but it is symbolic of the ease with which both technical possibilities and ethical questions have been swept into the normal routine of magazine life. It is perhaps time to stop and think it through. As an industry we stand on the brink of compelling our readers to treat all photographs as 'art', that is as imaginary, fictional constructions, whether they show television personalities shaking hands with people they have never met or the aftermath of some wartime atrocity. Libel will protect prominent people from damaging distortions, possibly. Copyright may or not protect photographers and picture libraries from having their photographs distorted. But who will protect the readers, who will never again be able to trust what they see?

The National Union of Journalists has recently begun a campaign for such photomontages to be labelled, probably with a symbol. The Press Complaints Commission has yet to consider the issue. As always, the PCC needs a formal written complaint before it can act. The few complaints it has received so far have been settled between the parties at an early stage.

This is an area in which editors should take the lead. Any montage, or electronically manipulated photograph (where the intention is to alter, rather than to correct losses of quality in the process) should carry two by-lines: 'Photograph by . . .'; 'Electronic montage (or enhancement, or treatment) by . . .' This both gives credit where it is due and tells the reader the truth, which is that the picture is a fiction. Of course, it may be a fiction designed to reveal a 'greater' or 'deeper' truth, but readers are perfectly capable of working that out for themselves.

Those who are using a montage to provide the momentary frisson of excitement that comes when the readers wonder whether something is real have nothing to worry about: that will still work. Only those who want to leave their readers in doubt or confusion, or positively to mislead them, will have anything to fear from such a scheme. The only real opposition is likely to be in-house: art editors and picture editors will not enjoy making it explicit to photographers and models that they have 'improved' on their original work.

THE COVER

This is not the place for a detailed discussion of design issues, which receive excellent treatment in the design press and numerous manuals and handbooks. But there is one area in which design has more impact on an editor's life than any other: covers. The question of covers, from the selection of suitable subject matter through to the positioning of the inevitable bar code, is likely to be the subject of unending discussion.

Newspaper-style covers are not really the issue here. There you will find that, by and large, content, the actual interest of the individual stories, overrides presentation, although that is no excuse for not producing an attractive and striking page. It is still important to find a striking main picture and to get your main news story into the right position, above the 'fold' so that it will stand out on a bookstall or, more likely, when it arrives in the post. You are likely also to include some kind of illustrated contents panel to ensure that even the most casual observer appreciates that this is a magazine with more in it than just industry news. You should ensure you 'flag' both interesting new material and popular regulars: columnists and the like.

Most of those reading this book, however, will be more interested in 'magazine-type' covers, featuring a photograph or illustrated image and a series of cover-lines, usually on an A4 or similar page rather than in a newspaper format.

A magazine's cover is its most prominent and useful selling tool. Many otherwise excellent publications are damaged by their editors' apparent inability to arrive at a suitable cover style. On the other hand good covers alone will not, in the long term, save an inadequate magazine. Finding a suitable cover style and sticking with it is made no easier by the undoubted fact that your covers are something upon which everyone will have an opinion, from the person who comes in to mend the photocopier to your managing director. Most of these opinions have regrettably little to do with reality.

There has been research on the importance of the cover to buyers, but it is of strictly limited use. The most famous report, commissioned by Comag, the magazine distributors, in 1990, has achieved a renown out of proportion to its actual value or relevance. Only 200 people were surveyed, 15 of them in any depth, and most of what they had to say was obvious. The survey discovered, for instance, that readers prefer an attractive, eye-catching cover to an unattractive one and that they don't care about the relevance of the picture to the subject matter. They want to know what is in the magazine, using the cover-lines for this purpose. But most people buy regular magazines irrespective of their covers: spontaneous buyers of unfamiliar magazines do so because they are going on holiday or, in the case of specialist titles, they want them for reference.

On the basis of these findings, Comag's report produced a set of recommendations on the ideal cover treatment which have mesmerised publishers (not usually editors) ever since. The key points would seem to be that there should be five cover-lines, which should not be meaningless and which should not obscure the cover picture. The cover picture must be clear and not crowded. Men expect the cover picture to have something to do with the content, but women don't. The cover subject should fill the frame and preferably be in the middle. Models must 'reflect the right image for the title', and 'their body language is vital'. Bright colours are preferable to dingy ones, but really there should only be three, preferably black, white and red. And people don't like free gifts obscuring the cover, but they will buy magazines that do this because they want the gifts.

What this research is actually saying is that readers prefer a competent cover to an incompetent one. A competent cover will not look crowded. It will look bright and not dingy. It will have the right number of cover-lines, and all of them will make sense. In short, it will look 'right'. It will have a certain inherent quality. But how that quality is achieved is largely irrelevant. The cover must have a sense of confidence and strength and must justify all the aesthetic decisions that have gone into its creation. But as to the means used to achieve that effect, it is almost the case that, as William Goldman famously said about the movie industry, 'no-one knows anything'. Certainly, any slavish attempt to follow a formula is wrong-headed.

Effective cover creation depends upon your being absolutely clear about what you are trying to achieve. The fundamental thing is for the cover to sell the issue, both to your regular readers, whom you want to buy this particular example, and to other people's readers, who might be looking for a change. Obviously those two objectives may not be entirely compatible, as we have previously discussed. And you may not have to sell your magazine: it may have a controlled circulation; it may be distributed solely (or overwhelmingly) by subscription; it may even be distributed without a cover price as part of some other package, with a newspaper for instance. But in every case you still have to 'sell' the issue. You may not have to persuade people to take the magazine off the shelf and up to the till, but you still have to produce a cover appealing enough for people to want to pick it up when it falls on their mat. The techniques are the same.

Sales, in terms of numbers, are not the only criterion of success, of course (although no-one ever wants to sell fewer copies, despite what they might say). You also have to sell to the right people, which means producing covers that embody not only the subject matter of your magazine but its spirit, ethos and standing. Clearly, this might easily conflict with your first objective. You can put 'SEX' on the cover in big letters every month (indeed, many do), but not if you are producing the official journal of the Royal Institution of Chartered Surveyors. Authority and immediate popularity do not always coincide.

Both of these objectives are perfectly acceptable when you are creating your covers. But you should bear in mind the way 'cover stories' are perceived among your staff. If you are in the lucky position of employing staff writers, you may find that the undoubted kudos that comes from having written the cover story is seen as a sort of reward structure. You should explain that it is not about that at all. The cover story is not the best piece in the magazine: it's just the best piece to sell on the cover. Nonetheless, some will take the view that not only certain writers but certain subjects should be placed on the cover in recognition of their inherent importance or merit, as if the cover were some kind of badge of honour to be awarded to deserving cases. This approach also should be discouraged.

A similar perception operates in parts of the outside world. If you have to run celebrity covers, you are likely to find yourself having to negotiate away your principal selling device on occasions. Certain 'artistes' take the view that they will only allow themselves to be interviewed by magazines which are prepared to put them on the cover.

If you enter into these kinds of Faustian deals, you will be expected to sign documents agreeing precise publication dates, for instance. Other demands invariably follow. As we have already seen, the celebrity concerned will often want to approve your choice of photographer, and then to approve a limited number of the actual photographs. You may, or may not, be allowed to send the writer of your choice. You may also be expected to sign all manner of conditions about the use to which any interview material is put. Some celebrities even ask for 'copy approval'.

At the end of all this, you may well have a usable cover story at a date that suits you and upsets your rivals. You will also have allowed your magazine to become part of the celebrity or studio's global marketing plan, all of which will have been worked out in detail months in advance. It is a moot point whether such 'contracts' are legally enforceable, but not a relevant one. If you break such a deal, even for perfectly sound editorial reasons, you can expect to be punished the next time you make an approach.

Some editors and publishers have been so keen to fill their magazines with film stars that they have tainted things for those who prefer to edit from a seated rather than a kneeling position. All such deals, especially those involving picture and copy approval, are in some sense a fraud on the reader. The cover of a magazine is not for sale (except in the case of certain giveaway publications where it is actually an advertising page), and this means that it should not be exchanged for 'access' or 'an exclusive'. Of course, this is an idealistic position. You will do what is necessary in your market, possibly through gritted teeth.

None of these things should divert you from your main task, which is to create covers that sell, thereby keeping your staff in work. Sometimes it is necessary to explain this harsh reality to those who think that covers are about 'supporting' various initiatives and organisations or about 'encouraging' various writers.

Subject matter

Subject matter is the fundamental decision in the process of creating covers that sell. Some covers, of course, especially in the women's general-interest market, are no more than attractive visual billboards upon which cover-lines are hung. There is often no connection whatsoever between the person pictured and the material inside the magazine. Sometimes the connection runs no deeper than the outfit the model is wearing: winter, summer, Christmas, summer holidays, and so on. In those cases there is no cover subject as such: the cover's success depends upon style rather than content.

Many magazines, however, will have a cover subject (or, less straightfor-wardly, several subjects). Naturally, the pool of subjects from which individual cover ideas can be selected depends entirely on the area covered by an individual magazine. This makes generalising difficult, but there are a few thoughts which may be useful. The first is the appeal to self-interest. Ask yourself what you can produce that will convince your readers that they have a positive, identifiable advantage over those who do not read the magazine.

You know your readers by now. What are the things they are really concerned about? And what ideas, stories and features have you generated that will really get them 'where they live', as the Americans say? You don't have to be a professor of psychology to know that in the general population this means money, family, sex, career, health, home – and not necessarily in that order.

These things in themselves rarely form the subject matter of either professional press magazines or specialist consumer publications. But stories about subjects apparently remote from those visceral concerns may well tap into them. A piece about new banking technology in a magazine for people who work in banks is really about job security. It does not do to become too rarified in your thinking about cover subjects: professional people and hobbyists are human beings too.

What you must do is offer something new, or unexpected, or surprising. The guidelines for what constitutes a news story can be helpful here: your cover stories should all be 'news' in their own way, even if they are only offering new recipes by a well-known cook or the first review of some piece of hi-fi equipment. You must be absolutely clear about what people want to know, and what they know already. Miscalculating here can kill a cover story stone dead, which makes it essential that you know not only what is happening in your subject area but also, in general terms, what your rivals are up to.

Some editors make a fetish of this, going as far as semi-criminal espio-nage expeditions to other people's offices and colour houses, but that is excessive. You should not be mesmerised by what they are up to: you must choose subjects on their own merits, and if other people do them at the same time, so be it. A successful magazine is an ocean liner: you set your course, you try not to collide with other craft (or icebergs), but ultimately other people have to get out of your way. You must obviously react to events in the real world but you should let publishing look after itself.

These things come into particular focus with 'people' covers. The use of an appealing person, one your readers are already interested in, is an obvious, easy, straightforward and endlessly seductive cover formula. With the reservations about celebrity work mentioned above, there is no reason not to pursue it. In an industry or specialist publication you will have to make your own stars, building up their editorial visibility over a period before you give them the cover treatment. If you need more than their name, and possibly a simple memory-jogging phrase, to sell them as a cover subject then you are too early. If your readers already feel they know exactly what they think, you are too late.

Editing, you might say, is about the manipulation of time and space. And in the case of cover 'stars', timing is everything. It is better to catch people on the way up when the readers are still interested in them, and that applies whether they are running ICI or presenting the National Lottery. Of course, you can catch them again on their way down, but that's a different kind of story and a less immediately appealing one. Even magazines for hard-nosed professionals should not scorn 'aspirational' (or 'directional', as the fashion fraternity say) features and cover subjects. Yes, you cater for the realities of their lives at the lower end of the professional ladder, but at the same time you show them what the big names are doing, and how they have achieved their present status.

Achievers always make a cover subject: those who might well achieve in the future are more tricky, and here one idea is to group them: 'The 10 best new bands', 'Tomorrow's award winners', 'High flyers'. Old chestnuts all, and invariably a blight on the future careers of those you identify, but a great way of making those at the fringes feel you identify with them.

Abstract subjects ('The future of accountancy', 'Be a better lover') do not lend themselves to simple photographic treatment. They need a more thoughtful approach, involving the creation of a genuinely expressive image. That should not rule them out, but their success depends upon the abilities of those coming up with the images and the willingness of your readers to use their mental faculties. This makes them tricky: allow plenty of time and have a fall-back position if the essential image fails to come. And all the time you should be thinking of how you can make a direct appeal in your cover subjects: 'How to . . .' 'The secrets of . . .' 'Winning at . . .' 'You can . . .' are all the start of strong cover-lines.

What makes a bad cover? Every editor has a store of horror stories, of covers sweated over and polished that died a death on the bookstalls. It is important to get a sense of perspective. You should examine your monthly or weekly figures in as much detail as is available to you, but you must take all factors into account. What was the weather like? What else was going on?

Were there any distribution problems? These are not things you can either do anything about or be held responsible for.

Everything else is likely to be your fault, however. There are not very many impossible cover subjects, in theory at least, except those that are ruled out by taste. But there are dull cover concepts and inept executions. You will find it a good idea to avoid depressing things that your readers can do nothing about (as opposed to depressing things that you are helping them overcome). That rules out a lot of the world's death and destruction, except in hard news magazines whose readers define themselves by their ability to confront such material without flinching.

The worst mistake you are likely to make in the selection of cover subjects is to provide your readers with too much of what they already know. Some editors call this the 'so-what' factor, and it is greatly to be feared. In practice, it might mean interviews with predictable people, instructional articles that don't inspire, previews of equipment they already know all about or analyses of professional problems they have already confronted and solved.

There is a particular problem about seasonal events: it may be a good idea to do a cover to mark Valentine's Day, or Halloween, but if you are approaching it with any sense of obligation, you'd do better to give it a miss. These feelings on the part of editor and staff are not easily concealed from the readers. Christmas covers in particular demand early consideration if they are not to be horribly predictable. Coming up with fresh thoughts in this context will not be easy, but that's what you are paid to do: and so are your team.

Cover treatments

At its best a cover is a perfect amalgam of image and type. Indeed, there are magazines which run images without type, but they exist in specialist markets appealing to the self-consciously artistic. Most magazines will settle on a picture with some kind of written label, to indicate an attitude to the material: a picture on its own, unless it is a particularly striking image, rarely expresses anything.

Several elements go into creating the average cover: the logo (sometimes erroneously known as the masthead); the image; the cover-lines; and the standing elements (price, barcode, date, etc.). The logo is really not part of the cover discussion. Almost invariably it stays the same from issue to issue, although some publications permit it to change colour and position and to drop behind the cover image.

The logo represents the magazine well beyond this particular context: it will usually be used in stationery, advertising and every other context too. It needs to be appropriately designed in the first instance, both on the level of basic technical efficiency (will it work in all the necessary circumstances?)

and on the level of 'appropriateness'. Once it is designed, it needs to be given appropriate legal protection and looked after: it represents your whole 'brand', to use the jargon, and you should not allow it to be applied to tacky merchandising.

On the cover, it should stay in one place and remain completely visible for maximum recognition and efficiency on the shelves; if these things are not vital to you, you can be more experimental. Art editors are obsessed with tinkering with the logo: you don't have to accept this unless you can see any point in it.

The standing elements, too, need to be neatly packaged. Bar codes in particular have to conform to tight technical specifications if they are to perform properly. At first there were some serious problems while designers tried to integrate them into their colour schemes, leading to chaos at the checkouts. Now, though, they generally appear in their absolutely standard size and shape, and everyone agrees to ignore them. More positively, you may feel that some sort of slogan under the actual logo is a good idea, particularly if you have something to boast about: 'Britain's biggest . . .' 'Europe's only . . .'. More tenuous claims often do more harm than good. Claiming to be the country's 'best-loved' magazine in a field on the basis of a survey you conducted yourselves is not calculated to enhance your authority.

Remember that all these elements must be seen in context. That means how they will work in a typical setting. Most bookstall magazines must have visual impact at a distance of at least three metres, although they will actually be read much closer. Logos should be at the top so as to be visible when they are racked, and should be recognisable when only half visible. If you need reminding about how magazines work in this context, you need only spend some time looking around a big newsagent or supermarket.

Cover image and cover-lines must also work at the three-metre distance, which is why so many magazines opt for a big face looking straight at the reader. But there are other approaches. One question is how much you change things from month to month or week to week. Should you change from illustration to photograph to montage to caricature, as the subject matter changes, or should you stick to photography, if possible all by the same photographer? There is certainly something to be said for enhancing basic recognition by sticking closely to the same formula, especially as far as typography and style of photography go. But you should be wary of producing issues that look identical to one another. You want people to recognise a new issue when it arrives without having to study the date.

Photography generally looks harder, more 'modern' and more 'classy', at least when you are using properly commissioned originals rather than agency shots or free pictures. Doing a cover shoot is expensive but at least you should get exactly what you want to express the particular idea, even if that idea is only a portrait of a person. Making a cover out of inferior photographic material forces you back on the ingenuity of your art editor.

Illustration can be very impressive, but it is difficult to keep up the standard and establish a style without using just one artist, and that may be undesirable. The same goes for caricatures. You may find it difficult to strike the balance between establishing a style and making all your issues look the same.

Expressing ideas, rather than merely showing people or things, is difficult and currently unfashionable. This is the style of the great era of magazines, from the mid-1950s to the mid-1960s, and it has never come back. It can be done by photography, illustration, photomontage or any combination of these, and simply requires an art director with imagination, an editor with nerve and a trusting publisher. Covers based upon images of objects rather than people are difficult to sell, with the obvious exception of hobby publications, which tend to use pictures of hi-fi equipment, cars, and so on. But even those areas are not as predictable as they have been: computer and photography magazines more often use pictures of people rather than hardware.

Most magazine covers now feature portrait photographs. Some will be famous (or at least known within the magazine's field), and here high quality portraiture should repay what it costs in terms of results. When viewing transparencies it is important to try and see them with the eye of the reader. You already know who the subject is, but is he or she instantly recognisable here? If not, you are in trouble.

Many magazines, particularly in the women's consumer field, will use simple face-on head-shots of anonymous models. The idea here is that the model has an attractive, appealing look that somehow corresponds to the way the readers see themselves. They have to like the person, or want to be the person. Thus high-fashion magazine covers will feature more extreme looks than the more middle-of-the-road titles, where the 'girl next door' is preferred.

In principle there is little more to it than that, but in practice these covers can be very problematical as every aspect of clothes, hair, make-up, posture and expression is subjected to minute analysis. Luckily some of the disgraceful superstitions that have bedevilled this process are gradually disappearing. If it ever was true that black cover models, for instance, are bad for sales, it is no longer true.

Interestingly, women's magazines rarely feature cover pictures of the opposite sex. When fashion-based men's magazines started in Britain they tended not to use cover pictures of women, presumably by analogy with the way the women's market had worked. This rapidly changed as soon as some brave soul took the apparently obvious step of using attractive and famous young women on the cover. Now that has become the standard treatment.

Cover-lines

Ideally, there should only be one cover-line. Your readers would buy your magazine because they were confident that it would contain the kind of things they were interested in, and the cover would give wonderful projection to a single brilliant idea. But relying on that kind of reader loyalty is now unwise. People have become what are called 'repertoire' buyers, selecting from a range of four or five titles. This choice will be made on the basis of what they believe the magazine contains.

There is no special magic about cover-lines, but you need to be clear about the point of them. With the exception of the main line, they are not there, like headlines and standfirsts, to label things that are already apparent to the reader. They are there to tempt and intrigue and invite further scrutiny. They should be positive and enthusiastic. It is very difficult to 'sell' a negative idea: 'How to avoid . . .'; 'Things not to buy . . .'.

Above all they need to be short, snappy, colloquial and absolutely straightforward. Sub-editors and editors very much enjoy writing puns and clever wordplay, and such material can be quite amusing in its place. You should discourage it on the cover, however. Readers need to look at the line once to understand what it means. They shouldn't have to spend time trying to work it out.

There need be no more than about four or five cover-lines, including the main line, as the Comag report suggests. That is because no-one will read more than that in the situation for which cover-lines are intended: on the bookstall. If readers want more than that, and they have time, they can look at the contents page.

The main line needs to be visible at the usual three-metre distance or so. The other lines need not be so big, but must all be clear. There are obviously any number of typographical treatments available. Some magazines use a sort of 'heading-and-standfirst' style: 'GOING TOPLESS: new convertibles for the summer'. This may satisfy the need to be both clever and informative, but it requires complicated typography and should be accompanied by a general reduction in the number of cover-lines.

Some magazines, notably in the women's general-interest sector, carry almost as many cover-lines as there are items within. This is obviously a calculated decision based on a study of the way their readers choose between what often seem to be identical magazine packages. It probably does not make sense for most other markets. In particular, editors should avoid adding more and more cover-lines simply to satisfy various parties in the office: promotions departments, disgruntled feature writers, even, in some cases, advertising departments. As usual, the only people who count in this context are readers and potential readers hooked by the brilliance of your cover concept and the simple eloquence of your cover-lines.

Technical questions

Put bluntly, your cover can be as artistic and full of impact as you like, but if your rivals have thicker paper, lamination, a fifth colour of ink and a cover-mounted free gift you are going to get nowhere. Once rarities, these things are now increasingly the norm as things get rougher on the bookstalls. In some markets, notably the computer field, the cover is increasingly becoming the place where you fix the free CD-ROM. Regrettable though this is, the cover still needs to be designed appropriately. As we have seen, Comag's research showed that people resented having covers obscured by gifts: unfortunately they do not appear to resent it as much as they dislike buying magazines without gifts.

DESIGN FOR ELECTRONIC PUBLISHING

At the time of writing, design for the new media is in its infancy. The stand-alone CD-ROM magazines that have been produced have concentrated on finding a suitable 'frame' within which to present various bits of acquired material, and these frames have ranged from basic adaptations of magazine typography to complete graphic 'worlds' with a logic of their own. There are many functional problems that are outside the scope of this book.

For instance, on-screen design has to be adaptable to different machines and monitors. It also has to include within itself the buttons and controls used to run it. How far should these be standardised? Should readers inserting a CD-ROM into their machines immediately know how to navigate through it, adjust the sound volume, quit the program, and so on? Sadly, no such standardisation exists at the moment, which is one reason, aside from the general 'flakiness' of the technology, that CD-ROM is looking increasingly like a false dawn. But those paper magazines who are using CD-ROM as some kind of adjunct will need to find an electronic analogue to their own paper design.

On-line magazines, however, are a more interesting phenomenon. Much of the Internet is a design-free zone. 'Mailing list' publications and Usenet discussion groups use simple 'ASCII' text, which readers may choose to read in any typeface they have installed on their machines. But most commercial publishing interest has revolved around the World Wide Web, and here *de facto* standards are evolving, because most Web page designers and readers have settled on Netscape Navigator and Microsoft Internet Explorer, as their preferred 'Web browser' programs. The browsers allow readers to move from Web site to Web site within a recognisable environment, ensuring that they never get lost. Individual Web sites, however, can be as radical in design and functionality as their designers wish.

As editor of a Web magazine, however, you should make transparency your main design objective. The technology is unappealing enough, without your adding another layer of confusion by the way you have set out your material. A Web magazine is only a magazine by analogy. It is more like a vast grid of pigeon-holes, each containing potentially interesting material.

The reader may start at the top-left hand corner, as it were, but can start anywhere else in the grid, either by accident or design. So you need to indicate a quick route back to the start (or 'home page'). Otherwise, readers can move around as they like, visiting the pigeon-holes (or pages) in any order. What's more, the pigeon-holes do not have to belong to the same rack: you can move to a particular page, only to find it belongs to some other site on the other side of the planet, conforming to a totally different design and editorial ethos. The reader doesn't actually know what's on any given page until it arrives, which takes precisely as long as it takes.

All this uncertainty is a great joy to the original 'netizens', the hard core of professional computer users and scientists who set the system up and use it as part of their work. It can be a considerable annoyance to the minority of Internet users who pay for their own telephone time, Internet access and computers.

These people, however, are the ones on whom the future of the Web as a publishing medium ultimately depends, since they have money to spend on other things than computer technology. As the Web matures to the point where people start reading the material, rather than looking at the pages briefly before moving on, site design will have to accommodate the desire to find things quickly and efficiently. While there are excellent searching tools for finding appropriate sites across the whole Web, individual site design often places dubious aesthetics well above functionality, making them frustrating things to use rather than merely to admire.

Magazines and books in the Western world all adhere to a recognised standard: by and large, you read them from the front to the back, using type designed to be legible and pictures intended to inform. None of these things can be relied upon in Web pages, each of which insists on its right to have its own internal logic, atmosphere and appearance. This is fine while people are looking around the Web for fun. It will be less acceptable if readers are looking for the kind of things they expect from traditional magazines: information, focus, a certain understanding of the way they are. In short, they expect magazines to accommodate them, rather than vice versa.

Finding a sensible way of doing all that, including getting potential readers to your site in the first place, keeping them there, developing a real relationship with them, and so on, is more a matter of editorial expertise and commitment than it is of facility with the programming languages used to generate the Web pages. Web designers are to today what QuarkXPress experts were to the recent past: they know how to design pages, on a technical level. But they have neither the training, experience nor judgement to decide what those pages should be about.

Whatever happens to the Web as a medium for commercial publishing (and at the moment it is an astonishing technology that has yet to reach the world beyond its own participants and enthusiasts) it certainly marks the end of typography as we know it. Many designers thought that the Apple Macintosh, introduced in 1984, brought that revolution, by turning type into a series of dots to be stretched and reshaped at will. But the Mac still ended with fixed marks on paper. Web page design has the potential to throw even that away.

In the time this book has been in preparation, the Web has changed from a series of pages featuring simple sans serif type on a grey background with the occasional photograph to a riot of colour and typographic experimentation. Already, readers of Web pages are finding new hierarchies. Since type was invented, you have been able to signal significance by making it bigger, bolder, or placing it in a more prominent position. In Web pages today, type is increasingly inclined to attract attention by blinking, or by moving around. But this is only the beginning. By the time this book has emerged from the print-publishing process, it will be common to click on an icon in a Web page to launch new programs on the viewing computer.

For all that, no-one has yet worked out a way of persuading people to read the Web pages they visit, or at least, not for any length of time. Those who work with computers are used to the experience, but most normal magazine readers will not appreciate reading from a monitor or even printing out to read later. Those few Web sites produced by traditional publishers and aimed at serious readers have had to keep their average article length very short. In addition, while it is often an attractive idea to create pages as composites of graphics and text, this can make them extremely slow to download on the kind of equipment most readers are likely to be using.

Those who are producing the most 'advanced' of the Web magazines are unapologetic about this. As Chip Bayers, one of the editors of *HotWired*, the on-line counterpart of *Wired* magazine, put it: 'We like to tell stories using words, pictures, video, and sound – in other words, all the tools given to us by the Web'. The fact that this makes the magazine difficult for those without advanced computer equipment and, more importantly, a faster Internet connection than that normally available to private households in Britain, is no disincentive. It is worth noting that such magazines' advertisers come very largely from the computer and telecommunications sphere, who are, of course, always happy to supply ever-faster machines and connections.

Editors should be looking closely at existing Web publishing operations, which vary from the basic to the elaborate and costly, such as Time-Warner's *Pathfinder* site. True editorial material, aiming to tell the truth irrespective of commercial and institutional pressures, will only be one option among many for readers wandering through the World Wide Web, alongside the dishonest, the inaccurate and the downright mischievous. We must, however, ensure that it has a prominent place in this new environment.

FURTHER READING

Evans, Harold (1978) *Pictures on a Page*, London: Heinemann.
Market Research into Magazine Covers (1990) Comag, West Drayton.
Owen, William (1991) *Magazine Design*, London: Laurence King.
White, Jan V. (1982) *Editing by Design*, New York: Bowker.

Chapter 8

The editor and production

The subject of production is hardly one to rouse an editor's passions. Nevertheless, it has to be mastered, if only so that you can entrust it to others. Production is central to the magazine editor's job. Editing a magazine is an essential part of a manufacturing process: it adds the value that turns a bundle of compressed tree pulp into an object worth buying.

As an editor you may not be responsible for the physical quality of that object, its printing and its binding, but you do require it to be done well, and on time, if your work is to achieve its optimum effect. That means the editorial part of the process has to be completed with the maximum efficiency. Editorial pages must be provided at the right time, they must occupy the right spaces and they must match the physical requirements of the printing process, in terms of size, shape and colour. This is a matter of copy-flow, scheduling and the flat-plan.

COPY-FLOW

Copy-flow is a complex matter. It determines the whole sequence of events from initial ideas to the final departure of whatever the editorial team releases, be that old-fashioned pasted-up pages and bags of transparencies, optical disks full of page layouts, words and picture-handling data, streams of electronic digits down the telephone line, or even, in the near future, finished printing plates.

There is no single linear thread. At various points in the process, things happen simultaneously. There will be numerous 'feedback loops' where work, once done, has to be assessed and if necessary done again. And, to add to the complications, the schedules for several issues will almost invariably overlap one another.

Given these difficulties, it is no surprise that most editors inherit someone else's sequence of events and decide to stick with it, rather than to start with a clean sheet of paper – or perhaps a stack of paper – and work out the most logical way of doing things. The tried and tested way may work, but it may also depend upon a particular combination of circumstances and relationships that will not always be sustainable. Complex and fast-moving systems have a way of 'just working' that gives many participants a sense of indispensability. Adrenalin can be addictive. But at the same time, the weight of work and responsibility is unlikely to be fairly or efficiently distributed.

Be warned, though. The shambles you inherit will be very convenient for some of your staff. When you attempt to replace it with something more logical, transparent and fair, you may find that things fail to work at all. The conservatism of people, even if it means sticking with the misery they know, should never be underestimated.

You might start your tidying-up process with a sort of flow chart, a working drawing that will let you take account of your resources: people, materials and time. These are such complicated matters that you cannot expect them to resolve themselves into a single neat diagram. Rather you need to try to isolate various aspects of the problem and deal with them one at a time. Separate sheets of paper might show you what all your people are doing at various times, where editorial copy is going in both paper and digital form, what proofing materials are being generated and the paths they take, and so on.

In the end you might be able to reconcile some of these elements into a single chart, festooned with different coloured inks, but it's fairly unlikely. This is an analytical process. You are trying to take apart an extremely convoluted and idiosyncratic complex of activities to see how it all works. Then, if you can, you put it back together in a more efficient and transparent form. Every magazine is different, of course, both in its staffing and in its actual technical procedures. The system described here is typical of that used on small to medium-sized consumer monthlies.

For now, forget that issues of your magazine overlap with one another and concentrate on the stages that go into the creation of a single issue. These stages overlap in time, and they may be repeated as material comes back round the system for re-evaluation and as circumstances change. What follows is an idealised mental picture of what happens.

The first stage is planning. There will probably be some kind of initial meeting. Who will be present, and what will they bring to it? You would expect to include your various section editors, and you would expect them to come with ideas but also more mundane information that helps you organise the issue ahead of you: the dates of significant events both for you and your readers, and so on. You should also write down what actual publishing information will be available at this stage: issue size ('pagination'), the likely advertising volume and editorial allocation, and any other variables which may encroach on your editorial allocation such as in-house adverts, offer pages and competitions. The meeting will generate thoughts on how that space is to be filled. By the end of it you should be well on the way to working out an approximate running order, for those pages which are not fixed and regular.

The next stage is commissioning and briefing. Here your commissioning staff set to work finding suitable writers, photographers, illustrators and picture libraries and giving them precise instructions, usually in writing. In-house contributors have to be 'commissioned' too, or at least thoroughly briefed.

Note that it is possible to commission photography and start library research at the same time as the accompanying writing, but that detailed commissioning of illustrators usually depends upon the writing having been completed. Illustrators may well respond to specific phrases and verbal images. Ask yourself whether you need to be involved in this process. It is often better to let commissioning staff operate on their own initiative within the guidelines, financial and otherwise, that you have set down. All parties must be well aware of 'copy in' dates which will have been set by your chief sub/production editor.

The next stage, which you might call copy-editing, starts as soon as the commissioned material begins to arrive. At this stage, good 'housekeeping' starts to become essential. It is a good idea to photocopy all original type-scripts and put them away safely, although typescripts as such are a dying phenomenon. Whatever form commissioned material takes, it needs to be drawn together and properly accounted for.

If it comes in on paper it must be either scanned or typed into the system and placed into the appropriate folder or queue. If it is sent in on a disc, this must be opened and the material moved to the correct folder. The naming of files within this folder should be the sole responsibility of one person, probably the chief sub/production editor, and should indicate the issue of the magazine they are intended for and the status of the copy itself.

The initial computer file should be printed out if no paper original exists. Many magazines use a printed 'top-sheet', stapled to that original, to track the progress of the story. Or there may be a 'job bag', a plastic or paper file holding everything of relevance. Different editors will tick or initial the top-sheet as the story makes its way around them. The top-sheet should also include author contact details and information about the original commission, for instance how long it is supposed to be and what it is intended for.

Later, relevant proofs and even transparencies will be added to this growing file of material, which will physically move around the office in a way that is supposed to keep track of the movement of the computer file it represents, which will also be making its way around the system. Depending on the time available to you and your confidence in your commissioning and editing staff, you may or may not read original copy. But you will certainly want to read the early edited versions of the story, and the original should always be available as part of the 'job file' or 'job bag'.

You and your senior staff should now be cutting and shaping stories, sending them back for re-writes, adding any extra panels and boxes, and writing headlines, standfirsts and other display matter. Some magazines have a single meeting at which all headlines are written in a batch. This is a matter of choice, but there is a danger of allowing these important elements to become 'samey', stereotyped and tired. Better, probably, to allow individual stories and individual editors to suggest their own headlines.

Sophisticated editorial systems can duplicate these procedures in computer form, and it is essential that you devise a file-naming system that facilitates it. These can take as their starting point a single word 'catchline', and then go through various numerically or alphabetically ordered variants.

The first copy-editing stage must be followed by a sub-editing stage, in which sub-editors check facts, construction, legality, grammar, spelling, house style and the rest. The copy will probably go to the chief sub-editor first, who will allocate it appropriately. Traditionally, sub-editors have had some involvement in more rewarding tasks such as rewriting and the writing of headlines, standfirsts and captions. Increasingly those tasks have moved up the hierarchy, leaving sub-editors to become more involved in copy-fitting.

By this stage, the art process will be under way. In earlier practice, there were two quite distinct processes: design and page make-up. Designers would design pages on paper, using pictures and typewritten copy and heading material provided by editors and sub-editors. Then they would pass their designs to skilled typesetters and finished artists to be made up into actual pages, either in metal (in living memory, but only just) or in photographic paper and film.

The arrival of the personal computer and page-layout software has removed this distinction. But the vestiges of the two stages still remain. It is usually sensible for designers to work on their designs, whether on paper or on screen, after reading the copy and looking at the pictures but before they import the real material into QuarkXPress or another layout program. Editorial design is always a compromise, but it should start as a visual statement into which editorial matter is brought, rather than as a mass of editorial matter which the design has to accommodate and prettify.

The art editor will allocate work according to the timing requirements of the production schedule. Once individual designers set to work, they have to select pictures in conjunction with the picture editor and relevant editors, scan them in or have them scanned in, depending upon the accessibility of the technology used, and then combine them with real copy to create spreads.

Obviously, the fixed elements of page design can be built into the system by the art editor and systems people. This can be as basic as determining the type area and the position of folios or it can be as detailed as laying down set design templates for particular parts of the magazine. Some larger publishing houses have long used centralised studios to 'design' many magazines simultaneously, and here templates are used extensively, which limits individual designers' creativity but has cost and time advantages. This is a long way from the 'editing by design' ideal, in which each spread is individually designed to reflect the materials incorporated in it. But it can, on the other hand, provide a welcome visual discipline and sense of identity for magazines which are produced by casual freelance designers rather than a dedicated and well-motivated team.

An art proof is generated at this stage. Colour laser-printing technology has now become sufficiently inexpensive to make it possible for such proofs to give a rough idea of colour balance as well as more normal visual and verbal matters. The proof, with any overmatter, which appears on a different sheet or outside the type area on the main proof, is then passed back to the art director, section editor and editor, who will be looking at the whole shape and feel of the spread as much as at details. The proof will then be returned for the artwork to be adjusted.

Next comes the copy-fitting stage. On receipt of a 'first proof' generated by the art department, the chief sub-editor will examine it before handing to a sub-editor to fit, rewrite where necessary and add any finishing touches such as captions, standfirsts, pull quotes and credits which have not been completed at an earlier stage. This will then be run out again, and a second or 'final' proof examined in minute detail. It will then go back to the chief sub-editor, who will give it a final check and then pass it around to all the appropriate editors. When they have added their final details and 'signed off' the page, these changes will be added on screen by the sub-editor. The page will then be given a final OK by the chief sub-editor and art director before being sent to the 'repro house' or 'colour house'. ('Repro', an abbreviation of 'reproduction', is the term used for the process of turning pages and photographs into the films used to make printing plates. The 'repro house' or 'colour house' is where this process takes place.)

The despatch stage involves assembling material to send off, by whatever means is favoured. Usually this will involve QuarkXPress pages with the right words and low-resolution scans in place. TIFFs, which are usually 'drawn' design elements created in different programs, usually go as separate files. It is essential that everything is logged as it leaves, whether as a 'SyQuest' or similar optical disk or via a modem. There are also, usually, physical things to be sent as well. Transparencies are usually sent by bike, along with proofs for the colour house to follow in the event of any difficulty.

At the colour house, the transparencies will be scanned in and then either electronically inserted into the pages according to the instructions contained within the QuarkXPress files or reunited with them as film. This is not a flawless process. Things can and do go wrong and colour houses are not immune from human failings. When things don't work, for instance, they have been known to open up the QuarkXPress files and adjust them. It is also the case that there are occasions on which you and your design staff will want to use the facilities of the colour house to adjust your picture material. The quality is much higher than is available on normal art department desktop equipment, which is why any adjustments to cover photography, for instance, have to be done on the colour house's equipment.

All these things make proofing critical. Traditionally repro proofs have been 'Cromalins', an expensive but extremely accurate way of reproducing exactly what should appear on the final printed pages. More recently cheaper forms of proofing, with lower resolution and colour accuracy, have been used. But unless money is extremely short, Cromalin quality is to be desired.

The Cromalins will be returned to the magazine for examination. This should allow enough time for changes to be made, but these are to be avoided for reasons of cost. Often the best that can be done is to scrape or patch the black film. If you are running the kind of magazine where such changes are common, you should ensure that your type is generally black on white. Changes at this late stage are to be avoided, particularly dramatic changes of cover picture or major feature material. In general, they should only take place in times of dire emergency. Serious legal problems are the first such occasion. Gross embarrassment, perhaps when someone dies or you have made a terrible mistake, is the second.

From this point, the issue is out of your hands. You may, out of interest, attend the occasional print run yourself and your publisher may be able to spare someone to observe what happens, but there is nothing much you can do about it. Nonetheless, if you are operating on a tight print schedule your office must be staffed at crucial times in the print process. Pages leave your colour house as film. They then have to be 'planned', or assembled into groups to make plates. The plates then have to be bolted on to the machines for printing.

At any of these stages things can go wrong. A classic problem is for a page to go astray between colour house and planning stages. You will receive a call asking what you want to do. The one solution is to have a made-up 'house ad' at the printers for precisely such eventualities. If they have time, however, you should be able to locate the page in the computer system and send it again. It is at times like this, when you are alone in the office and the telephone rings, that you realise what a good idea it is to know something about QuarkXPress or whatever layout program you are using.

That's the start of your flow chart. You need, though, to bring in two other factors. The first is time. How do all these little processes fit together in practice? How long does each task take? Which can be done simultaneously? Where does the pressure fall too much on the same individuals? If you draw boxes to represent individuals or departments, and join them with lines to represent the movement of copy and proofs, you should be able to see where those lines start to converge most insistently. You may need to find ways of dividing responsibilities differently.

The other factor is your computer system. You need to convert your theoretical copy-flow into a logical system of computer files, meaningful filenames and locked and unlocked folders. A piece of copy might appear first in a folder called 'copy in' on the main file-server. Editors might then copy that file to their own disks, edit it, then rename it accordingly, before placing it back in another file on the server, perhaps labelled 'copy to subs'. Sub-editors can then pull the file out to work on it before putting it back, renamed again, into 'copy to art'.

The art department are then free to pull it out, 'translate' it so that it can be used in QuarkXPress, add the 'style sheets' that control the typesetting rules, and use it in laying out their pages. Then they might drop the finished QuarkXPress files into a folder called 'finished layouts'. Sub-editors would then pull the file out for copy-fitting, send it back for proofing, then call it out once again for a final proof.

Eventually, once all parties are satisfied, the file can proceed to a folder marked 'to repro' until such time as it is copied on to an optical disk or sent down the wire to the colour house. There must be a comprehensible relationship between the movement of computer files around the office and the movement of any physical job file. People like pieces of paper, and the completion of any stage of computer work should be physically recorded on the job's top-sheet, if that system is in use. More sophisticated editorial systems may not need their own trail of paper, but they certainly need to be secure and reliable in operation.

SCHEDULING

As soon as you start to incorporate realistic time constraints in your copy-flow chart or diagram, you are on the way to scheduling. Your publisher or print-buyer should be able to tell you the exact timings inherent in the process once your magazine leaves the editorial offices. Bear in mind that these deadlines are fixed in accordance with advertising requirements as well, and cannot be changed at will.

A serious discussion with both printers and repro facilities (and you may have two of each if your cover is printed separately from the rest of the magazine, as is common) should allow you to get a feel for how things work at their end. This will translate into a series of dates and times for you to deliver your pages. Things are much more complicated if your magazine is only partly in colour, or if it is printed on several machines before being reunited at the binding and finishing stage, or if you have an add-on supplement to be printed and bound on at the same time. This will require extra time and your schedule will have to be brought forward to accommodate the printers.

Working backwards from those deadlines, and referring to the sequence of events you have laid down in your flow chart, you should then be able to create a schedule for a single issue. You work backwards through 'pages to repro house', 'final proof', 'first proof', 'finished layouts', 'copy-editing', 'all copy in' and 'commissioning of copy' right back to your original planning meeting. There may be extraordinary delays and complications. It is common for newspaper colour supplements to have a six-week 'lead-time' between putting the magazine to bed and its actually appearing on the streets. But within that there will also usually be a late section, allowing more topical material to be inserted as late as fourteen days before publication.

Once you have worked out realistic timings for a single issue, it is then simply a matter of superimposing more such schedules on to a single calendar. You must use a real calendar, which includes public holidays. At this point you must stop and take stock. It is easy to build yourself a schedule in which you are simultaneously 'passing' one issue, writing headlines in a second and holding a planning meeting about the third.

Be practical. It may be possible to do several wildly different tasks in the course of a day, but it is not possible to make several critical decisions simultaneously. In particular, you should try not to schedule anything at the same time as events which are affected by other people's time pressure. For instance, you must find time to study the Cromalins at precisely the moment they become available.

The important thing in drawing up a new schedule is to ensure that it works smoothly, painlessly and in a relaxed fashion almost all of the time. That way everyone involved in production will be have the resources to bring to bear when some genuine crisis or opportunity arises. If you do not habitually dither about your cover, you will be better placed to call on people's assistance when you decide you must change it because your cover star has been shot or because a much better story has suddenly presented itself.

Once you have the printing dates, and the schedule begins to take form, your own dates need to be worked out in detail. This will usually be the job of the chief sub/production editor, who will work back allocating a number of working days for each department – art editor, sub-editors and section editors – to handle the copy. These dates will then be recorded on a written schedule which must be distributed to each member of staff.

Often the feature content of a magazine will be divided into three or four sections. The priority of sections and their configuration may be laid down by the printers or may be just a device of the chief sub/production editor to even out copy-flow. When this is the case each section will have its own schedule, but the schedules will overlap. 'Section one' copy arrives with the editors on one date, followed by 'section two' copy days or weeks later. The editors have time to work on one section and pass it down the line before more feature material arrives on their desks to be edited. Each department will thus have a certain number of days to work on a certain amount of copy. This is to discourage people from leaving commissioning and editing until late in the production cycle. Chasing late copy or layouts is usually the job of the chief sub/production editor.

Schedules are built from the back, which is to say the point at which your material has to reach the printer. The process of print-buying invariably involves some compromise about the scheduling of printing: by fitting it around some more lucrative magazine contract, your printer will reduce your bill. The problem is that if your magazine fails to arrive on time for its print 'slot', your incompetence will have damaging effects not only on your own printing, finishing and distribution but on those of other magazines around you. That is why print contracts include punitive clauses about late arrival of material. In return, the printers will pay you compensation when their failures cause you difficulties further down the chain. All this becomes more complex as you go beyond simple four-colour printing to include external cover printing, finishing, binding, and so on. So you need a solid understanding of when your material needs to be with the printer, and, for your own use only, what the effects of lateness will be.

All parties in the production process must stick to the schedule or a backlog will be created. When this happens, the sub-editing department has to try and make up time. It is crucial to support your chief sub/production editor in enforcing discipline and in disputes over late copy and layouts. Missing your print deadlines can have expensive consequences.

FLAT-PLANNING

Flat-planning is the other production technique that an editor needs to understand, even though in practice it may be handed over to someone else. The flat-plan is a simplified map of the magazine, indicating what goes where, from the cover to the back page advertisement. Its purpose, in commercial publications, is to allocate spaces for advertising and editorial in accordance with sales that have been made or are confidently expected and the agreed ratio between advertising and editorial. In many large publishing houses the pagination of a magazine and the advertising/editorial ratio may have been worked out anything up to a year before when budgets were being allocated.

But a skilled editor also uses flat-planning to clarify questions of the order, prominence, size and shape of competing pieces of editorial material within the agreed editorial spaces, and to set the 'pace' of the issue.

Flat-planning proper requires detailed information from the advertising department about what types of advertising have been sold in which positions. Obviously, position determines the price paid. Restricting the available positions both improves rates and makes it feasible to produce an editorially appealing magazine. All these things will be laid down by either written rulings or custom and practice.

Long before actual flat-planning begins, you as editor can begin sketching out running orders and likely feature lengths. Indeed, you should get into the habit of visualising features as they will eventually appear even before you have commissioned them. Designers, too, will have sketched out likely 'shapes' of your big features even before they have the copy and photographs. From all this you should be able to establish a simple sheet indicating the order in which the main features will appear and their lengths and shapes. 'Cover story, driving the new Rover: 6 pages = 2 × spreads, 2 × single. Second feature; disposing of your Reliant Robin: 4 pages = spread and two singles.' And so on.

These are all purely notional at this stage, although you will want to commission or acquire suitable photographs to make those spreads a possibility. You will naturally want some shapes more than others. Features really need to start with some impact. You can get that with a spread, or by opening on a right-hand page (which is where the reader's eye naturally falls). You will not normally start anything on a left-hand page, but you can finish or continue features and sections there.

It is not surprising to discover that advertisers want the same spaces that you would like: right-hand pages. Naturally they don't want them to be facing other people's advertisements. They also like half-pages, vertically or horizontally, providing that you put editorial above or beside them. They do not normally want to be next to someone else's half-page advertisement, either.

The conflict between the editorial need to have some presence on the right-hand pages near the start of the magazine, so that browsers can tell that the magazine has something in it, and the need to sell advertising has to be resolved at the highest level early on. The advertising department should have a list of acceptable positions and sizes, in ascending order of price according to their prominence. But there must be a sensible upper limit: it will not normally do to sell every single right-hand page in the front half of a magazine. You in turn may be able to negotiate a notional flat-plan showing areas that are always reserved for editorial, so that readers will always be able to look in the same place for particularly important items, for instance the contents page and the back-page columnist.

American magazines, and some British glossies, use what is called a 'features well', meaning an area in the centre of the magazine devoted entirely to editorial material, without advertising of any sort. This is theoretically ideal, but is not to everyone's taste. British editors tend to prefer working arounds the obstacles presented by advertisements.

In the American 'features well', stories with little pictorial potential can end up as heavy spreads of text. American editors avoid that problem by starting features brightly with a colourful spread or two and then squirrelling the rest of the copy away in the back of the magazine where no-one will notice it except those who are already hooked, who will face a frustrating journey from page to page trying to follow it. This has not generally been considered appropriate or acceptable in Britain, although there are exceptions. It is particularly troublesome if the magazine suddenly has to go up or down in size. Every 'continued on p. . . . .' link will have to be changed.

In Britain, advertisements are generally placed between features – which presents no real problems at all and actually helps punctuate the magazine – and inside features. This is less desirable, but inevitable, in a competitive climate. Designers need to consider what advertising their pages will appear alongside and react appropriately. It is almost never the right approach to try to shout down an advertisement. Better to place your plain type against it and hope your readers are sufficiently engrossed to avoid being blown off track, which they should be. Worse problems come for a designer when the flat-plan somehow leaves two one-page editorial items opposite one another: it is then that wise editors will hope for another advertisement to appear.

Flat-planning is not a once-and-for-all event, although many magazines have a session at which problems are thrashed out. This can be a most useful occasion, on which advertising and editorial teams can meet and exchange views, or it can be the excuse for a lot of unhelpful bickering. You should have your notional running order in mind, as well as a full schedule of other editorial elements. Your advertising director or manager will tell you how many advertisements have been sold (or are confidently expected to be sold) and where they are. The advertising:editorial ratio established by your publisher will lead you directly to an issue size and indicate to you how many pages of editorial are available.

Of course, there is not always an exact fit. Issue sizes go up in fours (100 pp., 104 pp., 108 pp., etc.), whereas advertising is sold in units of a single page or less. For instance, if your advertising department sells sixty pages of advertising and you are working on a 60:40 ratio, you produce a 100-page issue. If they sell sixty-three pages of advertising, you either accept a reduction in the ratio to 63:37 on this occasion, hoping to average things up over a period, or you go up an issue size to 104 pages, at which point your ratio returns to approximately 60:40, leaving you with an extra page to fill which you may not have expected. The swings can be much greater than this, according to the time of year and the selling climate. With current high paper prices, publishers will usually opt to make you drop a few editorial pages.

Minimum and maximum issue sizes must be established, as must acceptable deviations from the agreed ratio. All this is controlled by your publisher, who will decide whether to go up or down an issue size and give you overall numbers of pages to work within. Issues will not normally be enlarged to accommodate extra editorial material, that being a cost, whereas they will be enlarged for more advertising, which is income. But extra editorial pages will be expected at particular times of year when advertising volumes are low but a solid presence on the shelves is required, or when particular events call for them.

Within these broad guidelines, however, it is for you and your advertising counterparts to agree the placing of advertising in and around editorial material. This may be complicated by several other factors. Full colour ('four colour') may not be available throughout the magazine in the standard press configuration used by your printers. In some places, only 'spot colour', meaning one or more of the standard inks used in the four-colour process, may be available. Advertisements which demand full colour must be accommodated in the appropriate sites. Your colour editorial must make what use it can of the remaining sites.

If, however, the demand for colour advertising sites cannot be satisfied by what is available and agreed within the standard flat-plan, more colour slots can usually be created at a price, which the extra advertising will more than cover; some of that extra colour facility may become available for editorial purposes. But you must remember that this will incur extra colour-origination costs, which you will be responsible for.

Another complicating factor is time. Not all magazines go off to the printer as a single batch of pages. Most are broken into sections to be sent off over a series of days, sometimes even weeks apart, to allow for more efficient pre-press work and use of the presses. You must take account of these sections in your flat-planning and scheduling. Individual features, for instance, should not fall across two sections, which may have entirely separate deadlines: if this happens the entire feature should be completed at the earlier date. Some types of material demand to go later rather than earlier, news being the obvious example.

Flat-planning, in complex cases, demands a clear head and good mental arithmetic. A blank plan of the whole magazine is used, and agreed fixed editorial sites and guaranteed advertising sites are filled in first: these will include your contents page and the 'first available right-hand' advertisement. Then you carry on adding more advertising and editorial until everything is accommodated. Start with the simple areas, notably at the back, before moving towards the problematical ones. Flat-planning usually starts at the ends of the magazine and works its way in to the centre. As each advertisement is included it should be crossed off the advertising schedule, as should your editorial items. Naturally this involves a lot of counting of pages to ensure that advertisements are not omitted or included more than once.

A crude flat-plan can always be adjusted at a slightly later stage, by mutual agreement. Indeed, there will generally be adjustments as more or less advertising sells than was expected. By this stage, changes to pagination will no longer be possible, which can mean infuriating last-minute adjustments to your cherished editorial schemes. If this becomes a regular pattern you should make appropriate protests. Creating more editorial matter than is actually used is extremely wasteful. Suddenly providing extra editorial because advertising falls short will result in your overrunning your budget. The ratio is an essential part of the magazine's publishing strategy and should be adhered to other than in exceptional cases.

Once drawn up, the flat-plan should be copied and distributed to art and sub-editing departments while you hold on to the master copy. If you agree any amendments with the advertising department, you should immediately issue copies of the new version, adding a note about the specific changes. The previous versions should be filed away where they can do no harm. The accidental use of more than one flat-plan is a common cause of production disaster. Ensuring the finished pages adhere to the agreed flat-plan is the responsibility of your production editor or chief sub-editor, advised by your art director and sub-editors.

HOUSEKEEPING

A good schedule, carefully policed, and a competent, workable flat-plan are the basis of a solid production regime. But magazines also depend upon the physical movement of material, and this needs to be logged and controlled. A system for signing off finished pages needs to be instituted and maintained. It is becoming increasingly common for individuals in industry to sign their work before releasing it for sale or to the next stage in the production process. There is no reason why magazine production should be any different.

Whatever the sequence of events before the final stage is reached, the finished pages should be signed off by the chief sub-editor or equivalent, by the art director or equivalent, and by you or your deputy. All three of you are actually doing different jobs. Your chief sub-editor is looking at the close verbal texture and providing a final check against typographical and factual errors. Your art director must approve both general competence and such matters as picture credits and copyright acknowledgements. You look at the whole thing for the impression it makes on the reader. You should not use this as an opportunity to simply second-guess other people's work, although if you find anything wrong, and it can be corrected in time, it is always right to send it back.

Of course, this assumes that there is something physical to sign. Most magazines these days leave the office in electronic form. You can sign a final laser proof, which should, if everything is set up correctly, give an entirely accurate picture of what will emerge from the printing process. You may get proofs from whoever turns your electronic pages into film, and these must be studied and signed off in the same way. The material that makes them up has long since left your hands, but replacement pages and picture files can be sent if necessary.

Someone needs to be designated to control precisely what is despatched, to log it out of the building and to check its safe arrival. These days that will be mainly photographic material and hard copies of text and design work for reference purposes. If material is going as SyQuest discs or similar, the contents of those discs must be recorded and checked against what is required. If material is sent electronically, one person should be responsible for sending it and recording what has been sent. Naturally there must be back-up and archive copies of all this material.

USING OUTSIDE FACILITIES

Despite advances in 'desktop' colour, it is still most common and most desirable to leave specialist tasks using expensive equipment to outside contractors. You do not need a high-end scanner, image-setters and the necessary computer power to run them in your office, nor do you want to have their expert operators on your payroll. It is as well to understand precisely what they can do for you, however, and at what cost. You should take the opportunity to visit your colour or repro house with your art editor at some agreed time and for a demonstration of what is possible. In particular they may be able to point out flaws in your production sequence, which may bring benefits in time and efficiency.

It is common for art editors to supervise the work done on covers and other high-profile pieces of colour repro. Be sure that there is no cost penalty for this and that results justify the close attention. The type of equipment used in colour houses may look like a big Apple Mac but it is radically more powerful and costly. Such interventions should be kept to a minimum.

At the other end of the process, a whole range of other trades and techniques are involved, including finishing, binding and distribution. Here you will tend to be in the hands of the experts, but as a customer you are entitled to expect good quality control. Keep an eye on complaints from readers about poor binding and printing and about late delivery. A simple way of keeping a modest check on these matters is to have subscription copies sent to your home, those of your colleagues and far-flung relatives. You will then begin to discover whether the system is running as smoothly as it might. Complaints about late delivery, faulty binding, bad printing and all the rest are really not your responsibility. But these are all things that have a direct effect on the satisfaction of your readers. As a conscientious editor you will not be able to ignore them.

PRODUCTION FOR ELECTRONIC PUBLISHING

The first publications using the new media, on-line and off-line, have simply modelled themselves on traditional magazine structures. They have editors and sub-editors, picture editors and designers. The principal difference comes at the final stage in the process. In on-line work, designers make up their pages in HTML, a high-level programming language, rather than in a page layout program. In CD-ROM work, actual production tends to be handled by outside specialists using professional multimedia tools. Both these may change as existing page production software is replaced by wide-ranging multimedia tools that will, for instance, allow page designs to be quickly converted into both on-line and off-line documents making full use of hypertext and multimedia technologies.

One important thing about on-line publishing, however, is that it does not require publishers to stick to a structure based on regular issues published at fixed dates. Issues and individual stories can be updated as and when new information becomes available. And on-line publishing is genuinely interactive. In the World Wide Web, for instance, page files can be left open for readers to contribute new information and lines of discussion. These two characteristics of the new medium, assuming they survive as it is brought increasingly under the control of commercial interests and the rule of law, seem likely to lead to new forms of editorial management and production planning. Clearly, not all editorial members of staff will be able to alter an on-line publication as and when they feel like it. Some system will need to be devised for regular controlled revision of material as well as for the generation of new pages. Whether the concept of weekly or monthly publication will survive, or whether all publications will move to a type of rolling production, remains to be seen.

Chapter 9

The editor and technology

Recently there was a discussion among a group of journalists about the skills they would require in future to enhance their chances of employment. Reporters, it was suggested, might need to know how to program computers, how to use databases and spreadsheets, how to write 'non-linear' or 'hyper-text' stories and how to practise what the Americans call 'computer-assisted research and reporting', which means using electronic research tools. Copy-editors (or sub-editors) would certainly have to know QuarkXPress, the page-layout program. But would they also need to know HTML, the language used for writing Web pages? And what about photographers? Would they have to understand electronic imaging and photo-manipulation?

Naturally, there were some objections to this technocratic future, largely from those who see such matters as distractions from the task of discovering interesting things and writing them up in an honest and appealing way. But the technophiles struck back: as an editor choosing between twenty or thirty candidates for a news job, aren't you likely to choose the one with computer-assisted reporting skills? Possibly, replied the technophobes, but really a wise editor would choose the one with the dirtiest shoes.

This seems to sum up the argument. Will the journalists of the future step into the dirty shoes of people who have been pounding the streets looking for stories? Or will they be wearing the elegant footwear of people whose mastery of desktop technology means they never have to walk further than the coffee machine?

What gives this argument a particularly ironical spin is that it was conducted not over a drink after work, or even at a conference, but in what is known as 'cyberspace'. The participants were arguing in JFORUM, the journalism discussion area that forms part of CompuServe, one of the oldest and most useful of the 'on-line services'. Even the most avowedly technophobic were sufficiently at home with the technology of modem and e-mail to engage in intelligent debate with strangers by sending written contributions down the telephone line to a central point where they were collated into a sort of conversation that any subscriber could read or take part in.

This is one of the most appealing aspects of the new technology: its potential for the advancement of dialogue on matters of common interest. The participatory nature of the new publishing media is what makes them different and, in some respects, better than the old. The technology we have to use to make them work, however, must not be allowed to stand between us and the human purposes for which publishing is intended.

Editors need to know about technology in their workplaces. Not on a technical level: actually servicing the equipment or debugging the software is one task they are unlikely to be saddled with. But they must know what the equipment will do and what it won't do, to such a degree that they can push it to its limits when necessary but otherwise forget about it. They need to find a way of making it all work invisibly, seamlessly, undramatically and reliably. That way they can get on with editing their magazines: finding the material people need and giving it to them in a form they can use.

CURRENT EDITORIAL TECHNOLOGY

Considering the lack of interest traditionally displayed by journalists towards technology, especially the technology of their own working lives, it is extraordinary that magazine publishing has changed so radically and, at least as far as most journalists are concerned, so painlessly and in such a short period of time.

Many current editors will have started their careers writing stories on typewriters, sub-editing them with pen and paper, laying them out on bigger sheets of paper, cutting and shaping pictures using bits of tracing paper and lots of arithmetic, and then sending the whole lot off to an entirely different set of people to turn into pages of metal type in a complex engineering process. That method of magazine production worked because of distributed human intelligence and responsibility. Lots of people worked as a team, at least theoretically, and people with specialised production skills (proof-reading, for instance, or type-setting) were required and allowed to get on with them, while we as editorial workers did what we do (or did) best: we worked with words and pictures.

The advent of computers, from the first mainframe-based editorial systems on, has changed all that. We have taken more and more control, more and more power, into our own hands. Instead of people who had to be persuaded, flattered, cajoled, bullied and bribed into doing things, we now pass on our instructions through extraordinarily complex software and hardware systems which do exactly what we tell them, no matter how inappropriate. Which means we always have to know exactly what we are doing. Machines have no common sense, no taste and no judgement. Although they can be programmed to simulate some of these things, they can rarely save us from ourselves.

Unfortunately, as editors or individual journalists, we all have more important things to do than study the impenetrable manuals of computer programs that are likely to be obsolete before we get beyond the introduction. Some companies have been reasonably assiduous about providing computer training, but most have not, preferring to rely on people's willingness to pick things up for themselves. But no-one, least of all an editor, can be expected to be up to date with all the software they are likely to encounter in their working lives. We have, by default, come back to relinquishing a lot of the control the computer was supposed to bring us. Only now, because of the power of the software and the unintuitive way most of it works, we are no longer able to comprehend much of what those working with and for us are actually doing. This is a slightly frightening prospect.

The great thing about magazine editing in earlier times was its simplicity. You could cut a story with the slash of a ballpoint. You could crop a picture with a pencil and a ruler. At the same time the technology of the day meant that there were many things you couldn't do. You couldn't write a headline that didn't fit and bend the type until it did. You couldn't change the leading in stories to cover up your inability to make intelligent cuts. You couldn't invisibly modify photographs to make them show things that didn't exist.

These constraints were in many ways a boon to creative intelligence. Because you couldn't do almost anything, you had to concentrate on those areas where you did have control: the fundamentals of words and pictures. They were also a guarantee of certain minimum standards. You did not produce ugly and unreadable type, for instance, because neither the technology nor the printers would let you.

Now we have to impose our own limitations and constraints to make the publishing task make sense. And that means using the power of computers to bring order and form both to the way our magazines are run and to the way they look. This is becoming more possible once again. It looks as if we are beginning to enter a period of consolidation in terms of the core editorial technology, which is to be welcomed. Processor speeds will continue to increase, and software to be updated. It is to be hoped that these lead to a period of stability and system reliability so that we can concentrate on editorial tasks.

The first generation of editorial computers, the mainframe- or minicomputer-based systems from the likes of Atex and SIII, were totally centralised, extremely reliable, very forgiving systems. They made it possible to track copy around the system and to observe what was happening at any time from a central point. But the first systems based on microcomputers, which started soon after the arrival of the Apple Macintosh in 1984, made no real provision for co-operative working. Individual machines would run different programs. When a story was written on one machine in a word-processing program, it would be moved to another to be laid out, using a page-layout program.

Later, simple file-servers were added, increasing the storage capacity of the system and its general security and reliability. But it is only in the last few years that publishers of larger magazines have been able to install complete systems that bind together their individual microcomputers in a way that gives editors the same kind of facilities that were taken for granted in the mainframe era.

The basic hardware and software tools

This may be a rash statement, but the multiplicity of software tools used for basic editorial tasks has been declining in recent years. This is a great improvement. Few of us have ever completely mastered Microsoft Word, and any future time we have for learning software is more likely to be usefully spent discovering how to do new things (using the Internet, for instance) than it is in learning new programs that will simply allow us to go on doing what we already do.

The need to find staff for editorial tasks without constantly retraining them has forced managements away from idiosyncratic solutions and in the direction of a number of *de facto* standards in the magazine publishing industry; these rarely coincide with the 'industry standards' we read about in the computer and business press.

For instance, at the time of writing, the computer (or 'platform') of choice remains the Apple Macintosh, now in its newer 'Power Macintosh' form. Apple were the first into the desktop publishing market, of course. But most of the important software tools are now available on the rival IBM-compatible PC platform and will run under the Windows 95 operating system. Most publishers have stuck with Apple, however, both because of the inherent elegance of the original hardware/software package and because most designers and journalists know and prefer it.

The decision by most of the national newspapers to go over to complete Macintosh-based systems seems to have ensured that that situation will continue, irrespective of the fate of the manufacturer itself. In any case, the next generation of computers will be capable of running any of a number of operating systems, which means that software skills honed on the current generation of applications will continue to be useful whatever happens to the hardware.

The two fundamental applications that editorial people use are word processing and page design and layout. In word processing, the favourite remains Microsoft Word, although many publishers have seen little point in updating it with the frequency that its manufacturers would like. For page design and layout, the standard is QuarkXPress. For a while there was a lively battle between QuarkXPress, Aldus Pagemaker and a number of smaller contenders. But QuarkXPress was the clear preference of graphic designers. The ready supply of QuarkXPress-trained designers (or rather 'QuarkXPress-familiar' designers, since formal training is not that frequent), coupled with publishers' unwillingness to pay for training themselves, has meant QuarkXPress achieving dominance.

Both QuarkXPress and Word are complex programs, but most users need never trouble themselves with Word's wilder excesses. QuarkXPress, on the other hand, becomes difficult very quickly, which may be another reason why those who have mastered it like it: contrary to the implied promise of most computer technology, it cannot be picked up and used by anyone within minutes. As an editor you should know the basics of QuarkXPress, if only so that you can open a spread and fit some copy in emergencies, but you will have to leave most of it to the experts.

Regrettably, a whole generation of sub-editors has emerged that knows little about sub-editing, in the traditional sense of checking facts and honing and polishing copy and headlines, but everything about QuarkXPress. This is understandable, since all those typesetting tasks which used to be undertaken by highly trained print workers have now been transferred to sub-editors and designers or to that strange class of person called 'Mac operator'. Picking up those technical skills has left them with little time or inclination to learn the craft of sub-editing, which is all about informed judgement rather than mastery of a set of instructions for operating a machine. In some cases, their entry to journalism will have come through some computer-related route and they will have neither training nor true journalistic experience. While they may get by in undemanding roles, they will need help if they are to get beyond that.

It seems imperative that all who work as part of an editorial team should understand that their principal tasks are to do with the shaping and focusing of editorial material. At the moment they happen to be using certain hardware and software tools, but those tools will change. Much has been said in recent years about the necessity for journalists in general, and sub-editors in particular, to be 'flexible'. This flexibility has usually involved their taking on non-editorial tasks previously undertaken by other specialists. To do this they have had to learn various computer skills.

But these should not be at the expense of editorial expertise: sub-editors, production editors, editorial designers and picture editors and researchers must continue to see themselves as editorial workers, making editorial judgements, rather than as machine-minders and production staff. In some magazines true editorial involvement has been removed from the production area and handed to a new class of section editors and commissioning editors. This is wrong on a number of levels. The exercise of editorial judgement in the page-making process is central to magazine work.

Some editors have always made it their practice to insist that new sub-editors and designers prove they can work without computers. This may seem reactionary, although it has the virtue of concentrating attention on the essence of the job rather than its technological trappings. And computers break down, and are stolen, even on press day, leaving those without a strong background in traditional skills at a loss. The important thing is to insist that your production staff are not dependent upon their machines. Electronic spell-checking, for instance, is not a substitute for the close attentions of a dedicated sub-editor, even if all parties are using an agreed dictionary including the idiosyncrasies of house style.

It is worth noting, however, that the march of software into areas once thought incontrovertibly human continues apace. Much translation, for instance, is now done by machine, although the odd human is necessary to weed out palpable absurdities. An electronic copy-editor, dubbed 'robo-sub', is also under development, permitting supervising editors to key in a percentage by which a piece is to be cut. The software then hacks away, using a complex set of rules to ensure the piece continues to make a kind of sense. The resulting edited material then fits the required space, although it may well have lost its whole point in the process. There are undoubtedly publishers who will be looking at this development with interest.

The incursion of technology into the editorial domain is not over yet. Increasingly, QuarkXPress, for instance, is being used as a way of controlling all sorts of tasks previously never attempted outside a colour house or typesetting facility. These are managed by small programs, known as Xtensions, built on to the core QuarkXPress software. There comes a point at which you as an editor will have to forget all about them (except, perhaps, if you are expected to pay for them out of your budget). You need to concentrate on the results of all this electronic wizardry, rather than how it is achieved.

The same, only more so, goes for the designers' tools: Photoshop, the photographic manipulation program, and Illustrator and Freehand, the two widely used illustration programs. There is no reason at all for you to touch either of these programs, but you probably should know what they can do so that you can talk intelligently to those who use them and so that you know the language. Part of an editor's job is being able to converse with specialists. In the same way that you need to know what 'privilege' and 'fair comment' mean when you talk to your lawyers, you may find it helpful to know approximately what a 'TIFF' and 'anti-aliasing' are all about.

Editorial computer systems

The arrival of true editorial computer systems based on microcomputer technology has been rather belated. Small magazines simply use the 'Finder' system of the Apple Macintosh, the 'office life' metaphor of files and folders, or its Windows equivalent, as a crude organisational structure. Finished stories are moved from one folder to another, then taken out and worked on again. They may be physically moved from one machine to another on floppy disc or on a basic 'AppleTalk' type of network. This is possible with simple text files, but pages created in QuarkXPress and visual material created in Photoshop and Illustrator require much more computer space and network muscle.

All but the tiniest magazines will, however, have a large 'file-server' computer where stories and pages sit when they are not being worked on. On that computer will sit folders labelled, for instance, 'Incoming copy', 'Copy for sub-editing', 'Copy to art', 'Finished layouts', and so on. People working on a story will pull it out of the file-server along a network, work on it on their own hard disc, relabel it so that everyone knows it has been worked on, then put it back in the next folder in the production sequence. Various fairly crude security and password methods are used to ensure that copy moves in the right direction, that some people have read-only access to particular files, and so on. This is not particularly sophisticated but it works perfectly well in small offices producing modest numbers of pages. It may be accompanied by some sort of messaging system allowing people to communicate by typed note. But in any case, such an operation is likely to be sufficiently small that people can simply lean across and talk to one another.

As an editor you must work with your company's supplier or systems people to ensure that the system conforms with your way of working rather than vice versa. But you should be prepared to take their advice on making the system logical, robust and efficient. You also need to take responsibility for making sure everyone using it, including any casual staff, understands how it works. Such simple systems tend to be relatively unforgiving and require great discipline from all those using them: stories can easily be lost, at least temporarily.

There needs to be a logical structure for file names to show each time a new version of a story has been created and to show which member of the team has worked on it. There have to be rules about procedure, since this loose type of computer network is not capable of imposing a real structure itself. And in both this case and the case of the network with no server, procedures should be put in place to ensure that everything is 'backed up'. Your systems people will tell you how and when this should be done, but it is your responsibility to ensure that it gets done. With the current epidemic of computer theft, it is usually essential to back up to something off-site.

This type of system does not, however, offer an editor the type of information about what is happening that was available with the earlier mainframe editorial systems. More complex systems, combining a file-server to store the actual material and a database to store information on what is happening to it, have started to become available. There is a system called P.INK, now marketed by Scitex, makers of the scanners used at your colour house. An early British system, produced by a company called Talbot, seems to have fallen by the wayside except for its base of established users, mainly in local newspapers. But given the dominance of QuarkXPress, it seems likely that the Quark Publishing System or QPS will corner an important part of the market for systems of this type.

QPS's expense and complication, however, mean that it is best suited to larger operations which might in the past have bought a mainframe-based system. Each user of the system has to 'log on', and is immediately recognised by it and given appropriate access, allocated various pieces of work and provided with all the necessary tools. Once someone has pulled a story up to work on it, no-one can open the same file until it is closed. But those with appropriate access privileges, notably editors, can look at what is happening to the story as it is being worked on.

One of the problems with QuarkXPress, especially for small publishers, is that it is ideal for designers but less than brilliant for anyone else. In particular, sub-editors need to adjust the text in QuarkXPress pages, to make it fit and to incorporate corrections and so on. To do that, their machines have to be running the whole program, even though they do not want to touch the page geometry, the style information, colours or any other part of the designer's box of tricks. Unfortunately, as they open the text box and fiddle about, they are quite likely to alter other things without even knowing what they have done. This 'damage' may not appear until a colour proof is produced.

QPS solves that by providing a built-in text editor, called QuarkCopy-Desk. Pages produced in QuarkXPress in a QPS system are made available to sub-editors, editors and writers using QuarkCopyDesk in a version in which only the text elements can be changed. QuarkCopyDesk also permits the 'notes mode' system beloved of those who grew up using Atex. This allows words and phrases to be marked in such a way that they are still visible on screen but are removed when the story emerges in proof and printed version. Editors can thus make suggestions to writers and sub-editors actually in the stories without the remarks finding their way through to print. It allows sub-editors to make cuts and rewrite passages while leaving the original still visible to the editor and writers.

Obviously whether you use such a tool, as opposed to making each edit of a story a completely different file and making your editorial comments on printed proofs or without reference to individual lines in a story, is all down to your style as an editor. QuarkCopyDesk is available as a separate item without the whole Quark Publishing System: this may mean that small publishers can save the expense and inconvenience involved in buying and installing XPress for sub-editors and editors who only ever need to use about one per cent of its capabilities. The 'notes mode' system is also available as an Xtension for QuarkXPress, where it is called 'red-lining'.

The Quark Publishing System will, incidentally, also provide information on how long particular users of the system have been at their screens, how many stories they have handled, how long they have spent on each, and so on. This type of information was also available in the earlier editorial computer systems. That such invasions of the necessary privacy of the creative writer are thought essential, and indeed, unremarkable, in editorial systems is an indication of the direction in which we have all moved in the years since computers arrived.

So long as all parties are aware of the capabilities of such systems, and do not make the mistake of thinking that anything they ever write on an office computer system is in any sense 'private', then there is perhaps no harm in it. The argument for collecting this type of information is that information itself is neutral: it is only the way it is applied that is good or bad. Let us hope, however, that no editors are ever party to judging their colleagues on the basis of such crude measures as the time spent actually tapping the keys or sliding the mouse. Real journalism will always have more to do with dirty shoes and a high telephone bill than an empty in-tray and a tidy desk top.

Archiving and library programs

Library and archiving programs are now the subject of a great deal of interest, principally because publishers, especially of large magazines, are coming to terms with the idea that their back issues and stored information represent, potentially, a good source of revenue. Unfortunately, these systems are at the same stage that page layout software was at five or more years ago, which means that no one system has begun to achieve dominance.

Electronic picture desks and libraries offer the possibility of selecting images on screen before passing them into Photoshop and QuarkXPress for incorporation into pages. The images themselves are scanned at high resolution and stored on either CD-ROM or optical disks, or can be sent down ISDN lines (a type of telephone line designed for the rapid transmission of digital information) from distant photographers and agencies. Low-resolution versions are made available for viewing and handling on screen and then those versions are replaced by the high-resolution versions at the output stage.

This technology was used first in newspapers, because of the costs involved and because the quality compromises are not so apparent with newsprint reproduction. But in some big magazine houses, notably IPC, similar equipment is now being installed, often as part of an effort to build up a valuable library of images and get maximum use from it. Where the various proprietary systems vary most is in the search tools they incorporate to allow images to be retrieved: obviously searching by attached caption is straightforward but other systems are being developed which promise to allow images to be retrieved by reference to their purely visual content.

Many smaller picture desks are using CD-ROM drives attached to standard desktop computers to view pictures offered in this form by agencies and libraries. Sometimes these CD-ROMs include in 'locked' form versions of the pictures scanned at much higher resolution. By keying in a code, the high-resolution version of the picture can be unlocked and used. Otherwise the real picture is despatched in traditional transparency form and scanned in at the colour facility.

It is true to say that many traditional picture editors and researchers are no more enthusiastic about this technology than their writing colleagues were when word processing was first introduced. This reluctance can be a frustration to those anxious to move boldly into the future, but strong picture-editing skills will continue to be more important and more rare than a relaxed attitude to technological innovation.

Text library systems are also at a fairly primitive stage. It is very likely, however, that the publishers of magazines will attempt, at the very least, to make available the full text of their own magazines for searching by their own staff and perhaps, at a price, their readers. It is already essential to have some kind of indexing system to allow easy access to material already covered; unfortunately, this has always required the services of an editorial librarian or archivist, and such people rarely form part of the tight staffing structure of modern magazines, even on a modest part-time basis. Out-of-house indexing is also a possibility but this too is expensive.

Since the text of magazines now exists in digital form at the magazine house, it would seem a fairly simple matter to turn it into a database for searching by staff. Unfortunately, it is not as easy as all that. Specialist software is becoming available in this field, but it has not yet reached maturity. Until it does, the old-fashioned card-index or paper-envelope methods are still required, but publishers are reluctant to pay for them. Sadly, there are magazines being produced today on which editorial staff have no way, except by memory, of recalling when they last wrote about any given subject. This is a false economy.

Those in-house library systems that do exist offer simplified versions of the searching tools used by professional librarians for interrogating commercial databases, usually of newspaper and magazine back issues. These are excellent devices but demand serious training and dedication. The commercial databases themselves charge per minute of connected time, and are thus an open-ended cost. This can be disastrous, especially when they are used by the inexperienced.

The cut-down versions that are becoming available for individual desktop use, as part of some editorial systems, are usually linked to in-house information sources rather than external sources for reasons of cost. They offer much more basic search tools, but even these are often beyond the easy grasp of busy journalists with so many other things to do. They are also, at their current stage of development, frustratingly slow.

Any thought of replacing genuine editorial library resources with this kind of technology is wrong-headed. The systems can complement these resources but they have a number of dangers. The first is simply that their current inadequacy leads journalists to 'check' facts by conferring with one another rather than by seeking out proper printed sources or asking for a librarian's help.

The second is that they have an aura of infallibility, simply by being computer-based, when the sources themselves may have been very inadequately compiled. A person checking previous appearances of a story by sifting through yellowed newspaper cuttings in a brown envelope can easily grasp that some might have gone missing. A journalist clicking through a string of stories on a screen is more likely to assume that everything on the subject is present, with potentially disastrous results.

In particular, despite their claims to be 'full-text' databases, many commercial services and CD-ROMs exclude material on various criteria, from non-ownership of copyright to legal contentiousness.

Desktop 'repro' and colour

The drive towards bringing more and more of the contracted-out aspects of publishing into the magazine's own premises has stalled recently. This is partly because it is in direct conflict with the modern management philosophy of 'out-sourcing' and keeping to 'core functions'. It is also because such things as repro and colour handling at a high level are extremely expensive, in terms of both capital equipment and the salaries of those needed to operate it. And few organisations would generate the volume of work required to justify truly professional scanning and repro equipment.

Thankfully, it remains much more cost-effective to have such work done by outside specialists, especially since there is continuing confusion over technical standards for the long-awaited 'desktop' versions. In any case, as and when such technology becomes more affordable and reliable, it is not likely to be operated by the editorial or art staff of individual magazines, at least not in the near future: a magazine house may have its own central reprographic facility but that is not something for which you as an editor should have any responsibility.

COMPUTER-ASSISTED RESEARCH AND REPORTING

This is an American expression for the use of computer technology in pursuit of stories and information. 'CARR' may become something of a specialism, simply on account of its potential complexity. But most journalists with any pretensions to writing about current events are likely to want to take on the burden of investigating computer-based sources themselves, in much the same way that generations of business reporters have taught themselves to use Companies House and interpret the documents stored there.

In the first instance, CARR is about using documentation stored in digital form on computer media. In its most reliable and straightforward version, this means the CD-ROM. Most public reference libraries will now have a selection of materials in this form: encyclopaedias of various types, back issues of newspapers and periodicals in full-text or abstracted form, statu-tory instruments, EC material, telephone and business directories, book catalogues, and so on.

Interrogating a CD-ROM database is not like looking at microfilm of old newspapers. Because you can search by key words as well as by date or issue number, it is easy to find things, even things you did not know exist. But because all you see, usually, is a featureless volume of text, it is less easy to interpret what you do see. Was a particular article a leader column or a news story? Was an item meant ironically or straight? Is this story a follow-up to something that does not appear in the database, and if so, what? The earlier story may have used a synonym for your search term, in which case it will not be found.

Journalists cannot afford to take everything at face value when they inter-rogate a CD-ROM database any more than they can when they speak to someone. Unfortunately the dumb insolence of computers means that those using them tend to take what they are given with gratitude and without due scepticism.

Worse, most library material on CD-ROM (consumer-market material is rather different) is produced in the Windows or DOS formats and conse-quently no one CD-ROM product interface resembles another. Switching, for instance, from the full-text version of the *Guardian* to the full-text ver-sion of the *New Scientist* is likely to provoke tears of frustrated rage in most journalists in a hurry. Nothing about the way the two products present their material is even similar.

Consequently this type of computer-assisted reporting is always much slower and more infuriating than it should be. But despite that, these devices are often a good way into a story or feature: not for the purpose of 'lifting' material, since everything contained within is copyright, but for suggesting lines of inquiry, people to talk to and new thoughts.

Oddly, considering its vast size compared with the average CD-ROM, the Internet and the on-line world generally are in some ways easier to use, although potentially costly. It is effectively impossible to describe what these things are about to anyone who hasn't tried them, but there is a basic division between commercial on-line services and the Internet itself.

The commercial on-line services, of which CompuServe is probably the best known, offer published information at premium prices, for instance newspaper and journal back issues from around the world. They are easily accessed using their own proprietary software, a normal desktop computer and a telephone line.

The Internet is different again, but here there has at least been some *de facto* standardisation on the Netscape Navigator and Microsoft Internet Explorer 'browser' programs for the World Wide Web. Accessing the Web is fairly straightforward once your computer and modem have been config-ured. Getting beyond that, and configuring the equipment in the first place, are, however, much more complex matters in which most journalists and editors will require expert help and advice.

Finding things in the Internet is not an exact science, by any means. A number of 'search' services of various degrees of professionalism are available. You type your search terms into a box on the screen, and the 'search engine' attempts to find them in the millions of documents it professes to know about. These include Web sites, naturally, which range from the massive resources of various government agencies around the world to the ramshackle efforts of individual enthusiasts. A broad inquiry will usually produce thousands of references. A very specific inquiry, using the search engine's idiosyncratic methods for narrowing the range of your inquiries, might produce ten or fewer.

But some search engines go beyond the Web, which is the Internet's glossy shop-window, into the areas of 'news groups', 'mailing lists', 'gopher' and 'ftp', all text-based aspects of the system. These are in some ways more useful if you are interested in finding people to talk to about the subjects you are researching, whether by e-mail alone or eventually by telephone.

This is perhaps better explained by example. You are writing a story about nursery education and you come across something called the 'High Scope' method of teaching small children. Your initial search directs you to various books and articles with the phrase in their titles: the books you might have to order, but the system might give you an e-mail number for their publisher. Some of the articles might be available on-line, at no cost.

One such article tells you the story of the programme from its inception to the present day. But you want more: a different search service, for which you have to pay, searches 'news groups', which is where people discuss issues of interest to them. In an education news group someone has recently used the phrase 'High Scope'. The contribution appears on your screen, together with the e-mail address of the person who made it: contributions to news groups generally include such information. You e-mail the person concerned, who is in the northern United States, to ask, politely, if he or she would mind sharing some thoughts on the method with you. The next morning, a reply is in your mailbox and you proceed from there.

Once your reporters have discovered this way of working, they may well, especially at the start, find it almost irresistible. But sound journalistic principles will continue to apply. The Internet is theoretically global, but predominantly American. You may not want your stories to be based on quotes from people in Arkansas whom your reporters have never actually spoken to.

Much of the material on the Internet is 'free'. This means, of course, that there is no guarantee of its quality, but then the same goes for much expensive information. You must remember, however, that there are costs: you will have to pay some kind of 'provider' to connect you to the networks, and you will have to pay telephone time. In addition, much of what you read or download is less than useless. The time spent sifting through it might be much better spent in making a few essential telephone calls or even in simply thinking. Data, which is what much of the Internet consists of, is not quite the same as information. And information is not the same as editorial matter.

Despite these reservations, computer-assisted reporting of various types is likely to grow, particularly as government agencies use the media for official communications. Those wishing to learn more should subscribe to the CARR-L mailing list within the Internet.

Information stored on computer and gathered by computer should not, however, always be taken for the truth. It will certainly not be the whole truth.

Chapter 10

The editor and the public

Freedom of the press is guaranteed only to those who own one.

A.J. Liebling

Few of us own a press, but the American humorist's remark should remind us of the privilege enjoyed by those of us who have regular use of one. With that privilege, however, comes responsibility, a responsibility that extends not only to our staff and readers, but to the wider society as well. The freedom we cherish is hedged around by restrictions. Some of these are petty and technical, but others are to the benefit of all citizens.

While we may chafe at some of the absurdities in British press law, we must all work within the law in such a way that we retain the capability of publishing what our readers require. Unlike journalists working in the United States, we cannot rely upon a constitution, or even a society, predisposed to support our activities. The British constitution's attitude to free speech in general is that it is an important principle but not one that should take automatic precedence over other rights, for instance that of property.

In recent times, free speech and press freedom have found some belated constitutional support in the European Convention on Human Rights. This at least establishes the fundamental structure of rights under which the British and European press operate. The Convention does not, however, have much to do with the normal daily practices of most working editors, acting only as the ultimate grounds for appeal in cases where high principle is at stake.

Most editors today live in a world in which freedom of the press is seen as a sectional interest rather than a general human right, and in which the activities of journalists are viewed with public scepticism and hostility. At some point these attitudes will have to be tackled, and the reputation of British journalism restored. In the meantime, realistic editors must be aware of the conditions under which they operate. To be an effective editor it is necessary to know and observe the legal and ethical restraints on publishing without allowing them to dictate what appears in our magazines. In other words, we must not allow ourselves to be defeated before we start.

PRESS LAW

Books on first aid for children invariably start with the same advice: summon adult help. Books on law for journalists take a similar approach: anyone one with a legal query is advised to fetch a lawyer. Sound though this is, it is not always practical. Nor is it universally applicable. We may indeed need professional advice, but for informed consultation rather than to be instructed on what to do next. We must retain responsibility for all our own editorial decisions: how to research and write editorial material, what to publish and how to deal with any problems arising from that publication. Of course, we will be better able to avoid falling into a position of helplessness if we take the trouble to learn what the law means for us in practice.

That way we can use legal advice to help us find safe, legal ways of saying what we feel needs to be said, rather than, as is so often the case, asking for guidance on what we might be allowed to say. It should be noted that libel insurance can place us in the latter position, since the lawyer's responsibility is to advise the insurers that nothing in our magazines is likely to attract successful litigation, rather than to assure us that what we wish to publish will be legally acceptable. This is a difference of nuance, perhaps, but it is important, here as everywhere else, that responsibility for deciding what to publish and in what form lies squarely with the editor and is not split or shared with anyone else, whatever their qualifications.

Libel is perhaps the most worrying area for many editors, with some justification, but it is not the only, or indeed the most important, legal question that we have to consider. Editors have legal responsibilities in their capacity as managers of people and as creators of products offered for sale as well as in their capacity as journalists. But it is in the strictly editorial role that they will encounter the most bewildering array of legal issues. These may include defamation; contempt of court; copyright; the law of confidence; trespass; passing off; trades descriptions; competitions law; the rehabilitation of offenders; obscenity; blasphemy; racial hatred; court, parliamentary and local government reporting; official secrets; and business law.

A book of this type is in no position to cover all these issues. An editor who is not confident in all of these areas, and few of us are, is advised to buy the leading textbooks on media law as each new edition appears and to read them regularly. It is also important to monitor the trade and national press for relevant legislation and court cases. Media law is currently in a state of ferment, particularly as the 'new media' become more important.

But theoretical knowledge must be supplemented by practical experience. When you have occasion to consult legal advisers, you must use this time wisely. Ask them to explain to you what is happening rather than simply follow instructions. Editing the magazine is your responsibility, and you must use your legal experiences, however painful and tedious, to help you do it better in future.

The four areas that cause most problems for working editors are defamation, contempt of court, copyright and the law of confidence. None of them is exactly straightforward, a reflection of the subtle intelligence of the legal minds drawn towards media law by the rewards to be earned from it.

Defamation

The law of defamation exists to allow people to defend their reputations and to gain compensation when those reputations are found to be illegally attacked. But a publication in which no-one is ever defamed is not worth reading. Your readers will expect to read about people and organisations behaving badly and being revealed as inadequate. Your task is to provide that material, the stories people don't want you to print, in a way that will not bring your operation to a halt under a welter of legal action.

By the time you become an editor, you should have the famous 'tests' for defamation inscribed upon your heart. A statement is defamatory if it:

• exposes the plaintiff to hatred, ridicule or contempt
• causes the plaintiff to be shunned or avoided
• lowers the plaintiff in the estimation of reasonable people
• or tends to make reasonable people think less of the plaintiff in his or her office, trade or profession.

You will also know the types of action people can take against you in this general area – libel, slander and malicious falsehood – and how they differ from one another. You will know that a plaintiff in a libel action has to show that a statement tends to injure his or her reputation, that readers of the statement would take it to refer to the plaintiff, and that the statement has been published, even if only to a third party.

And you will know how you defend your publication in a libel action: through 'justification', which means proving the truth or 'justification' of the 'sting', or salient point, of any factual allegation; by demonstrating that the item in question was 'fair comment on facts truly stated in a matter of public interest'; by invoking 'privilege'; or by any of several more obscure means.

Your task now is to ensure that this material is understood by your staff and contributors. They need not have the detailed understanding that harsh experience will have brought you. But they need to know enough to understand when there is a problem. This is difficult to ensure if you are taking on trust the legal training that those who write and sub-edit for you have received. It is important that the principles of libel (and indeed, all the legal questions considered here,) are known not only to reporters and sub-editors but to feature writers, columnists and even your key art staff: it is perfectly possible to libel someone in the way you crop a picture.

The current model of magazine journalism, in which a tiny number of staff assemble the product from the contributions of a large number of freelance writers of largely unknown reliability, has certainly been a boon to the legal profession. There are writers today, some of them well known, who think that the fact that a defamatory statement appears between quote marks and is clearly attributed to someone is a defence against a libel action.

Such ignorance places a tremendous responsibility on editors and sub-editors to 'clean up' copy in the production process. This is not the best approach. Sub-editors, whose training may have been no more thorough than that of the writers with whom they are dealing, are rarely in a position to do anything substantive about the potential libels they spot. A defama-tory statement cannot be made non-defamatory, in most cases, by 'toning down' the language in which it is made. Nor should it be. If a story or a statement within a story is accurate then it should be told boldly and starkly. If it is not, it should be removed. The 'toning down' approach leads to anodyne writing that may, paradoxically, be no less dangerous than absolute clarity.

What is required is a thorough examination of the material making up a story. Writing the truth, and being ready to prove it to be the truth, is the only absolutely solid way of dealing with libel actions. Of course, truth is a large and difficult concept, but we should start with accuracy, completeness and fairness and work up from there. These principles need to be drummed into both writing and production staff and systems put in place for ensuring that they are observed.

As editor, you can hand responsibility for these questions down as far as the individual writers, but you must decree the required standards and ensure that they are met. If they are not met, you must take appropriate action. If you are in the position of employing writers, you are entitled to keep a check on the way they research, interview and record their findings. You must ensure their notes are kept in a disciplined way, that tape-recording is used for contentious matters, and that all notebooks, tapes, printed sources and the rest are retained and stored: a libel action can be launched anything up to three years after publication.

Freelance writers represent a particular problem. You have no real way of knowing about their expertise, their training and their character, except per-haps by long-term familiarity. Few such writers would take kindly to being asked to present their notebooks and tapes for your inspection. Unfortu-nately, if there is a problem, much worse is likely to happen to them. It may well be worth producing a guide for your writers, outlining the standards you expect from them. This would include instructions on using notebooks and tapes and keeping them safely in case of subsequent trouble. Such a guide can even be sent out with your commissioning letters.

Attempting to off-load your libel responsibilities on to your writers, by expecting them to indemnify you against any libel costs, is not an accept-able practice in magazine publishing, although it is traditional in book publishing. A commission does carry an implied obligation on writers to assist in fighting any resultant legal action. In any case, most libel plaintiffs will sue author as well as editor and publisher, so co-operation between all parties becomes essential. A libel action is a most unpleasant experience for everyone concerned, so it is vital to stress to your contributors at this stage the importance of avoiding any such eventuality.

A professional approach demands the checking of all facts and approaching any witnesses or informants with a high degree of scepticism. But the physical evidence backing up a story takes on extra significance if you should be unlucky enough actually to attract a libel writ. As proceedings develop, all of this material, plus anything deemed material in the way of interim versions, layouts and notes in your computer system, will have to be handed over. When the evidence for your big story is revealed as no more than some scribbles on the back of an envelope, you are likely to suffer more than embarrassment.

Solid journalistic practice is a much more sound foundation for avoiding legal trouble than attempting to fix or fudge things on a verbal level. Where a story makes serious allegations, it is becoming more common for it to be supported by written statements from sources, signed in the presence of a solicitor, although this has not yet become standard practice. Stories in general should be balanced. Your writers should speak to all relevant parties, and you should ensure that they do not become emotionally involved to the extent that they could be accused of 'malice', in its peculiar legal sense. Malice here means publishing something you know to be untrue, or not caring whether it is true or not.

There is even some danger of a reporter's incurring an action for slander, the oral version of libel, by the way he or she chooses to go about investigating a story. But in a slander action the plaintiff has to show actual monetary loss except in five special cases: accusations of a crime for which the punishment is imprisonment; accusations of having a contagious disease; suggestions that the plaintiff is no good at his or her job; attacks on the plaintiff's creditworthiness; and attacks on the sexual conduct of a woman or girl.

Naturally you should always keep your ear open for evidence of malice in its lay sense: journalists are no more immune from self-interest and petty dishonesty than anyone else, but it is essential that they don't exercise these qualities in your pages.

Sub-editors do have an important role to play in the prevention of libel actions. They should be alert to potentially hazardous material and ready to take it up either with the author or with the commissioning editor responsible. But they must also see that things are worded in the most appropriate way. Stories should be clear. People who are identified should be identified unambiguously, to avoid dragging in others with similar names. Innuendo, where words have a special defamatory meaning to certain groups within the readership, and double-meaning should be removed by careful sub-editing. Terms with precise meanings should be used carefully: your writers and sub-editors should not bandy around such words as 'bankrupt' unless they know what they mean.

The sub-editing of 'opinion' columns, 'angry' columns and 'humorous' columns and the like is a much more subtle matter. Here judgements have to be made about language, but they must be based on the formula of honest comment on a matter of public interest, based on facts that have been truly stated or accurately alluded to. The law protects outrageous opinions, but takes a dim view of the mingling of inaccurate facts and comment in the same column or phrase.

This is particularly important for those publications which review products, whether babies' pushchairs or cameras. You must make a judgement about how 'robust' your magazine's criticisms can be. You must also ensure that any 'objective' methods of testing used are operated with the greatest care and that those doing the reviewing have absolutely clean hands.

Any suggestion that your reviewers might be doing consultancy work for rival manufacturers, unless this is boldly declared, will certainly be interpreted as malice. Reviews have to be fair and seen to be fair. As editor you must have systems for avoiding foolish mistakes that might lead to unnecessary libel actions. Anything tricky in new copy should be brought to your attention, although you don't necessarily want to have to sort it out personally.

In the end, you must take responsibility for what is published. This does not, however, mean that you must never publish anything defamatory. A magazine that never brings anyone into hatred, ridicule or contempt, that never causes anyone to be shunned or avoided, or that never makes anyone think less of a person in their office, trade or profession, is a dull read indeed.

You won't find much of this in legal textbooks, but any editor knows that the libel question is a matter of judgement and risk-assessment. It's a 'percentage game'. How likely are these words to cause offence? How likely are they to lead to a solicitor's letter? How likely are they to lead to a writ? How likely is the libel action to go to court? And what is the outcome likely to be?

One of the unattractive aspects of Britain's libel laws is that defence of a reputation is only available to the rich or those who can find someone else to pay their bills, there being no legal aid for a defamation action. Which means that editors look not only at the strength or otherwise of a story written about someone, they look at how likely that person is to be able to do anything about it. In practice this means that they are less willing to libel the rich, the powerful and the well-connected than they are to traduce the poor and the weak.

It is not quite as clear-cut as that, however. A relatively poor individual may belong to a wealthy organisation, for instance a trade union or a professional organisation, that will pay for legal action. On the other hand, you can gamble that certain types of rich people will not sue, either because they are prepared to accept robust criticism, even abuse, as the price of their social prominence (increasingly unlikely), or because they have something to fear by going near the courts. There is also the question of the prospective plaintiff's general character. At one stage it was common to assume that you could say anything you liked about people with 'no reputation to defend': they would not go to law for fear of having that demonstrated to them. This is not something that can any longer be relied upon.

On publication, there should be a clear system for dealing with complaints and queries, particularly those that contain a hint of legal menace. All complaints should be passed straight up to the editor. Only you should have the authority to promise any kind of correction or, crucially, any apology. In particular you must prevent staff trying to 'sort things out' by cunningly weaving some kind of correction into a new story: if anyone is going to do that it has to be you, and it is risky.

People who have been inaccurately written about will generally want a simple statement putting the story straight. Factual errors in themselves cannot cause a libel action unless they have defamatory implications. Consequently they do not actually have to be corrected, although they should be, unless they are very trivial.

If you are confident that a complainant will be satisfied with a correction, and you are sure that your magazine got the story wrong, then place a plain correction in the next issue. You must be careful not to suggest that anyone else, either a source or the author, got it wrong, however, unless you want to make an enemy of either of them. A correction may sometimes head off a solicitor's letter, which will save you money, but is not usually enough to appease a seriously aggrieved complainant.

An apology may do the trick, but here complications start to arise. It may be safe in a case of accidental defamation, where you did not realise that the words would be understood to refer to the complainant or where some circumstances of which you could not be aware have made the words defamatory. In these cases you have no defence, so you have nothing to lose.

The problem of apologies in general is that they mean admitting a fault, which may destroy your defence. If you do print an apology, you will only be safe in doing so if the complainant agrees in writing that the apology, and any payment you might make towards costs, settles his or her claim against you. If the complainant won't agree that, then you could easily apologise, destroy your own case in the process, and still have to go to court. These are deep waters, and it is important that anything resembling an apology is only printed on legal advice.

If you choose to negotiate yourself, you should head any letters 'without prejudice', which means that they are not binding unless they include a full and final agreement. That at least should enable your lawyers to sort things out if you get into a mess. There is a saying that may be relevant: 'A man who is his own lawyer has a fool for a client.'

If the libel action against you goes further, however, you will pretty soon find yourself called upon to make a serious and honest assessment of your chances of success. Newsroom bravado (or even editor's office bravado) soon withers under the harsh light of legalistic inquiry. You and your writer will have to produce all the evidence upon which the story was based, and at some point, during the process of 'discovery', it will all have to be handed over to the other side, including irreverent jottings, insulting catch-lines or filenames, early versions, ill-transcribed tapes of interviews, crass dummy headlines and more. Journalism does not usually emerge well from this kind of scrutiny, which is why it is essential that good practices and legal aware-ness are universal throughout your editorial team.

The process of defending a libel action invariably involves completely re-researching the original story. Journalists generally have little enthusiasm for looking backwards, but here they will have no choice. It is at this point that you discover the extreme unwillingness of your sources, even those who are quoted in the story, to give you the necessary assistance when lawyers and courts are involved. This is a problem which can be confronted earlier by asking them for written statements at the time of original publication. If they refuse then, too bad. If they agree, you have effectively guaranteed their involvement if anything goes wrong. Unnamed sources are, as usual, less than useless here. If they form a central part of your case, the courts are likely to try to make you name them, which is not what you want at all.

At this point, many publishers and some editors will want to settle with the plaintiff for fear of greater losses at a later point. Libel insurance com-plicates matters, since it often doesn't even start to apply until your costs look like reaching a certain level, and at that point the insurance company takes over your defence and decides whether or not you can fight.

It is important, however, not to crumple too easily. Publications which gain a reputation within the legal business as a 'soft touch' can expect a constant string of vexatious complaints. No matter how small and how trivial, these usually end up costing money, if only in terms of your time.

The whole magazine industry received a salutary lesson in the *Yachting World* case of 1994. The magazine's review of a new trimaran resulted in an action brought by the yacht's manufacturer. *Yachting World*'s publishers, IPC, subsequently agreed to pay substantial damages and costs.

In the immediate aftermath of the case, however, IPC introduced a libel checklist for its journalists. They were told to log the date and time of all telephone calls; to date and sign all contemporaneous notes; to ensure that the other party in any story was aware of their intentions and was agreeable to any product test or article; to double-check with their original author any facts taken from cuttings; to refer any worries about an article to their editor and then in turn to the company lawyer; and to avoid 'ambivalent catch-lines and irreverent jottings', which could turn out to be disastrous as documents connected with a story have to be disclosed.

These requirements sound excessive at first sight, but there is little in them that goes beyond the normal good practice of an efficient news team. Where magazines get into trouble is in softer areas, where feature writers may not be so aware of the dangers.

Proposed changes in defamation law.

The Government has recently introduced a new Defamation Bill to tackle some of the complexities of current British libel law. The new Bill is intended to bring the law up to date in the technology it covers and to improve and simplify its procedures. In practical terms, it is not likely to affect the way editors approach legally tricky stories. But it does offer new approaches and lines of defence if you face a defamation action. The proposals include:

- a modernisation of the defence of 'innocent dissemination' available to those who have been involved in distributing defamatory material without having had control over the substance of what is published
- an 'amends defence', allowing publications to bring an action to a swift close in cases where they recognise that they have defamed someone and are prepared to pay damages
- a reduction in the time limit for beginning a defamation action, from three years after publication to one
- a new 'summary' procedure, allowing judges sitting without juries to deal with straightforward and less serious defamation claims.

Clause 1 of the Defamation Bill extends what is called the defence of 'innocent dissemination'. Previously this was available to those, such as distributors and newsagents, who handled publications that may have contained defamatory statements but who could not be held responsible for their content. Now it has been extended to printers, but also to those processing and selling film and sound recordings and electronic media and to those broadcasting live programmes or operating 'communications systems' who have 'no effective control' over those using them to make defamatory statements. This is intended to cover commercial on-line services, the providers of Internet services, and any future technological developments along those lines. No such defence is available to authors, editors or publishers.

The 'innocent dissemination' defence, however, does not protect those who knew that the material they were handling was defamatory, or who ought to have known. Defendants must still have taken 'reasonable care' in relation to the publication of the material. What this will mean in practice has yet to be determined. It does not require printers, distributors and others to take any editorial or libel-reading role: indeed they must not because in doing so they will lose their right to be considered 'innocent'. But they will continue to need reassurance that some responsible person – the editor and his or her legal adviser – is in charge of determining that the publication is legally safe.

In particular, in determining whether a person took reasonable care, the court can have regard to the 'previous conduct or character of the author, editor or publisher'. Those publishing satirical magazines and those with a record of malice or recklessness will continue to have difficulty with their distributors and Internet providers.

Clauses 2 to 4 detail the 'offer of amends'. This would seem to offer a swift and reasonably predictable way of dealing with accidental libels: those caused by mistaken identifications, wrong photographs, the erroneous attribution of quotes, and so on. A person who has published a false statement alleged to be defamatory can resolve matters by making an offer of amends to the complainant, which must include a suitable correction and apology, but also compensation and costs.

Currently, a publisher admitting to a mistake and offering an apology risks the complainant's pressing on in an attempt to collect damages from a jury. The new system promises to take such cases, where publishers are willing to admit fault, away from juries. The sums of money in compensation have to be agreed by the parties, but if they can't agree, they will be determined by a judge without a jury. The judges should make more predictable awards than has been the case with libel juries.

The offer can be made at any point before you as editor and publisher submit your defence, but not later. As soon as the aggrieved person accepts the offer, the defamation action comes to an end. If, on the other hand, you make the offer and it is not accepted, the fact of its having been made is available as a defence if the defamation action proceeds. You do not have to use it as a defence: you can also use it in mitigation of damages. But if you use it as a defence, you may not rely on any other defence.

You cannot use this defence if you knew, or had reason to believe, that the allegations you published were both false and defamatory. The court will presume that this was not the case. If, however, the plaintiff manages to convince the court that you published knowing or having reason to believe that the allegations were false and defamatory, your defence falls. Because you have used the 'offer of amends' as your defence, you are not allowed to use any other. This would put you in a very dangerous position.

The Bill seems to have been framed in such a way that the 'offer of amends' will be widely available as a defence to those who published without malice, got it wrong, and are prepared to admit fault and apologise. Few editors publish defamatory material if they know or have reason to believe that it is false. But those who can be shown to have published maliciously or recklessly and seek to use the 'offer of amends' procedure will find themselves in great difficulties.

It seems possible that this new procedure will deal efficiently with many of those libels which stem from mistakes. Cases in which magazines are not prepared to retract, apologise and pay compensation will continue to go before a jury, as will those in which the plaintiff can show that the publication was malicious or reckless.

Clauses 5 and 6 deal with the reduction of the time limit during which defamation proceedings must be begun. This changes from within three years of publication to within one year. There are exceptions, however. For instance, the court can set aside the time limit if the plaintiff did not know about publication in time to begin the action within the time limit. The time limit for malicious falsehood actions also becomes one year.

The new 'summary' procedure comes in Clauses 8 to 11. For the first time this brings all defamation actions before a judge at an early stage so that he or she can decide whether the case can be dealt with in summary fashion. If the judge decides that the claim has no 'realistic prospect of success' he or she can dismiss it. On the other hand, if the judge decides that the magazine or newspaper will not be able to defend itself with any 'realistic prospect of success' he or she can make a summary judgment. Unless the plaintiff asks for summary judgment, the judge can only do this if he or she is satisfied that the summary procedure will provide adequate compensation for the wrong the plaintiff has suffered.

If the judge disposes of the case summarily, he or she can award damages up to £10,000, can restrain the defendant from publishing or republishing the defamatory material, and can demand a declaration that the allegation was false and the publication of a suitable correction and apology. The wording and positioning of this is to be agreed between the parties. If they do not agree on the wording, the judge can order the publication of a summary of the judgement. If they do not agree on positioning and timing, the judge can direct the defendant 'to take such reasonable and practicable steps as the court considers appropriate'. The summary procedure does not apply if the judge concludes that there is a defence with a reasonable chance of success or if there is some other reason for there to be a trial.

Among more minor points, the Bill amends the defence of 'privilege' to cover all types of publication and to include fair and accurate reports of public proceedings not only in Britain but across the world. There also several more technical clauses concerning stories about wrongful convictions and about the basis of entitlement to damages. The Bill also rules that courts no longer have to determine whether a statement is 'arguably capable' of bearing a particular meaning. The test now is whether a statement is 'capable' of bearing the meaning.

At the time of writing, the Bill had been introduced in the House of Lords but no timetable for its progress had been announced. The only aspects that seemed likely to be controversial enough to slow the Bill's passage were the provisions about 'innocent dissemination', which the on-line services and other providers of electronic information feel do not go far enough in protecting them from libel actions. They are dealing with many millions of subscribers, all of whom have the potential to write defamatory statements. They have proposed instead that the law provide them with a short period of grace during which they can remove any offending material from their systems before becoming liable for a libel action. This seems unlikely to prove acceptable.

Editors are advised to familiarise themselves with the provisions of the new Defamation Act as it comes into force, which may already have happened by the time this book appears.

Contempt of court

A libel action can be extremely alarming, but it does not have the air of threat that comes with a contempt of court case. Contempt is a criminal offence, carrying a maximum penalty of two years' jail and an unlimited fine. Cases are heard by High Court judges, sitting without a jury, even though the offence in question may simply be one of publishing scandalous material about a judge. No wonder editors, by and large, are careful about contempt.

Contempt of court means interfering with the proper conduct of justice in such a way that someone will be prevented from having a fair trial. There are two types, in effect: 'strict liability' contempt, where a contempt can be committed quite accidentally; and various types of deliberate contempt, from interviewing jurors about their deliberations to 'scandalising the court'.

Editors whose publications carry any kind of crime coverage or law reporting should know the rules. Every other journalist should know that contempt is committed when a publication 'creates a substantial risk that the course of justice in particular proceedings will be seriously impeded or prejudiced', and that the danger period starts when a case becomes 'active', which is to say as soon as an arrest is made or charges are laid against someone.

There is a great deal more to it than that, of course, and editorial staff need to be encouraged to think carefully and clearly when they are dealing with any material that makes specific reference to events in the criminal courts and legal system. This is an area in which expert advice is essential, especially in view of the potential penalties. As an editor you should make it your duty to provide anyone working for you with a very basic summary of the law's demands as they affect them. At the very least, this may be enough to prevent such headlines as 'Rapist released on bail', sometimes composed by junior sub-editors.

Copyright

The subject of copyright has been explored in chapters 7 and 8 in the context of commissioning and buying rights. But it has many other implications. Copyright is the right to reproduce an original work. Normally it belongs to the person creating the work but it can be sold ('assigned') to someone else, or various 'licences' to use the work can be agreed. Copyright in a work created by an employee belongs to the employer; until 1988, journalists were in a privileged position, in that copyright in their work belonged to their employers only for the purpose of newspaper or magazine publication. The rights to use the work in book form, for instance, belonged to the individual. This has now been removed.

An infringement of copyright occurs when a 'substantial' part of a work is reproduced. A 'substantial' part need not necessarily be a high proportion of the actual words: it can be a small but very important part. It is important to note that there is no copyright in ideas, only in their expression. The work in question need only have been put together with some element of skill to receive copyright protection: it need not be artistic. It has long been established that railway timetables and television schedules are copyright materials.

The relevant defence for magazines and newspapers wishing to reproduce 'substantial' parts of copyright material is called 'fair dealing'. The use of reasonable extracts from the work of others is permitted when it is for research or private study, criticism or review or the reporting of current events. Criticism or review need not actually be of the copyright material in question: it is a general permission for that type of work.

In all cases, the title of the source material and its author must be identified in the text, and it must be used 'fairly'. This is the most subjective part of the law. Here the question of your motive is important. For instance, large portions of another magazine's interview with a star must not be lifted and reproduced simply because you have not been able to secure such an interview yourself and wish to compete. This is very important in the vexed area of 'cuttings jobs', those features which are largely composed of quotes and observations first used by other writers.

Such features may indeed be considered either 'criticism or review' or part of the 'reporting of current events'. But if the borrowed materials amount to a 'substantial' part of the original work they must be properly attributed, and the new work created must not be intended to compete directly with those works it has drawn upon. This is particularly relevant in the case of 'instant' features devised to 'spoil' someone else's book serialisation or cover story: in this case any borrowing should come from other sources than the one your feature is intended to compete with.

There is also a suggested upper limit to the volume of borrowing. The Society of Authors and the Publishers Association have arrived at an agreement that reproduction of text for the purposes of criticism or review will not require permission if the amount borrowed consists of

• a single quote of fewer than 400 words from a prose work
• a series of quotes of fewer than 300 words each, totalling no more than 800 words

and if the total does not comprise more than a quarter of the original article being quoted. This agreement is not actually enshrined in the law, so it may be possible to use more material legally. But to do so, and to use such material outside the 'criticism or review' area, may well invite a solicitor's letter.

Satire and parody is an interesting case. It is difficult to parody something, especially a picture, without using a substantial part of it. In this case a fair dealing defence could apply, provided that suitable attribution is included. Theoretically the 1988 Copyright Act also gives copyright protection to the extempore words of any speaker once they are recorded, either on tape or as notes. The person making the record, however, provided he or she has not been specifically forbidden from doing so, has the right to reproduce them for the purposes of reporting a current event or making a broadcast.

Editors should be aware of the 'moral rights' created by the 1988 Act, even though most of them are specifically ruled out for employees and for anyone who gives consent for his or her work to be published in magazines, newspapers or other periodicals. They are: the right to be identified as the author; the right not to have the work subjected to 'derogatory treatment'; the right not to be falsely named as the author of a piece of work; and the right not to have one's own private photographs published.

These rights may not be sold but they can be waived, and publishing organisations often produce contracts which try to insist upon this being done even in contexts where the rights don't actually exist. It is worth noting that the rule against 'derogatory treatment' of copyright works is another difficulty for satirists and parodists, although there has yet to be a relevant court case.

Infringement of copyright is a potentially rather serious matter. Compensation is usually limited to profits the copyright holder has lost as a result of the infringement or to the fee you would have been charged if you had acquired the material legitimately, but for flagrant and deliberate abuses the court is entitled to award additional damages. It is sometimes tempting to 'lift' a photograph or line-drawing that can't be found elsewhere, but you are likely to be found out and made to pay compensation. This is a matter for negotiation between the respective lawyers, which already makes it an expensive way of acquiring illustrative material even before an actual sum in compensation is agreed.

More serious, though, is the use of injunctions to prevent the use of copyright material which is intended to form the core of a news story or feature. You may be intending to build a major piece on the basis of leaked documents, but if this is discovered by the copyright holder, various legal manoeuvres become possible. These include an 'Anton Piller order', named after the first case in which it was used, which gives the copyright holder the right to search your premises for his or her material. In this particular case you have no right to be represented at the hearing leading to the order, and may know nothing about it until the copyright owner's solicitor arrives. This is a type of 'prior restraint' and must be resisted by legal means. There is a sort of 'public interest' defence against normal copyright injunctions, but no real defence against an Anton Piller order.

Copyright is an immensely complex area of the law and is likely to become more so. Material only falls outside copyright by reason of its advanced age: as of 1 January 1996 copyright expires seventy years after the end of the year in which its author died, but there are numerous exceptions. Editors should take it as a general principle that every piece of publishable material belongs to someone and has to be legitimately acquired or licensed before it can be republished or used in any way. The same, of course, applies to the material which we ourselves create. Between acquiring material at one end and attempting to control the use of material at the other, we are all in for a busy time.

Confidence

The law of confidence is a growing problem for magazine editors. People in a contractual relationship with anyone else, particularly their employers, are obliged to keep confidential anything they learn as part of that relationship. As journalists, however, we may desire to publish precisely that kind of material. The law of confidence exists to prevent one party in such a contractual relationship breaking that confidentiality, for instance to give documents to a journalist.

The injured party, usually the employer, can seek an 'interim injunction' from a High Court judge, prohibiting publication of the material prior to a full court hearing. This can be a year or more later, by which time the document's value as news material will have been destroyed. In the meantime, the injunction may well play havoc with the magazine's production, printing and distribution schedules.

The magazine can defend its wish to publish on public interest grounds. But there is a great danger that the judge will also order the return of the documents, which may have marks that reveal their source. Editors who fear such an order are advised to act swiftly to remove any such identifying marks. Destroying or mutilating such documents can be a contempt of court if the order to return the documents has already been made, but not before that, so it might be a wise precaution.

The classic situation is that a reporter receives a document and then telephones the company to which it relates in an attempt to ascertain its authenticity. This is obviously good practice, but is often followed by an injunction banning publication and demanding the document's return and the identification of the source.

Precisely this happened in 1990 when Bill Goodwin, a trainee reporter in his first weeks on the Miller-Freeman (then Morgan-Grampian) business-to-business magazine the *Engineer*, received a tip-off about a computer company. He duly rang the company to check and found himself faced with first an injunction prohibiting publication and then an action to make him reveal his source. He refused and was fined £5,000 for contempt of court. He subsequently sought a judicial review of the case in the European Court, backed by the NUJ and his employer.

In 1996 the court ruled that the British Government had violated his human rights. Goodwin's counsel suggested that as a result of the judgement the Government would have to give journalistic sources greater legal protection.

Until such time as this comes into effect, stories based on confidential documents which may have been illicitly obtained will continue to present a problem. Journalists may have to write them without informing those whom they are about. Their response must come in the next available issue. This is the only instance in which this is an acceptable practice.

Despite the Goodwin case, the courts already give some recognition to the journalistic principle of not revealing sources of stories. The 1981 Contempt of Court Act, for instance, says that courts should not insist on the revelation of sources except where it is 'necessary in the interests of justice or national security or for the prevention of disorder or crime'. Of these four cases, the 'interests of justice' have been given the widest interpretation, but questions of 'national security' still represent the fastest route by which an editor or reporter can be sent to prison.

Data protection

Any organisation holding 'personal' information about individuals on a computer or computer system is subject to the 1984 Data Protection Act. The definition of 'personal' information is extremely wide, covering just about any fact or opinion that is linked to an identifiable individual.

The Act gives individuals rights over that information: it has to be 'fairly and legally' collected, open to inspection and corrected if inaccurate. To hold such information on computer without registering with the Data Protection Registrar is a criminal offence.

Individual freelance journalists *may* be able to escape the Act's scrutiny under what is called the 'word processor exemption', which states that the Act does not apply to information entered onto a computer for the sole purpose of editing the text and printing out a document: it is then supposed to be removed. But the Data Protection Registrar has made it clear that the Act's provisions certainly apply to journalistic information processed and held within an editorial system or electronic library.

In effect, and with the enthusiastic support of the current Registrar's office, the Act is a form of privacy law, although it was not seen as such on introduction. Potentially it could be used by any member of the public who expects to be written about or who feels information has been collected in ways that are not 'fair'. In practice, it has not been, because it makes no provision either for gagging writs or serious damages.

But a forthcoming European Union directive threatens to tighten up the provisions of the law. In return there will be a 'journalistic purposes' exemption. The precise nature of this has yet to be determined, but it runs contrary to the British tradition that journalists have neither greater nor lesser rights than the rest of the population.

Editors must ensure their current data protection practices are sound and legal and should prepare themselves for serious threats to come.

Other laws

There are a great many other legal areas that editors may need to know about, depending on the areas in which they operate. They include:

- trespass, which affects the way reporters and photographers go about their business
- trades descriptions, which cover advertising features and theoretically require cover-lines to be an accurate account of the contents of a magazine
- the Rehabilitation of Offenders Act, which has implications for the way you report on people's criminal pasts
- competitions law, affecting the way you run any editorial or promotional contests, which are supposed to be games of skill
- indecency and obscenity: indecency offends those who see it, whereas obscenity corrupts their minds
- blasphemy, an offence against specifically Christian beliefs, for which there has been only one prosecution since 1922
- racial hatred, another rarely applied law
- court reporting, which requires expert knowledge of complex procedures
- election and parliamentary reporting, which have their own rules
- local government law, which provides investigators with rights as well as restrictions
- business law, particularly in respect to the way the demise of companies is reported
- official secrets: it is an offence to publish material you know to be covered by the Official Secrets Act, if you also have reason to believe it will damage the interests of the security service or the United Kingdom.

THE LAW AND ELECTRONIC PUBLISHING

It is worth noting that the impact of the new media, particularly the on-line technologies, has yet to be felt on the law. The proposed new Defamation Bill makes some attempt to consider the role of the on-line services in making material available for publication rather than actually publishing it. This has not, however, been resolved. In the United States, case law has determined that America On-Line is a publisher, because it maintains that it edits material to conform with family values, whereas CompuServe is more akin to a library or bookstall.

The position of the Internet itself has not yet been made clear. There is no doubt that there is plenty of indecent material in the Net, by any standard. Racial abuse, blasphemy and any number of other offences against established editorial ethics are also prevalent, including that overriding obligation not to publish anything that could reasonably be foreseen to cause injury or harm to the reader. Nor does one have to look very far to find hair-raising libels and contempts. The first Internet libel cases are beginning to clarify the extent to which Internet service providers can claim to be innocent distributors. Anyone producing any kind of Internet publication, however, has the full responsibilities of any publisher.

Traditionally law has been constrained within territorial boundaries. The stringency of British libel laws, for instance, and the generosity of our juries to plaintiffs, have made Britain a haven for foreign nationals wishing to sue both British publications and foreign publications circulating here in small numbers. At the same time, the US courts, to take another example, have refused to enforce libel judgements made in English courts against US citizens, because of the 'repugnance' of English libel law to the American constitution.

The Internet professes to know no territorial bounds. But English libel law makes it clear that the publication takes place wherever an offending remark is read, rather than produced. The older generation of Internet enthusiasts have expected the world's legal systems, including the right to the protection of intellectual property and the right to have one's reputation protected, to give way to the free-for-all quality of the new medium. This seems fairly unlikely. The Communications Decency Act, currently stalled in the US courts, would make the Internet as regulated as daytime television.

But legal solutions alone will not be able to turn cyberspace into a territory as regulated and controlled for publishing purposes as the United Kingdom. It would seem difficult to prevent British Internet users from having access to sites and pages, however libellous and obscene, that have been created in accordance with the laws of the territories in which they physically reside. On the other hand, much of the material that appears to come from abroad has actually been copied, for technical reasons, to server computers in the UK, where British laws can be applied.

Technological wizardry has created this situation, however, and technology, ultimately, is likely to solve it. Encryption software intended to prevent the copying of intellectual property in the on-line world is now being tested. This will control access to pages and sites and prevent the free duplication, breaking down and reuse of graphical and verbal elements within them. Our current Internet, in which information is wild and free, may then come to seem as remote, anarchic and exciting as the Wild West.

In the meantime, those publishing on the Net are advised to conform to

the legal and ethical norms of their home territories. This may seem somewhat tame, but it may well be the safest approach.

CD-ROM publication has much more in common with traditional book
and magazine publishing. Material on CD-ROM cannot easily be unlocked
and copied, unless it is designed to be so. True pirating, the copying of
complete discs with professional manufacturing equipment, is not relevant
here. But anyone publishing CD-ROMs must be aware that they are entering
a new world of copyright negotiation, dealing with rights with which they
are not familiar, particularly if they are including video clips containing
music and performance.

Another problem is more prosaic. CD-ROM discs have some potential for
disturbing the computers upon which they are played. Editors must ensure
that any such publication is accompanied by suitable denials of liability,
backed up as necessary by insurance against product liability action. This is
not usually a problem with printed magazines.

PUBLIC COMPLAINTS

Complaints against your magazine will not all take legal form, principally
because of the cost of taking legal action, which is prohibitive when legal aid is
not available. There are a variety of other remedies available to complainants,
but in the first instance the onus is on you to provide a fair and equitable way
of dealing with them. Larger organisations could consider having an 'ombuds-
man' of the type appointed by some of the national newspapers. Most of these
people report, however, that they do not have enough to do. Complaints are
generally resolved by the editor, which is exactly what should happen.

The 'right of reply'

It makes sense to publish corrections of factual errors without being asked.
Far from damaging your reputation for accuracy, this should, if carefully
handled, actually enhance it. Beyond that, you should consider your attitude
to the so-called 'right of reply'. There is, of course, no such right, although
various parliamentarians and industry bodies have tried to create one. It is,
however, a matter of natural justice that a person who has been substantially
attacked should be given reasonable space to respond. Depending upon the
seriousness with which you take your letters page, this could well be the ideal
forum for such a response. The idea of 'equal prominence and size' for such
responses is not a sensible one in practical terms. Wounded responses to
attacks do not necessarily make good reading.

There are more serious objections. What type of reply is to be offered, and
to whom? Is the right of reply to be limited to a point-by-point rebuttal of
factual inaccuracy, or is it to be a rhetorical response to the accusations, not
of the magazine itself in most cases, but of those quoted within its stories.

And if those thus contradicted are unhappy, are they too to be given the right of reply to a reply?

Good editors will do everything within their power to keep relationships happy in their area of the press. Sensible letters in response to criticism, amended as necessary to remove libellous remarks, should always be published. Genuine controversy should be allowed to rage for its natural life, then allowed to die: 'This correspondence is now closed.'

The Press Complaints Commission

For those complainants who are not satisfied with your own peacemaking efforts, but who have neither the finances nor appropriate grievances to take to law, there is the publishing industry's own supervisory body, the Press Complaints Commission.

The PCC was set up following the critical Calcutt Report on the press, with the express intention of heading off potential legislation by demonstrating how the press could regulate its own behaviour. Established and dominated by newspaper interests, it nonetheless has a supervisory role over the whole world of periodical publishing. Members of the public may complain against breaches of the PCC's code of practice. The code makes editors responsible for ensuring that the activities of staff and 'as far as possible' of freelances conform to its guidelines, which cover various aspects of reporting and editing practice.

An editor facing a PCC complaint will be contacted by the organisation and invited to reach a settlement with the complainant. If that fails, the PCC will carry out its investigation. You as editor must provide a written response to the complaint, which goes to the complainant, and then may come back for further comment, and so on. You and your staff may be interviewed by the PCC's staff, as may the complainant, but there is no hearing and no confrontation between the two parties. In the end the PCC makes a ruling. These adjudications are published quarterly, but even editors who are found to have breached the code are not required to publish them in their own publications.

It is certainly possible to be sceptical about all this. For a busy editor it is a time-consuming distraction. For an aggrieved member of the public it may represent a poor remedy for distress or embarrassment. It will be interesting to see how long the PCC lasts before the Government gives in to demands for action to curb the excesses of a small section of the press. That will not be a great day for the rest of us.

FURTHER READING

Robertson, Geoffrey and Nicol, Andrew (1992) *Media Law*, Harmondsworth, UK: Penguin (new edition due September 1997).
Welsh, Tom and Greenwood, Walter (1995) *McNae's Essential Law for Journalists*, London: Butterworths.

Chapter 11

The magazine business

THE PRINT MAGAZINE TODAY

It is not easy to define a magazine. A dictionary will tell you it is a periodical containing articles, stories, etc., by various people. But so is a newspaper. And advertising magazines, such as *Exchange and Mart* or *Loot*, contain no editorial matter.

Finding a definition that covers everything from *Hello!* to *Laboratory Equipment Digest* is one of the problems that bedevils attempts to quantify the magazine market, both within Britain and abroad. *Willings' Press Guide*, a trade directory, lists about 12,000 periodicals in Britain. *BRAD* (*British Rate and Data*) lists more than 7,000 magazines that take advertising. Neither lists the countless small-scale local and hobby publications, from parish magazines to football 'fanzines'. Outside Britain, *Willings* lists nearly 12,000 'important' magazines. *Ullrich's International Periodical Directory* lists 147,000 'serials', as the librarians call them, although few of them are of a type that would fly off the shelves at W.H. Smith.

One way of getting to grips with these unwieldy numbers is to break them down by type and by frequency. This information is the starting point for those trying to make them work.

Business-to-business magazines

'Business-to-business' magazines is the current jargon for what used to be called 'trade' magazines. They currently outnumber consumer magazines in Britain two to one. Despite this, their profile outside the industry is low, simply because few of them appear on bookstalls.

There is no such thing as a typical business-to-business magazine, any more than there is a typical business. At one end of the scale come glossy general publications aimed at a broad range of people working in business. These have more in common with consumer magazines than with much of the business press, and are usually edited by people with wide journalistic experience both within and outside the business market. At the other extreme come those aimed straight at the specifiers and purchasers of particular items of equipment, with titles and editorial material which are baffling to anyone else: here relevant industrial experience is essential.

In between come all the rest. Some magazines are 'industry' orientated, designed to appeal to a range of people within that sector, while others direct themselves at particular professions within an industry or towards particular technical interests. Weeklies will often have a broad appeal within, say the computing or advertising industry. Monthlies tend to define themselves more narrowly, to particular professional groups.

Circulation method is crucial to an editor's strategy. Broadly, the distribution of business magazines falls into three categories: paid-for (where sales may be on the bookstall or by subscription); institutional (where distribution is to members of professional societies or associations); and free (which is usually in the form known as 'controlled circulation', in which copies are distributed according to a carefully nurtured mailing list).

Where paid-for magazines and controlled-circulation titles are battling in the same market, they will have subtly different objectives. Controlled-circulation magazines survive by convincing their advertisers that they are read: their circulations don't change except by expanding or cutting back the mailing list. Paid-for magazines must have solid sales, both for the sake of circulation income and for keeping their advertising rates high. Consequently, the controlled-circulation title will often go all out for impact; the paid-for title can more safely concentrate on being 'the journal of record'.

Institutional magazines present a different set of problems. There the close relationship with the parent organisation may create difficulties for the editor's freedom of action. Publishing objectives need to be clear and in this case they may not be. Is the magazine a service for the reader, or a way of making money for the society, or some combination of both?

The business press's readers can be very demanding. Not only that, but the individual industrial communities served are small, and relationships with a title can be intense and long-lasting. Editors will be expected to play a role in that community.

One potential problem is that editors are often publishing stories about their advertisers; this can demand careful handling, especially on controlled circulation titles where editors are regularly reminded that advertising is providing the great bulk of the title's revenue. Things are more comfortable when advertisers have a more oblique relationship with the subject matter of the magazine: drug companies, for instance, support magazines for medical doctors but the magazines do not directly write about drugs.

In the strictly scientific field, quite different editorial objectives and procedures operate: papers submitted are subject to searching 'peer review' before being published, to ensure their acceptability, and without exception the journals are edited by those who share the vocabulary and expertise of their readers and writers. Nonetheless, while 'journalistic' values may be inappropriate, many aspects of the editorial process still apply.

Consumer magazines

When members of the general public think about magazines, they tend to have consumer titles in mind. At last count there were more than 2,000 titles published in Britain. Every year more are added, while a few die. Publishers and editors are increasingly adapting to a world in which magazines appear, thrive briefly to meet a particular need, then disappear.

This is true also in business magazines, where the buoyancy of a publishing market reflects entirely the buoyancy of that sector within a nation's economy. New technologies and industries require new magazines. Older sectors struggle to retain their viability, and their appeal to publishers reflects that. The most successful publishers are those who anticipate new markets, but they are also those who know when to leave dying ones.

In the consumer sector, most of this kind of 'churning' operates within what is called the 'specialist' area. These are titles aimed squarely at enthusiasts for a particular leisure pursuit or people with a particular demographic interest: magazines for sports enthusiasts, collectors, hobbyists, people with young children. Some of these pursuits are more short-lived than others.

Publishers who know this area, and who can operate at speed, aim to catch enthusiasms before they peak and leave them before they die. There are plenty of examples: skateboarding; mountain-biking; computer games tied to particular 'platforms'. Editors working in the specialist consumer market may temperamentally gravitate towards those areas which seem likely to be always with us (the major sports, home interests, babies) or they may work in the more volatile sectors. In the latter case they need to ensure that, while displaying suitable enthusiasm for the subject matter, they are developing the kind of editorial skills that adapt to abrupt changes of direction.

General consumer magazines find their readers from a broader sweep of the population and by a more subtle process. Some titles, obviously enough, have a clear target, if a broad one. The biggest sector in Britain during the late 1980s and early 1990s, in terms of number of titles, was the 'county' magazine. These appealed nominally to a 'family' readership, although in essence they were aspirational products aimed at those with expensive houses and an interest in self-realisation through property. The housing boom fostered them, and the collapse destroyed them. Currently there are a great number of magazines aimed at the elderly, a measure of the surprising volume of disposable income in that area.

But consumer magazines, even within the same market, differ widely in the way they address their readership. Readers of major women's magazines, while increasingly volatile in their reading habits, will usually identify themselves with a particular title or group of titles. These magazines do not announce their target audience in the same way that a magazine for a particular computer's owners would: they make their claim through tone of voice and the balance of content.

Nonetheless, they have to be focused to appeal to an identifiable group within the general market in which they operate. This is the key task of the general consumer magazine editor, and it is something that is much more difficult to grasp, though not necessarily to carry out, than producing a magazine for people whose overriding interests you think you know, as is the case in the controlled-circulation business press and specialist consumer press.

Of course, editors can succeed simply by producing a magazine in their own image. Despite the claims of scientific marketing, this still can work, and publishers recognise its success. A happy match between editor, subject matter and readers can be a head start. This may seem obvious. But it is surprising how many editors find themselves running titles with which they have no natural sympathy. Indeed, many consider it a mark of professionalism to be able to do so. But in general consumer magazines, especially, the connection between editor and readers needs to go deeper and operate more efficiently than anything that is possible through calculation. The case for instinct remains strong.

Newsletters

A newsletter is a basic print publication without advertising and, usually, without pictures or elaborate graphics. It operates on a purely editorial proposition: that the information contained within will be so valuable that it needs no overt presentation or adornment and that it is worth the whole cost of its production (and more, of course, in the case of commercially published examples). This is an extremely difficult act to sustain.

In the past, industry newsletters did well by simply presenting a 'digest' of information available from other sources. Readers paid for the convenience of having someone else do their necessary reading for them. A good industry magazine may well do at least as good a job and may be available free or on a normal magazine-style subscription. But the very 'unprofessional' look and feel of newsletter production provides an aura of authenticity, of 'unvarnished truth', that is attractive to some readers. As editors, we need to acknowledge that there are times when our cherished editorial skills – selecting, shaping, projecting – are not valued. If we are honest, we will also recognise that there are times when they are not appropriate.

At the same time, a newsletter cannot succeed if its content does not convince. A specialist industry newsletter will only justify its price, which is often out of kilter with its perceived value, if it offers insights that are only available to working practitioners in the field. They may need editorial assistance from trained and experienced journalists, but if they are succeeding they rarely need advice on the fundamentals of subject matter. Newsletter publishing is a natural for on-line treatment. Readers' indifference to production values means that they can see the advantages of publication via 'e-mail' or 'mailing list' when it brings them new and vital information quickly and at low cost.

Contract publishing

Sometimes a commercial or other organisation may wish to publish a magazine or periodical for its customers or members. The job of producing the title in question is then handed over to a contractor who employs an editor and staff for their technical skills.

In many cases the publication carries no outside advertising and is predominantly a vehicle for the organisation's chosen message. It may use a wide range of editorial techniques to make that material interesting to its readers. As always the central relationship is between the editor (or the editor's employer) and the customer, but in this case the customer is the organisation paying for the magazine. It is a moot point whether 'editorial' exists at all in that context: it may have the appearance of editorial matter and may attempt to achieve the same effects, but in essence the content will be what the contracting organisation wants it to be.

More sophisticated versions of contract publishing see an organisation simply using its position in a particular industry and exploiting it through publishing techniques. An aircraft company will not allow outside commercial publishers to distribute magazines on its planes. It may, however, choose to publish such a magazine itself, and sell that captive readership to other advertisers. Hence the success of *Hot Air*, the magazine published by the Virgin airline. The most recent development has been the production of 'customer' magazines by supermarket chains, some of which have a substantial cover price and compete directly with magazines produced by major publishers. Success is not guaranteed: some chains have withdrawn their magazines after disappointing sales.

In these cases an editor must then produce a magazine that meets normal editorial criteria: that is, that it is sufficiently interesting to the people who receive it to make them read it. If they read it, the advertisers will be satisfied, and the supermarket or airline and the contractor will make money. In this context, the editorial relationship, between editor and reader, is more genuine.

As the profitability of the operation increases, so should the editor's freedom of action, but in practice that depends a great deal on everything from the number and type of advertisers to the personal relationship between the editor, the publisher and the marketing executives in the parent company.

There are those who believe that editorial freedom is like virginity: you are either free to edit or you are not. While admirable in theory, this rarely accords with the experience of editors in any field.

House journals

House journals and in-house publications of all types are sometimes produced by contract publishers, working closely with the management of the organisation which requires such a magazine to be produced. They work better, however, when they are produced from within the organisation, but professional editorial expertise can be of tremendous benefit.

Communication is one of the great themes of contemporary management. At its worst, the house journal is simply the contemporary equivalent of the threatening message on the notice board or the blunt Tannoy announcement: another form of shouting. At its best, however, it acts as a genuine 'local paper' for a community defined by a common employer. This requires both a maturity on the part of management, which may not, initially, see why it should pay for a publication that it doesn't directly 'control', and a strong editorial vision. The challenges for any house journal editor are no different in kind from those facing any editor: you must make the journal read, and the best way of doing that is to make it loved.

Non-profit and amateur magazines

Magazines which are published with the intention of making a profit are only a part of the picture. Many more publications are produced because people have a message they want to impart, or information that they need to get across, or a particular view of the world that they want expressed, and they don't mind paying to do it. All of these will have some sort of editor, even though the person doing the job may not have that title or even have considered it an appropriate description of the position.

With no need to compromise with commercial aspects, advertisers or even readers, this might be considered very close to the pure editorial ideal. In fact, the opposite can be the case. Publishing which serves the person or organisation originating the material rather than the reader is a form of vanity publishing. Editorial skills can be employed to make the message sharper, to increase its impact, and so on, but these may well bring conflict with the message's originator. And without a reader in mind, those skills will be operated in a vacuum. Editing should always be a dialogue, not a monologue.

Amateur publishing can be an entirely admirable pursuit. In some cases it leads on to publishing for profit, though it doesn't have to to be justified. Hobby publishers, producing 'fanzines' and the like, are often much closer to their readers than professional editors and publishers can expect to be.

They can begin and finish publishing with little fuss, their costs minimal and their obligations uncertain.

With the rise of electronic publishing, too, the hobby publisher can achieve astonishing results, limited only by time, imagination and skill. Hobby publishing at its best is constantly finding new markets, new readers, new topics and new ways of writing about things. In practice much of what is produced is simply an inferior imitation of the worst of commercial publishing, but no professional editor should ignore or scorn the non-professional publishing world.

NEW DEVELOPMENTS IN PRINT

Print is not dying. Not yet, anyway. The electronic media, while capable of new miracles every day, have yet to find a means of delivery that will make them accessible and acceptable to most people in most situations. You cannot roll up a computer and stuff it in your coat pocket when there are no seats on the bus and you need both hands to hold on. You cannot read it in bed or on the train. You can't scribble in the margins of the articles or rip out the things you wish to keep.

Of course, these objections apply equally well to television, and when television first came into its own it cut a swathe through the newspaper and periodical industries. But today's magazines are, with a few honourable exceptions, the product of the post-television world. Even those which predate television have learned to adapt to its presence.

Magazines today are not, by and large, a leisure experience in themselves. The days when families would sit at the table and read *Picture Post* or *Life*, either as a group or one at a time, are gone. Magazines are an adjunct to work, in the case of the business press, or, in the case of the consumer press, they work with and around other forms of leisure. They are designed to fill in the gaps.

Today's magazine reader finds the time to read while travelling, while waiting to travel, while listening to music or watching the television with one eye, in bed or in the bath. Sensible editors have realised this. Those catering for more leisured sections of the population (the retired) or, those who spend a lot of time on trains and planes (the wealthy), can afford to make greater demands, as, paradoxically, can those dealing with the young, whose busy lives sometimes include intense involvement with their chosen reading.

But everyone else is working hard at their products' accessibility and manageability and for this the electronic media have no immediate answer. Nonetheless, the pace of change in electronics is such that no-one can afford to be complacent about what can and cannot be achieved. The phenomenon of 'convergence' between previously disparate industries – telecommunications, television, computing, cinema, publishing – means that companies in many areas are working on precisely this problem.

Before print gives up, however, it has a few tricks left. One hope is the production of 'personalised' magazines, designed for a much narrower target group. Across industry generally, the concept of mass production is under attack. The new enthusiasm for service drives this on, but great break-throughs in database technology – the manipulation of lists – have made it a practical possibility. Many magazine publishers have powerful databases already: indeed, in some cases publishing seems to be an adjunct to database collection rather than vice versa.

Linking databases to computer-controlled printing equipment allows adjustments to be made to the finished product. Different geographical areas get different advertising inserts. Different demographic groups might receive different add-on supplements or promotional material. Magazines can be assembled differently according to the information in the database. This goes well beyond dropping in those letters 'personally' addressed to the subscriber.

Approaches such as these still conform to a traditional model of publishing. Printed material is mass-produced at a central point. It is then distributed. But we may one day produce material which the reader has delivered electronically to the home, where it is simply printed out. The technology for this is with us today and getting cheaper.

The twist that makes this both an Opportunity and a Threat (to use the management jargon) to editors is the intelligence of the device that loads down the material. It could simply be a channel through which completed mass-produced identical magazines are poured into the world's homes. This would be most convenient for the publishers, freed from those paper and ink bills. There may be some takers for such a service.

On the other hand, people might prefer to be able to specify in advance the subject matter they are interested in and then have their home computer seek it out, download it, assemble it into a practicable and even beautiful form, and print it out. Already you can buy software that will let you do precisely this, albeit in fairly rudimentary form, using the resources of commercial on-line services.

In this version of the future, readers would still have a printed magazine to take around with them, to scribble notes on and fold up and file and all the rest. But the material stays in the machine: they can store it for reprinting at any time. They can search the whole volume of downloaded material, as it accumulates, at computer speed. They can produce their own annuals and yearbooks and clippings and send them to their friends (copyright permitting). And all without chopping down any unnecessary trees.

This proposition depends upon the consumer's taking an extremely close interest in the material on offer. The passivity of many readers – the extent to which they trust the professionals to assemble a product that they will enjoy – should not, perhaps, be ignored.

BEYOND PAPER AND INK

While foresters, printers and many publishers have a considerable investment in the continued success of paper, we as editors have no fundamental interest in any particular delivery method. We have an investment in written language, but that's a different question. Our essential service to readers is likely to survive and indeed prosper in a world in which delivery is by electronic means.

The question is whether the 'magazine' as an idea will exist in an electronic environment. The answer must be that it will. Computer technology is so diffuse that the only way to navigate through it is by means of a series of metaphors. This is recognised in the interfaces the majority of us use to communicate with the machines on our desks: the little pieces of paper, the folders, the filing cabinets, the waste bins. They use an 'office life' metaphor.

The magazine is a real product, but it will also work as a metaphor. It has a cover, it has a contents page, it has content. You can drop in where you like, and start where you like. You can flick through the things you don't like and concentrate on those you do. You can cut things out and file them away. You can read a piece once and dump it, or you can go back again and again.

When the electronic media can do all those things, in a way that anyone of any age and level of education can handle at a first attempt, without having to read a manual or go on a course, then it will be in a position to challenge paper and ink. This may happen sooner than we expect.

One of the reasons we as editors are so well placed in the current techno-logical turmoil is that we are already working in the digital domain, by and large. Before 1980, most British journalists had never seen a computer, except possibly on visits to the typesetters. By 1985, people were writing on personal computers and the first minicomputer-based editorial systems were being installed. Since then we have seen, in rapid succession, the near-universal spread of direct input of written material by journalists, on-screen layout, microcomputer-based editorial systems and networks and, most recently, electronic picture desks, cameras and even desktop colour 'repro'.

A whole professional generation has come through with no sense of type as a physical object at all: it is simply a pattern of electronic impulses. Increasingly, the same is true of pictures: the advent of the electronic picture desk and photo library, already current in some of our biggest newspapers and magazine houses, means it is perfectly possible to be an editor, picture editor, layout artist or sub-editor and never put your hands on anything resembling an actual photograph.

Words have been in the digital domain for ten years. Layout elements joined them about eight years ago. Pictures joined them more recently. Once these elements have entered the digital domain, things become possible which would never have been imaginable when the slim corpus of editorial philosophy was being thrashed out in the newspaper offices of Chicago and Fleet Street and the magazine factories of Watford and Covent Garden.

Having learned to find our way around the digital world in our own offices and studios, we currently translate all our efforts back into the defiantly analogue world of ink and paper. It works. But the world is moving towards electronic delivery. Our philosophy, our skills and our product – the magazine – may hold the key to making the digital domain as comfortable, as useful and as accessible to the average family or business as the local library or the local newsagent, without diminishing its potential.

Electronic publishing works on a rather different basis from that of print publishing. Despite the 'surfing' analogy that is often used to describe the process by which people move from page to page or 'site' to 'site', most people using electronic publishing are likely to make use of computer search tools. In other words, they will decide what they want to read about, and then the computer will present them with a selection of the electronic publications in which such subjects appear.

At this point, the traditional trust between reader and editor will come into its own again: the reader will discover that a particular electronic magazine has a reputation for accuracy, fun or provocation and will choose accordingly. This is one reason why publishers are interested in exploiting existing magazine titles in cyberspace rather than creating new ones.

What seems unlikely is that readers will wait patiently for the next issue of a favourite magazine to appear in the electronic news-stand, once a month, and then flick through it to find the kind of things they have been led to believe will be there. Certainly readers are less likely to read from beginning to end even than they are at the moment. But whereas now readers flick through, backwards and forwards, until something leaps out, the readers of the electronic magazines, it seems likely, will either select from a menu (an electronic contents page) or will simply search for the things they are interested in by typing key words and waiting for the machine to find them.

The concept of reader loyalty will be tested to the extreme, since readers using the Internet can consult anything that is openly published on the networks instantaneously. True, some publishers will start to demand registration and fees, but readers will still expect to pick and choose from the output of several, if not many, and those which are cheap and/or free will get the most page traffic.

The 'bookmarks' and 'hotlists' of current 'Web browser' programs are lists of electronic sites, culled from the entire range on the networks, to which individual readers expect to return. They are, in a sense, rudimentary magazines compiled by the reader from the output of many publishers. They can be changed at will, stored for later use and passed around to other friends and colleagues.

In an office setting, in the same way that someone might photocopy three or four articles on the same theme and circulate them to colleagues, it is a simple matter to do a search on a particular subject, turn the results into a list of bookmarks and distribute that around the office network for people to call up at their convenience. If there is time, the 'editor' of the bookmarks might prefer simply to collect the relevant material from the individual pages and form them into a single document, whether in plain text or some more complex and visually appealing form; theoretically, this activity will take account of copyright law.

In this new world, editors may well lose, for many of their customers, one of their most important tools, the ability to structure material on the pages for the purposes of directing their readers' attention: to say that this should be read first and that later. People who want that will still be able to get it, electronically as well as on paper. But many will not want it.

At this point, the question of what the readers will want goes deeper than mere subject matter: readers may well assemble their own packages of subject matter for themselves, making much editorial agonising obsolete. But other aspects of reader choice will loom larger. The way things are written, tone of voice, the way the material addresses the reader, the selection and ordering of material within the individual story will be central. And the material's veracity, reliability, completeness, currency will be more important than ever. Whatever publishing medium is employed, the trust between editor and reader will need to endure.

Every editor should be looking now at the new electronic media and asking where they will lead. There will be few magazine editors in the years to come who will not be expected to have some involvement with these new publishing methods. This is rather an alarming prospect for those who value ink and paper, and there is a tendency for editors to ignore it in the hope that it will go away.

It will not. All that will happen is that the new media will be run by people with different skills from our own, perhaps without a solid appreciation of editorial values. This would not be so bad if the 'traditional' paper-based media were able to carry on as normal. But American research has tended to suggest that the amount of time and money that families spend on media products stays as a constant proportion of their household incomes: any growth in electronic media will come at the expense of print publishing. We must provide electronic services for our own readers before we lose them to other people.

Sadly, much of the discussion over the future of the media has been conducted on a low level. Scepticism on the part of print journalists and publishers about some of the claims made for the electronic media has been condemned as self-interested propaganda for the status quo. There may be an element of that, but increasingly print publishers are attempting to place a foot in both camps, often at the cost of considerable discomfort.

The common denominator of the new media is that they are intended to be read via a personal computer or television, whether on the screen or by printing out. Beyond that, and certain ways of structuring their editorial material, they have little in common. Rather than a single approach, they represent a whole series of different technologies at different levels of maturity. At the one end of the scale there is the pleasingly basic world of e-mail. At the other there is 'multimedia', an extraordinary amalgam of words, pictures, graphics, moving pictures and sound.

For editors in commercial publishing, the technologies that are most likely to impinge on their professional lives are CD-ROM in its numerous variants (and successors) and the Internet. Later we can expect other media which attach themselves to the domestic television rather than the personal computer, for instance 'interactive TV', 'video-on-demand' and 'satellite digital'.

Today the principal 'off-line' electronic delivery device, meaning one which does not require connection to any information store outside the home, is the CD-ROM, a development of the audio compact disc, which is becoming familiar to all of us. 'On-line' publishing is a very different proposition, not so much technically as philosophically. It supplies the same kind of digitised material as CD-ROM, and may look similar at the point of delivery. But it requires the reader to establish electronic contact, by telephone line or some more advanced equivalent, with some central point for delivery to take place.

Interest in the 'on-line' world today revolves around the Internet and, to a lesser extent, the commercial 'on-line' services. At a much later stage 'video-on-demand' threatens (or promises) to replace (or greatly modify) television and the video rental industry as much as the print industry.

The likelihood is that none of these technologies will replace print. But they are becoming an important adjunct to print today, and their successors will affect our whole industry. We must incorporate them into our thinking now, while we have the opportunity.

CD-ROM

A CD-ROM is an acrylic disc that looks identical to music CDs but carries not music but anything up to 600Mb of digital material. Placed in a special drive in a personal computer, it opens up to reveal anything from a dictionary or a purely textual version of a year's newspapers to a series of moving-picture clips, sound files, still pictures, programs and pieces of text.

CD-ROM's versatility as a storage medium is one of its charms. Some publishers have rushed to embrace it because it seems to represent a touch of stablity in a bewildering new world. It is manufactured, like a print magazine, and has to be distributed and sold in shops. It is a consumer product. The problem is that its perceived value is low. When visually identical discs are given away with every other computer magazine, how are publishers to persuade people that it is worth paying hundreds of pounds for the

Encyclopaedia Britannica, or even £15.99 for a 'multimedia' magazine using the technology?

Three models seem to be emerging for the use of CD-ROM in magazine publishing. The first is simply to produce a stand-alone product on disc. Two appeared on the British market during 1995: *Unzip*, backed by IPC, and *Blender*, produced by Dennis Publishing. These are youth titles, priced to compete with audio CDs rather than with traditional magazines. *Unzip* boasted that it contained four to six hours of material: probably more than some print magazines in the same market. Only one issue has so far appeared.

The discs are capable of holding a great deal of material even if, as seems to be essential for maximum market penetration, a certain amount of space is used up in ensuring that the discs will play on both Windows and Macintosh machines. The costs of creating suitable material to use the space are vast, which is why those which have so far been released have relied heavily on material supplied under licence by commercial concerns: film and record companies, other CD-ROM producers, and so on. Much of the editorial input comes in the shape of written or spoken commentary on this promotional material.

A second approach is to produce a print magazine with a CD-ROM attached, but with the CD representing perhaps a dominant part of the package. Several of these are available, principally aimed at buyers of CD-ROMs themselves, but again they seem less than satisfactory as editorial packages. The bulk of the appealing visual material is made up of clips from other products, once again, although on occasion there have been attempts by the magazine's own editorial staff to produce their own short 'movies', more to demonstrate the potential of the medium than for any strong editorial purpose.

The third approach, however, is proving more successful. This is simply to use the CD-ROM as an adjunct to a printed product. This can be as simple as supplying a CD-ROM full of 'shareware' software with a computer magazine: given that almost all computer magazines now do this, the competition between them has now returned to the level of their magazines' editorial quality, which is where it belongs.

Other magazines outside the computer area are beginning to use the device for 'adding value', especially where this comes in the shape of material that is editorially unappealing in a print context. This might consist of valuable but visually dull technical information in the case of a professional journal, or an index to back issues.

But particular markets have found ways of exploiting the device that are both commercially effective and editorially appealing. *Creative Review*, a magazine for creative people in advertising, for instance, uses it to display current commercials, music and multimedia that it would otherwise simply be writing about: it becomes an illustrative medium. The magazine can also use the CD-ROM to give away such things as complete typefaces.

In this particular case, the CD-ROM disc is used as a subscription-building device. The discs are only available to subscibers, who far outnumber the magazine's bookstall buyers. And the costs are offset by carrying advertising material supplied by those who want to reach the magazine's readers, for instance picture libraries and computer suppliers. This too is in 'multimedia' form. Readers have to select it if they want to look at it, which means that it has to be much more directly informational than traditional advertising. This is one of the themes of 'new media' advertising.

The editorial role in the creation of such a product is surprisingly large. Journalists have to find the right visual and 'movie' material and negotiate the necessary licences to use it. They then have to view it all in its original videotape form and write appropriate reviews and commentary. Some kind of running order has to be established (although the reader doesn't have to follow the suggested sequence) and the material has to be selected and adjusted to fit the storage capacity of the disc. Original source material (on professional videotape or 'unlocked' CD-ROM) has to be acquired to be processed into the form used on the disc. An editorial designer may design the 'interface' or screen image within which the various elements will be seen, to ensure it is in keeping with the visual identity of the parent magazine.

But the actual production of the CD-ROM is beyond the capabilities of editorial staff, at least for the time being, owing to the rather demanding nature of the software used to assemble it. In a multimedia environment, captions and headings are animated, and the movies themselves are controlled by the clicking of icons on the screen. All this is assembled at a production house using a multimedia 'authoring' program. The currently preferred example is Director by Macromedia, but this is an area that is likely to become more competitive in the future.

In particular, Quark Inc., whose QuarkXPress program has become the effective standard for magazine design, is about to produce a multimedia authoring program for CD-ROM and the Internet intended to be used by editorial designers and others. Whereas Director is aimed at those used to working with time as a starting point, including those from a television graphics background, QuarkImmedia has a page as its controlling metaphor.

Whether this will encourage editors and their staff to take on such a fundamentally new role remains to be seen. Whether they do or not, producing a CD-ROM has many aspects which remain squarely within the editorial ambit, particularly if the disc is more than merely a selection of sample movie 'clips' supplied by others. Obviously, normal editorial criteria must apply to the selection of material and to any new writing and graphic material included. The editor must make absolutely sure of the legality of any agreements for using material, and must ensure that its copyright status is correctly explained on the disc and its packaging.

But beyond that there are several problems posed by the nature of the medium itself. In the first place the editor must ensure that the disc is tailored to suit the computers used by his readers. This is not as clear as it might be. Increasingly the plastic CD disc is being used to carry material for machines which are completely incompatible with each other. Any attempt to cater for more than one machine (IBM-compatible and Macintosh being the obvious pairing) must be very carefully planned and organised for maximum space efficiency. It is not economical to produce two entirely separate packages on the same disc. The two machines can both use certain types of movie file, for instance. All this needs to be carefully thought out by your technical advisers.

Unfortunately, even if the disc is produced for one platform only, its reliability in use is not guaranteed. You will need to take a view on the sophistication of the computers available to your readers and plan your disc accordingly. Moving video images only fit on the CD-ROM disc because they have been electronically compressed, usually in a system known as QuickTime. This requires a recent computer to work properly, and you may have to supply the program on the disc.

Even then, though, neither the quality nor the reliability of CD-ROM is particularly outstanding. People have been encouraged to think that CD-ROM is like an audio disc: you load it on to your machine, it plays, and then you take it off, with the machine untouched. CD-ROM is not always like that. Each time you load a CD-ROM on to a computer, it loads various files into the machine's hard disk. Good practice demands that they are removed when the CD-ROM is removed, but that is not always the case. These stray files may, by accident or malice, interfere with the proper running of your reader's machines. Over a period, especially if they use lots of different CD-ROM discs, the problems can become severe.

Because of the individual nature of every personal computer, you as an editor can expect a rate of failure from your CD-ROM discs of quite a different order of magnitude from the kind of manufacturing problems we sometimes experience with paper magazines. Wise editors accompany their discs with a legal disclaimer: permanent damage is rare, but you can't be quite sure. There should also be a telephone number of a hotline for those who have been unable to make the CD-ROM disc work, or worse. Readers of computer magazines have a high tolerance of software failure, but as the technology struggles into the wider market that pattern cannot be expected to be repeated, and you should be aware of the capacity of technological failure to damage the reputation of your magazine.

The CD-ROM is a fine device for storing large quantities of text, compu-ter programs and still pictures. And when it works, multimedia on CD-ROM can have a certain charm. But it is hard to avoid the feeling that its appeal is not that it is done well but simply that it is done at all. To produce any kind of moving picture from a single plastic disc is a technological miracle, on one level. Looked at dispassionately, however, its quality is not yet good enough to permit comfortable viewing for more than a few minutes. Even then there is the problem of producing material that will bear viewing more than once.

Consequently, observers of the nascent multimedia industry are increasingly seeing multimedia CD-ROM as an 'interim' technology. A much higher capacity disc, currently in development, will allow true, high-quality, full-screen, full-motion video. In the meantime CD-ROM allows everyone from content producers to consumers to 'practise'. This may be a sufficient reason for you to experiment with it, despite its potential for causing you problems. It will not be replacing the printed magazine, however.

ON-LINE PUBLISHING

The CD-ROM is what is called an 'off-line' device. The reader has the CD-ROM player in the office or at home and purchases CD-ROM discs to play on it. Increasingly, though, the attention of periodical publishers is turning to what is called 'on-line' technology, where material, written, visual and multimedia, is brought to your home down a telephone line.

Unlike the CD-ROM and the conventional magazine, this is not a 'closed' technology whereby a complete item is manufactured and sold and then supplemented by further editions in subsequent weeks or months. The essence of on-line publishing is that it is a continuous, 'rolling' process. You may for convenience produce 'editions' of your on-line magazine or newsletter, but it can be continuously updated and changed from the moment it is launched. In some cases, this can even be done automatically. A business magazine might, for instance, want to include a continuous read-out of current share prices of companies in its industrial sector. Setting up such a system is a contractual problem, involving finding the right supplier of information, rather than a technological one.

The other key aspect of 'on-line' publishing is that it is genuinely 'interactive'. CD-ROM technology is sometimes called 'interactive', in that you can make choices between various options in the software. But 'on-line' publishing permits genuine interaction between human beings. The image of the Internet as a pursuit for obsessives, passively sitting at their screens in isolation from one another, is something of an illusion. The Internet is actually built on conversation: communication between strangers, using the written word, pictures and graphics but also, increasingly, the spoken word, sound and moving pictures.

All this is most unlike our current model of publishing, in which we give people what we think they want, once a month or once a week, and learn their attitude to it only through our sales figures and the occasional 'letter to the editor'. Any publisher attempting to make the Internet conform to that model is missing the point. The rise of the World Wide Web, which permits the creation of pages and whole magazines with a strong family resemblance to their print counterparts, has led many publishers astray. They are spending large amounts of money and time producing products with little thought of their economic viability, which is the ultimate guarantor of their editorial integrity.

The Internet was not designed for commercial interests. It has its background in a scheme to ensure the survivability of American military communications by allowing individual chunks of information to find their own way round the country even if the direct route was broken. From that beginning, it grew into an academic network across much of the Western world. Today, particularly since the development of the World Wide Web, it is attracting vastly more commercial use, to the outrage of many of its founders.

The World Wide Web

The Web is a series of computer storage 'sites' that keep their material according to a commonly agreed format. When a reader's computer contacts one of these sites via the telephone line, and that reader is running one of the 'browser' programs, his or her computer displays a series of 'pages'. These pages contain text, photographs and graphics and, increasingly, sound and moving images.

The key to understanding the Web is that it is not so much about creating objects as about building the links between them. An initial 'home page' created by a publisher will link to further pages of its own, or to movie clips or sound files: clicking on a word or panel will bring that material to you. But it may also link to sites and material created by other people: the Internet has a 'sharing' ethos that has yet to come to terms with the matter of copyright. Further, the Web browser programs allow users to download copyright material, notably graphics, and disassemble them into their component computer code for their own purposes. This practice has yet to be tested in the courts.

The programming language used to make Web pages, HTML (Hyper Text Mark-up Language), was designed to allow readers to decide on typefaces and styles that suit their particular equipment and eyesight. Increasingly, though, the creators of Web sites are designing them in such a way that they dictate the way they are seen: in that respect it is coming to resemble mainstream publishing.

The question of income generation, however, remains a conundrum. Publishers are launching their own Web sites with great enthusiasm. They often ask readers to register, but they have not, as yet, generally started trying to charge people to look at them. People will pay to look at certain things on the commercial on-line services, usually stored versions of print publications.

But there are two problems about the Web and the Internet generally. One is a mere technological worry about secure credit-card transactions. The other is that the prevailing ethos is opposed to paying for information. Those attempting to charge readers for information will simply find they slip away to look at information that may be less good but that is definitely free.

There is, as yet, no obvious way of attracting readers to an Internet site in the first place, except by advertising in other media. There is no shop window. There are no shelves upon which publications aiming at similar interests can sit. Each Web site has precisely the same degree of impact in the Net as any other: you look at them all one page at a time.

Readers use a variety of searching tools to find particular page titles, strings of text and other indicators. And they 'surf', following tip-offs from other enthusiasts or by pursuing the links built into the various home pages. This seems unlikely to produce a steady flow of readers, especially for publishers trying to charge when there are plenty of people who do not. Those who do publish on the Internet must devote considerable effort to the task of ensuring that their site is known to all the main 'search engines'.

Anyone who uses the Internet at all, with the possible exception of private e-mail, is a publisher in one sense. All those contributions to 'news groups', the vast number of discussion areas on everything from operating systems to lingerie, are public, although they may not appear so to some of the participants. Submissions to 'mailing lists', another way in which information and disinformation is disseminated, are also public, although people who want to read mailing lists have to make the effort to subscribe to them (usually at no cost) and can be refused. Every enthusiast with a single Web page and every participant in a CompuServe or Microsoft Network discussion area is also a publisher.

Commercial publishers entering this area are latecomers at someone else's party and will find that the early arrivals have their own way of doing things. These often make more sense than simply trying to adapt existing practices and material to a new medium. Editors who are asked by print publishers to look at on-line work will tend to find themselves producing either a new stand-alone publication or some electronic analogue of an existing magazine. In both cases, the chosen mechanism is likely to be either the Web or, less frequently, some area in a commercial on-line service where access can be easily controlled and admission fees extracted.

Publishers entering this strange new world have convinced themselves that 'content is king', and that consumers will pay for it. This may eventually prove to be the case. Certainly people have been prepared to pay for some of the content that is available in the commercial on-line services, notably back issues of magazines and newspapers. But as the Internet becomes more accessible, while remaining largely free, that position looks increasingly untenable.

At this point advertising comes into the equation. It is perfectly possible to incorporate advertising into Web pages. Some existing Web publications do precisely that. It costs readers time and money to download the graphic that indicates the presence of an advertisement, and more time and money to go to the advertisement itself. It has been argued that a new type of 'informational' advertising will evolve, which people will read because it is inherently interesting. Of course, readers don't have to read advertising via a publisher's Web site: they can go to the advertiser's site. But if the advertising is cunningly worded, and placed among editorial matter they want to read, they may prefer to reach it that way. This is vaguely analogous to traditional publishing.

Some publishers of 'controlled circulation' journals, which go free to qualifying readers, see the Web as being similar to their own existing practices. They will not charge for entry to their pages. Nor will they, necessarily, sell advertising within those pages. But readers may be required to provide information about themselves as part of the registration process, and that may be passed to advertisers. But that's only the start. As readers move around a Web site, they leave a trail of information: which sections they read first, what days and times they log on, how often they visit the same section, what other sites they have visited. This information, too, could be legally sold to advertisers, provided it is presented as an account of groups of unidentified readers rather than individuals.

At best, the readers will receive a lot of junk mail. At worst, this would seem to have more serious implications. When a reader purchases a magazine, no-one knows it's been bought or which bits have been read. When readers access an Internet page, these pieces of information are collected as part of the process. If the readers have not registered, the 'server' computer which runs the site knows only which 'domain' they come from (a single domain may have hundreds of individual users). But if the readers have registered, then it knows their names and any other information that was extracted at the time of registration. All server systems can collect this information. Only the Data Protection Act controls its use.

Some high-profile Web publishers solemnly declare that they will not use information thus collected for the purposes of advertisers or anyone outside their own organisations. In practice there is little control over the use of such material, particularly in the United States, where there is no Data Protection Act to provide even a nominal brake on the exploitation of computerised personal records. The collection and sale of such information may prove irresistible to some involved in Internet publishing, but it represents a radical alteration in the contract between publisher and reader. There may be a niche here for print publishers: the magazines which do not invade your privacy.

At present, many publishers are 'dipping their toes' into the Internet. There are many boasts about commercial success but little actual evidence. Publishers will probably have to forget about trying to make it into another way of distributing their existing products and concentrate instead on its own special qualities. These have more to do with continuous accessibility to authors and readers and with creating genuine two-way communication.

In practice, commercial publishers have tended to concentrate on creating attractive pages and sites in the World Wide Web, with liberal use of pictures and graphic elements. The verbal content itself, rather than its wrapping, has tended to be less impressive. The existing hardware and software means for accessing the Web make reading continuous text rather arduous.

Publishers have compensated by making articles short and breaking them up in a way that makes them computer-efficient but difficult to follow. In one case, the British Condé Nast publishing company has set up a Web site that demands that would-be readers download a special program to help in the presentation of the on-line versions of such magazines as British *GQ*. This would seem likely to create more problems than it solves.

In general, those producing Web sites to complement their print magazines have tended not to risk damaging their existing products by offering anything too interesting. The sites have tended to offer snippets of articles from current and past issues, plus a plethora of thinly disguised 'house advertising' for the publisher itself. This is not universally the case: some extremely wealthy and adventurous publishers, notably Time Warner in the US, have placed many of their magazines on-line for reasons that have not quite become clear. Certainly there is no immediate economic justification for it.

Technically it is not difficult to produce a basic Web site. The page creation language, HTML, is simpler than most programming languages, at least to start with. Predictably, as commercial interests come to dominate the Web, pages are becoming more complex and the programs used to create them are slipping out of the reach of amateurs.

Commercial software suppliers will, however, be producing products designed to assist. Adobe PageMill is the favoured Web editor. And QuarkImmedia is intended to help QuarkXPress users feel at home with 'hypertext', the key organisational device of the Web, as well as with multimedia. This means that you should be able to entrust the task of creating Web pages to your sub-editors and designers rather than giving it, as you might at present, to computer enthusiasts with no understanding of editorial communication.

Hypertext

Hypertext is the important buzzword, although it has been around for a surprisingly long time in computer terms. It means organising material in such a way that it is stored as a series of individual documents or sections of a document, which you access by clicking your computer mouse on various on-screen graphical devices, including buttons, panels and text that has been highlighted in various ways. The most obvious example of hypertext in action is the 'help' file found with most computer programs. Click on a term in the index and you will immediately be taken to that section of the manual.

This system has had its uses in individual computers but found a new life with the invention of the World Wide Web. Rather than the highlighted and underlined text (or 'hot link') taking you to another document on the same computer, a link in a Web page is quite capable of taking you to a different document in a different computer on the other side of the world.

Hypertext is, on one level, extremely appealing. But it is a new way of reading. Careful construction to ensure a consistent and gripping narrative becomes rather pointless when readers can and will read a story's many aspects in whatever order they choose. This may have profound implications for coming generations' ability to think. Certainly it has implications for those creating on-line magazines. These tend to use short blocks of text chained together by hypertext links. You must do what you can to see that they are read in the correct order but at the same time you must accept that they probably won't be.

The unpleasantness of reading on the computer screen, the interests of the people who designed the Web, and the searching abilities of computers mean that on-line publications tend to be used in quite a different way from normal print publications. Those accessing Web sites don't read them, at least not in the traditional sequential way. They may flit around looking at what is on offer, particularly anything visually appealing. They may download areas of text to their own computers with the sincere intention of reading it later. Or they may use search tools to find the snippets of 'information' that they feel they want without worrying too precisely about its context.

It is one of the contradictions of the Web (and the Net generally) that while publications designed for it tend to be visually startling and verbally minimal it is also full of vast areas of simple text. These are among the most useful things on it for its original users. If you want, for instance, to find out about the ways in which Shakespeare uses a word, you have only to go to one of the full-text sites and do a search.

Commercial publishers, however, are moving in the other direction. They want to catch the attention of the casual 'surfer', and if that means tiny snippets of text accompanied by flashing headlines, moving captions, video clips and sound in real time, so be it. Like CD-ROM, on-line publication is seen as a 'multimedia' exercise, despite the vast costs involved in the creation or licensing of such material and the great uncertainty of ever recovering any of that money from readers or advertisers. Recently one British publisher was boasting about the success of its site, which had attracted 100,000 'hits' in its first month and 150,000 in its second. On average, it was said, each reader had spent between three and five minutes looking at the site.

This is not, however, the level of attention that we are used to from our readers. It is difficult to imagine our advertising staffs convincing anyone to take space in a print magazine whose readers looked at it for less than five minutes a month. We may well find it sensible to stand aloof from multi-media madness at least until its economic basis is established.

In the longer term, the so-called 'video on demand' technology being pioneered experimentally around the world may represent a more practical basis for multimedia publishing. Here the vast computer files required to store full-length feature films are kept at giant central servers and 'down-loaded' to individual homes at high speed over fibre-optic cables. Multi-media magazines, downloaded in the same way, then become a much more realistic technical possibility: they will make their material available almost instantaneously, rather than painfully slowly. Their economic viability is no more certain, however, than that of their Internet counterparts. And even if that problem were to be solved, most editors would have a limited interest in a new form of communication that threatens to downgrade still further the act of reading.

This is not, however, to say that on-line publication itself is a mistake. On the contrary, editors who make the effort to deal with it on its own terms are likely to find it extremely useful, challenging and even profitable.

Mailing lists and e-mail magazines

The fundamental strengths of on-line publication are its qualities as an editorial medium. The first is the ease and speed with which it can be up-dated. The second is its 'two-way' nature, which makes it both a device for 'broadcasting' to thousands of individuals and a way for those individuals to answer back, either publicly or privately.

Viewed in this light, both 'stand-alone' and 'complementary' on-line pub-lications make sense, but they do not have to be flashy Web sites with vast costs and unquantifiable readerships. A stand-alone magazine for a particu-lar market might well work better on a mailing-list basis. Producing a mailing-list magazine is not much more difficult than writing any piece of text in a word processor. It is then distributed at fixed or indefinite intervals, to those who have asked for it. These are people who are prepared to supply their e-mail addresses and then take the trouble to open the mail when it arrives and load it on to their hard disks.

It is a safe assumption that they are interested in the content: few people will continue to receive mail-out material they don't read. This makes them genuine readers, which in turn makes them people whom advertisers can be invited to reach, although only in a way that is sufficiently unobtrusive and useful in itself. The key thing is that the content, not its packaging, will have to be vital to those readers' lives. It will have to be news and it will have to be accurate. Only an editor can provide these things.

It is worth noting that some of the stand-alone Internet magazines which claim to be making money operate on precisely this basis. Consider the case of the British publication *PowerPC News*, which is produced on both a mailing-list and a Web basis. Its success is built on its mailing-list version. It claims that each fortnightly issue is read by 50,000 people. Subscribers are not sent the whole issue, merely the contents page. They then retrieve the items they are interested in. The mailing-list version, which consists solely of ASCII text, goes out three days before the World Wide Web version.

Subscribers are also promised 'PowerFlashes', brief news updates between issues of the magazine. The magazine also offers advertising, which it calls 'commercial information', but subscribers have to ask for it. The magazine's mailing list is obviously a powerful commercial tool, but APT Group plc, the magazine's parent company, promises not to sell or release the list to other companies.

There are, of course, people making money by going to the opposite extreme, producing state-of-the-art Web pages with every multimedia device available. But a look at their advertising indicates that a great deal of it comes from those with a vested interest in an ever more complex technological future for the Web and indeed the world: manufacturers of 'server' computers and software and suppliers of telecommunications links.

These people are not necessarily too concerned that their advertising expenditure immediately pays for itself. The same goes for the 'prestige' advertisers whose presence in some of the Web sites seems more intended to demonstrate their commitment to the future than to gain them any extra business. Such publishing ventures don't necessarily offer much guidance to people operating in a less technologically based market niche.

On-line magazines to complement print publication are also a viable idea, especially if publishers are prepared to let them run as a cost, for reasons of technological chic, rather than insisting on their breaking even. It is appealing, perhaps, to publish the full text of a necessarily truncated interview on the Web or to reproduce more photographs from the cover shoot. But this is a kind of vanity publishing without any real future. Sooner or later the bills will have to be paid, even if publishers manage to bully freelances into handing over their work for nothing.

It is more sensible to use the on-line publication to do things which print publishing, however lavish, cannot do. This might mean using the Web site or mailing list to provide news outside the normal time strictures of the print magazine, allowing a monthly to become effectively a daily for news purposes. The idea is that this will become an extra service for readers, binding them closer to the magazine. At the same time the Web site can become a discussion area for subjects provoked by the magazine and its writers. This is slightly more tricky to accomplish, technologically and editorially, but there is no reason why articles in the Web site should not be accompanied by 'threads' of argument, as seen in Internet 'news groups' and commercial on-line service 'forums'.

This has implications for commissioning. Writers would be required to answer reasonable comments on and criticisms of their articles. At the same time, Web magazine editors, guided by the law, would have to make decisions about the way those comments, criticisms and other contributions would be edited, if at all. But the effect would be to encourage readers to return to the site regularly, to declare their interests, and to feel as if they were participants in a dialogue rather than passive consumers. Once again, that would make them an attractive, quantifiable group to offer to advertisers, but again, only to those capable of producing advertising that was appealing and informative in its own right.

As stated earlier, any Web site generates prodigious quantities of information on the people who access it, especially if they have been made to register. But finding a way of using that information that is both commercially sound and morally justifiable is more complex. It would seem a minimum requirement that people are explicitly asked about the way in which information about them, from demographics to e-mail addresses, is sold to advertisers.

This is a different conception of editing from that understood by the print editors of the past, who were content to put together a magazine, put it on sale, and then move on to the next one. Now there will be a requirement for continued dialogue. But this may well be an enriching experience for all of us, readers and journalists alike. And it would seem essential if the Net, and particularly the World Wide Web, is to develop as a publishing medium beyond what it seems to be at the moment: a series of billboards, each pleading 'Read our print magazine.'

In the end, we will probably not have the choice about whether we get involved with the Internet or not. Business publishers first, and consumer publishers later, are in danger of finding their readers drifting off in the direction of new electronic publications, which can be set up with comparatively small costs. The danger is not that they will convincingly imitate print publications, but that they can provide the same kind of things that readers need from print magazines in a faster, more involving way.

Video-on-demand

If the Web looks commercially immature, 'video-on-demand' is even more remote. This is the technology, currently on small-scale test in several parts of the world, that allows householders to 'download' the video or television programmes they want to see from massive central computers. At the same time, provision is made for all manner of 'interactive' involvement with those same computers. Sports viewers will, for instance, be able to select their own camera angles, or so it is said.

Several magazine publishers are contributing to the experiments, by providing magazine material that can be accessed for viewing on the television screen by the same process. The actual material will be similar, probably, to that being pioneered on the CD-ROM interactive magazines, although quality and reliability will benefit from the powerful computers likely to be used. Whether magazine pages viewed on a television screen will in any sense be able to compete with television itself remains to be seen: in any case, the economics of the system in its television and video aspects are anything but clear. The central computer storage and power required goes beyond anything ever assembled for civilian purposes.

EDITING IN THE INFORMATION AGE

We are, by general consent, entering the 'age of information', in which all the world's knowledge will be available at the speed of light. The disadvantages of this, of course, are blindingly obvious. The more raw 'information' that becomes available, the less likely we are to be able to find our way through it. The Internet is a classic example of this. While there may be massive amounts of 'information' available, few people know what it is, where it is or to what degree it can be relied upon. Anyone who has explored the world of the 'Usenet news groups', for instance, knows that to call much of the material found there 'information' is a wilful distortion. The Internet only works at all because researchers have devised powerful software tools, or 'engines', to search it: there is, however, no index or catalogue.

Internet afficionados profess to support a vision of the future in which individuals will freely seek the information of their choice. This will free them from the 'tyranny' of a 'mass media' that makes decisions for them. Readers in certain fields may indeed wish to seek out material on their own special interests, taking its accuracy and probity on trust. But most of the raw information held in the Internet's vast array of computers will never have the appeal of a magazine directed towards a particular reader. There is a sense in which skilled editors come to know their readers' needs better than the readers themselves.

The skills of the editor will be more necessary than ever as the information explosion continues. Readers who are pressed for time will, if we have earned their respect for our professionalism, be prepared to delegate to us the task of seeking out, shaping, verifying and producing the information, elucidation, analysis and entertainment they need. We will continue to form a bridge between the interests of our readers and the world of raw information.

An editor and the editorial team bring words, graphics and pictures together to produce something that is more than the sum of its parts. The magazine that they create is an entity in its own right. At its best it is capable of bringing enlightenment and entertainment to thousands, even millions, of people. In all the talk about new sources of 'information', it is sometimes forgotten that magazines, as presently constituted, have one other purpose. When lots of people read the same magazine, they have something to talk about. The new technologies have yet to find an equivalent to that.

FURTHER READING

Lambert, Steve and Ropiequet, Suzanne (eds) (1986) *CD-ROM: The New Papyrus*, Redmond, Washington: Microsoft Press.
Wiggins, Richard W. (1994) *The Internet for Everyone*, Maidenhead, UK: McGraw-Hill.

National Union of Journalists Code of Conduct

1   A journalist has a duty to maintain the highest professional and ethical standards.

2   A journalist shall at all times defend the principle of the freedom of the press and other media in relation to the collection of information and the expression of comment and criticism. He/she shall strive to eliminate distortion, news suppression and censorship.

3   A journalist shall strive to ensure that the information he/she disseminates is fair and accurate, avoid the expression of comment and conjecture as established fact and falsification by distortion, selection or misrepresentation.

4   A journalist shall rectify promptly any harmful inaccuracies, ensure that correction and apologies receive due prominence and afford the right of reply to persons criticised when the issue is of sufficient importance.

5   A journalist shall obtain information, photographs and illustrations only by straightforward means. The use of other means can be justified only by over-riding considerations of the public interest. The journalist is entitled to exercise a personal conscientious objection to the use of such means.

6   Subject to the justification by over-riding considerations of the public interest, a journalist shall do nothing which entails intrusion into private grief and distress.

7   A journalist shall protect confidential sources of information.

8   A journalist shall not accept bribes nor shall he/she allow other inducements to influence the performance of his/her professional duties.

9   A journalist shall not lend himself/herself to the distortion or suppression of the truth because of the advertising or other considerations.

10 A journalist shall only mention a person's race, colour, creed, illegitimacy, disability, marital status (or lack of it), gender or sexual orientation if this information is strictly relevant. A journalist shall neither originate nor process material which encourages discrimination on any of the above-mentioned grounds.

11   A journalist shall not take private advantage of information gained in the course of his/her duties, before the information is public knowledge.

12   A journalist shall not by way of statement, voice or appearance endorse by advertisement any commercial product or service save for the promotion of his/her own work or of the medium by which he/she is employed.

Press Complaints Commission Code of Practice

The Press Complaints Commission is charged with enforcing the following Code of Practice which was framed by the newspaper and periodical industry and ratified by the Press Complaints Commission.

All members of the press have a duty to maintain the highest professional and ethical standards. In doing so, they should have regard to the provisions of this Code of Practice and to safeguarding the public's right to know.

Editors are responsible for the actions of journalists employed by their publications. They should also satisfy themselves as far as possible that material accepted from non-staff members was obtained in accordance with this Code.

While recognising that this involves a substantial element of self-restraint by editors and journalists, it is designed to be acceptable in the context of a system of self-regulation. The Code applies in the spirit as well as in the letter.

It is the responsibility of editors to co-operate as swiftly as possible in PCC enquiries.

Any publication which is criticised by the PCC under one of the following clauses is duty bound to print the adjudication which follows in full and with due prominence.

1. **Accuracy**
(i) Newspapers and periodicals should take care not to publish inaccurate, misleading or distorted material.
(ii) Whenever it is recognised that a significant inaccuracy, misleading statement or distorted report has been published, it should be corrected promptly and with due prominence.
(iii) An apology should be published whenever appropriate.

(iv) A newspaper or periodical should always report fairly and accurately the outcome of an action for defamation to which it has been a party.

2. **Opportunity to reply**
A fair opportunity for reply to inaccuracies should be given to individuals or organisations when reasonably called for.

3. **Comment, conjecture and fact**
Newspapers, while free to be

partisan, should distinguish clearly between comment, conjecture and fact.

4. **Privacy**

Intrusions and enquiries into an individual's private life without his or her consent including the use of long-lens photography to take pictures of people on private property without their consent are not generally acceptable and publication can only be justified when in the public interest.

Note – Private property is defined as (i) any private residence, together with its garden and outbuildings, but excluding any adjacent fields or parkland and the surrounding parts of the property within the unaided view of passers-by, (ii) hotel bedrooms (but not other areas in a hotel) and (iii) those parts of a hospital or nursing home where patients are treated or accommodated.

5. **Listening Devices**

Unless justified by public interest, journalists should not obtain or publish material obtained by using clandestine listening devices or by intercepting private telephone conversations.

6. **Hospitals**

(i) Journalists or photographers making enquiries at hospitals or similar institutions should identify themselves to a responsible executive and obtain permission before entering non-public areas.

(ii) The restrictions on intruding into privacy are particularly relevant to enquiries about individuals in hospitals or similar institutions.

7. **Misrepresentation**

(i) Journalists should not generally obtain or seek to obtain information or pictures through misrepresentation or subterfuge.

(ii) Unless in the public interest, documents or photographs should be removed only with the express consent of the owner.

(iii) Subterfuge can be justified only in the public interest and only when material cannot be obtained by any other means.

8. **Harassment**

(i) Journalists should neither obtain nor seek to obtain information or pictures through intimidation or harassment.

(ii) Unless their enquiries are in the public interest, journalists should not photograph individuals on private property (as defined in the note to Clause 4) without their consent; should not persist in telephoning or questioning individuals after having been asked to desist; should not remain on their property after having been asked to leave and should not follow them.

(iii) It is the responsibility of editors to ensure that these requirements are carried out.

9. **Payment for articles**

Payment or offers of payment for stories, pictures or information, should not be made directly or through agents to witnesses in current criminal proceedings or to people engaged in crime or to their associates – which includes family, friends, neighbours and colleagues – except where the material concerned ought to be published in the public interest and the payment is necessary for this to be done.

10. **Intrusion into grief or shock**
In cases involving personal grief or shock, enquiries should be carried out and approaches made with sympathy and discretion.

11. **Innocent relatives and friends**
Unless it is contrary to the public's right to know, the press should generally avoid identifying relatives or friends of persons convicted or accused of crime.

12. **Interviewing or photographing children**
(i) Journalists should not normally interview or photograph children under the age of 16 on subjects involving the personal welfare of the child, in the absence of or without the consent of a parent or other adult who is responsible for the children.
(ii) Children should not be approached or photographed while at school without the permission of the school authorities.

13. **Children in sex cases**
(1) The press should not, even where the law does not prohibit

it, identify children under the age of 16 who are involved in cases concerning sexual offences, whether as victims, or as witnesses or defendants.
(2) In any press report of a case involving a sexual offence against a child –
(i) The adult should be identified.
(ii) The term 'incest' where applicable should not be used.
(iii) The offence should be described as 'serious offences against young children' or similar appropriate wording.
(iv) The child should not be identified.
(v) Care should be taken that nothing in the report implies the relationship between the accused and the child.

14. **Victims of crime**
The press should not identify victims of sexual assault or publish material likely to contribute to such identification unless, by law, they are free to do so.

15. **Discrimination**
(i) The press should avoid prejudicial or pejorative reference to a person's race, colour, religion, sex or sexual orientation or to any physical or mental illness or handicap.
(ii) It should avoid publishing details of a person's race, colour, religion, sex or sexual orientation, unless these are directly relevant to the story.

16. **Financial journalism**
(i) Even where the law does not prohibit it, journalists should

not use for their own profit, financial information they receive in advance of its general publication, nor should they pass such information to others.

(ii) They should not write about shares or securities in whose performance they know that they or their close families have a significant financial interest, without disclosing the interest to the editor or financial editor.

(iii) They should not buy or sell, either directly or through nominees or agents, shares or securities about which they have written recently or about which they intend to write in the near future.

17. Confidential sources

Journalists have a moral obligation to protect confidential sources of information.

18. The public interest

Clauses 4, 5, 7, 8 and 9 create exceptions which may be covered by invoking the public interest. For the purposes of this code that is most easily defined as:

(i) Detecting or exposing crime or a serious misdemeanour.

(ii) Protecting public health and safety.

(iii) Preventing the public from being misled by some statement or action of an individual or organisation.

In any case raising issues beyond these three definitions the Press Complaints Commission will require a full explanation by the editor of the publication involved, seeking to demonstrate how the public interest was served.

Glossary

Terms which have their own entry are printed in SMALL CAPITALS.

ABC   Audit Bureau of Circulation, the organisation which provides independent confirmation of a magazine's sales.

ad/ed ratio   the ratio of advertising to EDITORIAL in an issue of a magazine.

ad-get feature   an EDITORIAL FEATURE commissioned to encourage advertisers to take space alongside.

advertisement feature   the approved term for ADVERTORIAL.

advertorial   an advertisement written and designed to resemble EDITORIAL material.

all rights   the right to republish a piece as often as required in any medium and in any territory.

angle   the particular point of interest within a news story, either to the writer or to the readers.

appraisal   a formal meeting in which an employee's performance is assessed and discussed.

artwork   (a) the visual elements on a page, excluding text; (b) the physical components of a page, including HALF-TONES and typesetting, prior to being turned into FILM.

ascender   the upper strokes of LOWER CASE letters such as b, d, h, etc.

ASCII   American Standard Code for Information Interchange. Pronounced 'Askey' and used to mean plain text in digital form without formatting.

assign   to sell COPYRIGHT material outright.

attribution   connecting a quote or information to its source. A note 'attrib?' in copy is a request that a quote be linked to a speaker.

back issue   an earlier copy of a magazine.

background   the context in a story or FEATURE.

back up   to back up is to make another copy of computer documents in case the originals are lost or damaged. 'Back-ups' are the copies themselves.

bad break   where automatic HYPHENATION produces ugly or misleading results, e.g. 'therapist' becoming 'the-rapist'.

band   a wide plastic wrapper or band allowing an extra supplement to be attached ('bound on') to an issue.

bar code   a machine-readable serial number placed on a magazine COVER.

baseline   a notional line along the bottom of a row of type. DESCENDERS fall below the baseline.

bind   to fasten pages together to make a magazine.

blob par   a paragraph started with a black dot or BULLET. Used to emphasise extra points of interest.

bleed   to print beyond the boundary of the page after trimming. Pictures are said to 'bleed' or be used 'full-bleed'.

body copy or **body text**   the main text of a piece.

body type   the typeface in which the BODY COPY is set.

bold   heavy type.

bookmarks   a list of favourite WORLD WIDE WEB pages stored in a BROWSER PROGRAM.

boost   a BOX telling readers what to expect in the next issue.

box   an area of type marked out by rules.

brainstorming session   a meeting intended to produce ideas.

brief   (a) instructions to a writer, photographer or designer; (b) a short news item.

bromide   photographic paper produced by a typesetting or imagesetting machine.

browser or **Web browser**   computer program used for reading WORLD WIDE WEB pages.

budget   a statement of expenditure and income allocated to a department for a given period.

budget forecast   a forecast of expenditure and income for a department in a given period.

bug   an electronic pick-up used for recording telephone calls.

bullet   a black dot used for emphasis or in lists.

bureau   an outside facility used to produce BROMIDES or FILMS from electronically assembled pages.

business-to-business   the current term for trade magazine publishing.

bust   to be too long for the space allocated. Used of HEADLINES, STANDFIRSTS and CAPTIONS.

by-line   the author's name when used on the page.

caps   capital letters.

caption   a piece of text associated with a photograph, usually to indicate what it shows.

caret mark   a mark used in COPY MARK-UP and PROOF-reading to indicate that something must be inserted.

cash-flow   a chart indicating income received and cash spent.

cast off   to calculate the space occupied by a piece of text.

casual   a freelance journalist employed on a temporary basis.

catch-line   a short identifying name given to a story as it passes through the production process.

CD-ROM   compact disc used to display words, images, sound and moving pictures on a computer screen.

centred   a form of typesetting in which space is distributed at both ends of each line.

centre-spread   the middle two pages of a SADDLE-STITCHED magazine.

chapel   a branch of the National Union of Journalists based on a single magazine house.

classifieds   small advertisements grouped together.

clip art   pictures not subject to COPYRIGHT restrictions, usually obtained in digitised form.

close   to send an issue to the printers: 'The issue is closed.'

collate   to assemble the pages of a magazine into the right order.

colour   (a) printed using the FOUR-COLOUR PROCESS; (b) descriptive writing.

colour house   where photographs are SCANNED and united with electronically generated pages and type to produce the FILM required to make printing PLATES.

colour separations   the four separate pieces of FILM created when full-colour material is put through the FOUR-COLOUR PROCESS.

column   (a) regular article; (b) a section of type set across a fixed MEASURE and running vertically down the page.

column rule   a vertical line separating COLUMNS.

commission   a contract asking a FREELANCE writer or photographer to produce a piece of work.

connect-time basis   the pricing of electronic media according to the time a reader spends connected to them.

contact sheet   a sheet of photographs made by pressing the negatives directly against the photographic paper. The prints are the same size as the original negatives.

contacts   journalistic sources.

contacts book   a book of sources' telephone numbers.

contempt of court   illegal interference with the course of justice.

contract publishing   a form of publishing in which professional publishers take a fee to produce magazines on behalf of a commercial organisation.

controlled circulation   a form of free distribution in which copies are sent to readers on a mailing list.

copy   all written material.

copy-edit   to sub-edit written material for consistency, accuracy, grammar, spelling and house style.

copy-fit   to ensure edited material fits the allocated space.

copy-flow   the movement of journalistic material during the editing and production process.

copyright   the right to reproduce a piece of creative work, usually held by its creator.

cover   the first page of a magazine.

cover-line   words used on the COVER to entice readers.

cover-mount   a free gift attached to the COVER.

credits   details of photographers, authors, stylists, providers of clothes, etc., to go alongside photographs.

Cromalin   a proprietary PROOFING system for proofing FOUR-COLOUR material from FILM rather than printing PLATES.

crop   to alter the size and shape of a photograph.

crosshead   a small HEADLINE in the body of the text

cross-reference   a reminder to readers that further information on a subject is to be found elsewhere in an issue.

customer magazines   magazines published by large organisations to give or sell to their customers.

cut   to delete a section of text.

cut-out   a photograph in which the subject has been 'cut out' and the background discarded.

cuttings   previously published articles, either a writer's own or other people's.

cuttings job   disparaging name for a FEATURE or PROFILE written without extensive new research or interviewing.

database   information organised and stored in a computer.

date-tied   only relevant if published at a specific time.

deadline   the time by which a journalistic task is expected to be completed

deck   technically, one complete HEADLINE, no matter how many lines it occupies. A subheading beneath it in a different font or size would be a second deck. Often used, erroneously, to mean a single line of headline type: a two-line headline is thus called a two-deck headline.

defendant   a person or organisation subject to a legal action.

delete to cut a character, word or line. Indicated by the symbol: δ

departments a useful American term for the elements common to every issue of a magazine: EDITOR'S LETTER, news, products, etc.

descender the tail of certain LOWER CASE letters (p, q, y etc.), descending below the BASELINE.

desk a department of a magazine, e.g. features desk, news desk, subs-editor's desk.

desktop publishing (DTP) computer hardware and software to permit the typesetting and make-up of pages, complete with photographs, on screen.

diary the routine events covered by a magazine's reporters. Hence 'off-diary' stories are those that are out of the ordinary.

diary column (a) a gossip column; (b) an account of someone's week.

dingbat a typographic symbol available from the keyboard.

disc or **disk** a computer storage medium, available in fixed 'hard disc' or portable 'floppy disc' form.

display ad an advertisement that uses more than simple type and appears outside the CLASSIFIED section.

display type large type used for HEADINGS, etc.

domain a group of computers through which individuals access the INTERNET.

double-page spread (DPS) two pages opposite one another, whether used for a single EDITORIAL item or a single advertisement.

drop cap a large letter at the beginning of a paragraph, usually at least as deep as two lines of BODY TYPE.

dropout a fault in camerawork or PLATE-making meaning light areas of a picture lose all detail.

duotone a black and white picture reproduced by printing in black and one other colour.

dummy (a) a mock-up of a new publication; (b) a complete set of PROOFS in correct order; (c) a reduced-size, plain paper mock-up of the current issue showing the location of display advertising etc.

edit (a) to cut, check, rewrite and otherwise improve an article; (b) to be an editor, either of a whole magazine or of a section.

editorial (a) the journalistic content of a magazine; (b) the EDITOR'S LETTER.

editor's letter introductory remarks by the editor

electronic mail (e-mail) a means of communicating by typing messages into computers.

em (a) a unit of measurement, becoming archaic. An em, properly called a pica em, is 12 POINTS. It represents the space occupied by an upper-case M in 12 pt type; (b) historically, an em in any type size is the width of an upper-case M in that size. Thus a 9 pt em is 9 pts wide, an 8 pt em 8 pts and so on.

embargo a ban on publication before a specified date.

en half the width of an EM in any type size. Typesetting jobs were measured in ens, the en being the average width of a character in any type size.

ends written at the end of a piece of original COPY to indicate that it has ended.

end symbol a typographic device (usually a black square or BULLET) used in magazine pages to indicate that a piece has finished.

exclusive a story or interview that is unique to a particular magazine.

expenses costs incurred.

facing matter an advertisement that is 'facing matter' is one that is placed opposite EDITORIAL.

fair comment a defence to certain LIBEL actions.

fair dealing   the permitted use of COPYRIGHT material.

feature   a piece of writing that is longer, more discursive and contains more 'colour' than a news story.

fifth colour   an extra colour, often day-glo or metallic, used to create a striking effect beyond the means of the normal FOUR-COLOUR PROCESS. Often used on COVERS.

file   any document created on a computer.

filename   the name given to a computer document.

fill   to rewrite a piece of type, whether a HEADING, STANDFIRST, CAPTION or BODY TEXT, to fit a given space.

film   material produced by imagesetting machines and colour separation equipment and used to make printing PLATES.

first rights   the right to publish an article once in Britain. This is the standard commission, unless the writer agrees otherwise.

fit   to CUT a piece of writing to match a fixed space.

fixed direct costs   costs incurred in production but not proportionate to the volume of production.

flannel panel   the magazine's MASTHEAD, including its address, telephone numbers, staff box and copyright notice.

flash   a design device for drawing attention.

flat-plan   a plan of the magazine, indicating where every advertisement and every piece of EDITORIAL will appear.

focus   concentration on the identity of a magazine.

focus feature   a label sometimes used for AD-GET features.

focus group   (a) a small group of readers and potential readers assembled for research purposes; (b) key editorial staff in some magazine houses.

folio   page number.

follow-up   a return to a story to encompass new developments.

footer   a line, often including the magazine's name, that appears at the bottom of every page.

format   (a) the size and shape of a page, e.g. A4; (b) to format text is to apply to it all the typographic specifications laid down in a magazine's design. This should happen automatically when text is transferred into a LAYOUT program.

fount or font   traditionally, a set of characters in one TYPEFACE and one size. Today it tends to mean a typeface in its complete range of sizes and italic and bold variants.

four-colour process   a printing technique that uses four colours of ink (cyan, magenta, yellow, black) to simulate full colour.

freelance   a self-employed journalist, either writing at home or working as a casual sub-editor.

furniture   (a) design elements common to every page of a magazine; (b) regular features and fixed items in the magazine as a whole.

galley proof   a proof produced as a single column of type, before page make-up.

gatefold   a page, usually the inside front COVER, which folds out to accommodate a large advertisement. Occasionally used for editorial.

gone to bed   the magazine is at the printers and cannot be changed.

graduated tint   a TINT which changes in density or hue from top to bottom or side to side.

grid   the underlying structure of the magazine, determining COLUMN widths and image area. Now usually exists only in computer form.

gutter   the gap between two COLUMNS or two adjoining pages.

h & j   HYPHENATION and JUSTIFICATION. Now usually encountered as rules built into DESKTOP PUBLISHING programs.

half-tone   an illustration or photograph after it has been broken into dots for printing.

hard copy   words on paper before they are typeset.

header   a line of type that appears at the top of every page.

heading or **headline**   an area of DISPLAY TYPE that draws the reader's interest to a feature. Need not be at the top of the page.

hold over   to keep an item for the next issue or some future date.

hot links   words and graphics on a page of computer text that can be clicked to take the reader to a different page.

hotlist   a list of favourite WORLD WIDE WEB pages held in a BROWSER program.

house ad.   an advertisement placed in a magazine by its own publisher.

house journal   a magazine produced for employees of an organisation.

house style   a set of rules about disputed spellings, matters of punctuation, capitalisation, use of numerals, etc.

HTML   Hyper Text Mark-up Language, a computer language used for the creation of WORLD WIDE WEB PAGES.

human interest   a type of story or feature concentrating on emotional aspects of individual lives.

hypertext   a method of displaying text in computer systems, allowing the reader to navigate by using the mouse to click on words and images.

hyphenation   the insertion of a hyphen into a word as it breaks at the end of a line. Controlled by dictionaries built into desktop publishing programs but subject to manual override.

icon   a drawing on a computer screen used to indicate and manipulate files, disc drives, etc. By extension, similar drawings used as illustrations and graphics in page design.

image area   the part of a page which is normally inked.

imprint   the names and addresses of the publisher and printer and any other legally required information.

indentation   (abbreviated to 'indent') a shorter line than usual, leaving a white space at the beginning or end. Used to mark paragraphs.

injunction   a court order.

insert   an advertisement or announcement that is inserted between a magazine's pages.

interim injunction   a court order banning publication in advance of a court hearing. Used to prevent publication of material based on breaches of confidence.

Internet   the international network of linked computers.

intro   abbreviation for 'introduction': the author's opening paragraph. Not to be confused with the STANDFIRST or SELL, which are written by editors and sub-editors.

justification   (a) adjustment of the spacing between words and characters. 'Justified' type is set so that lines are full out at both ends; (b) proving the truth of an allegation when defending a libel action.

justified   see JUSTIFICATION.

kern   to reduce space between two letters to make them fit neatly. Computer systems do this automatically, but it can be manually adjusted.

kicker   an introductory HEADING in small type above the real headline.

kill   to drop a story or FEATURE.

kill fee   a payment in respect of a story that has been dropped at an early stage.

landscape   a picture with a horizontal emphasis.

layout   designs for pages, SPREADS and LONGER features; printed versions of those designs.

lead   (pronounced 'leed') the most important and prominent story on a news page.

leading   (pronounced 'ledding') the vertical space between lines of type. Measured in POINTS.

legal   a potential legal problem or query: 'We've got a legal on this story.'

letterspacing   adjustment of the space between individual letters to improve appearance. Also known as 'tracking'.

libel   a defamatory publication or statement.

licence   an agreement to use COPYRIGHT material within negotiated restrictions.

lift   to acquire writing or pictures from some other published source without paying for them.

line drawing   an illustration that uses lines rather than areas of continuous tone.

listings   details of events, entertainment, etc.

literal   a typographical error.

logo   abbreviation for 'logotype': the magazine's name, in the typographic style used on the cover.

lower case   small letters, as opposed to capitals.

manuscript   original COPY on paper.

mark up   to prepare typewritten COPY for typesetting.

masthead   the panel including the magazine's name, address and telephone numbers and often its staff box. Incorrectly used to mean TITLEPIECE.

measure   the width of a column. Measured in PICA EMS.

media pack   details of a magazine's circulation, readership and technical specifications. Used to attract advertisers.

mf   abbreviation for 'more follows'. Written at the end of individual pages of COPY.

model release form   a form to be signed by a photographic model, indemnifying the magazine against various legal claims.

mono   in black and white.

mug-shot   simple identifying picture of an individual person.

multimedia   bringing together words, images, sounds and moving pictures to be accessed on a computer.

Netscape Navigator   the dominant WEB BROWSER program.

newsletter   a magazine with basic production values distributed by subscription.

next week/month box   a BOX or PANEL indicating what the magazine's next issue will contain.

nib   news in brief: a one-paragraph news story.

NVQ   National Vocational Qualification: an industry-wide in-service training scheme.

off-line   an electronic medium that does not require a connection to a remote computer.

off the record   a statement made subject to restrictions as to how it is reported.

on-line   an electronic medium that requires connection to a remote computer.

on-line service   a commercial organisation selling information to those connecting to its remote computers.

on spec   a feature offered for the editor's perusal, without obligation.

on the record   a statement made without restrictions as to how it is reported.

orphan   the short line at the beginning or end of a paragraph appearing at the bottom of a COLUMN. Best avoided.

outs   photographs submitted for a LAYOUT but not used.

overheads   costs not directly related to a magazine's production.

overmatter   type in excess of the space allowed for it.

overs   see OUTS.

ozalid   a type of PROOF.

page rate (a) the price of a page of advertising; (b) the sum an editor can spend on a page of EDITORIAL.

page traffic measurement of how well a given page is read.

pagination the number of pages.

panel an area of type enclosed by RULES and often backed by a TINT.

Pantone a proprietary colour-matching system. Fifth colours are sometimes called 'Pantone colours' because this is the system used to define them.

par/para abbreviation for 'paragraph'.

paste up to create pages from BROMIDES of type and HALF-TONES, ready to go before the camera. Effectively replaced by DESKTOP PUBLISHING programs.

peg the event to which a story or feature has to be tied to make it topical: 'The peg for this is the new school term.'

perfect bound a method of BINDING, using glue, that creates a magazine with a hard, square spine.

photo-montage a photograph assembled out of several originals or extensively retouched.

pica 12 pt type. A pica EM is a 12 pt em. The pica em is used as a unit of typographical measurement.

picture by-line a by-line incorporating a photograph of the author.

pixillate to treat a picture electronically so that the subject is unrecognisable. Used to protect anonymity in stories where this is legally necessary, and in imitation of television practice.

plaintiff a person or organisation bringing a legal action.

planning meeting a meeting dedicated to future issues.

plate an ink-bearing surface used in the lithographic printing process.

point the fundamental unit of typographical measurement. There are 72 pts to the inch and 28.35 to the centimetre.

portfolio (a) group of magazines owned by a single company; (b) a folder showing examples of a designer's work.

portrait a picture with vertical emphasis.

post-mortem a meeting to discuss the previous issue or issues.

pre-plan a meeting to discuss future features.

pre-press print planning, FILM assembly, PLATE-making and other activities required before printing.

preprint a section of a magazine printed in advance and then inserted into the issue.

print run the total number of issues printed.

prior restraint legal action preventing publication.

privilege a defence to some LIBEL actions.

profile a portrait in words, usually of a person but occasionally of an organisation, a place or an object.

proof a printed copy of work in progress, for checking purposes.

pull quote a quote extracted from a FEATURE or news story and given visual emphasis by typography.

qualitative research research dealing with readers' opinions, aspirations and feelings.

quantitative research research based on demographic and statistical aspects of the readership.

ragged right type that is not JUSTIFIED, but is 'flush left' or RANGED LEFT. Each line is of a different length, giving a 'ragged' appearance.

ranged left type that is not JUSTIFIED but is lined up on the left.

ranged right type that is not JUSTIFIED but is lined up on the right.

readership   the total number of people reading a magazine, based on research into how many people see each copy.

register   the correct alignment of all four colours of ink. Printing can be 'in register' or 'out of register'.

regulars   the repeated elements in a magazine: contents page, EDITOR'S LETTER, news, letters, etc.

repertoire buyers   readers who choose from a range of magazines.

reportage   term used for 'gritty' investigative news features, with appropriate photography.

repro   abbreviation for 'reproduction', meaning high-level SCANNING of colour pictures and their reuniting with type and page LAYOUTS to make the FOUR-COLOUR FILMS required for colour printing.

repro house   also known as COLOUR HOUSE. Facility specialising in reproduction and colour work.

retouch   to improve or alter a photograph. Now done electronically.

revenue   income.

reverse out   typically, to show white type emerging from a black background. Sometimes known as a 'wob', for 'white on black'.

right of reply   procedure for correcting published errors. Not yet incorporated into English law.

ring-round   news story or FEATURE based on telephone calls seeking instant reactions to events.

river   white space forming an ugly river-like pattern through a column of type.

roman   the standard upright style of type.

rough   a designer's sketch leading to a finished layout or giving guidance to a photographer.

RSI   repetitive strain injury, a crippling condition affecting some of those who work on screen.

rule   any line appearing in printed matter.

runaround   type which is set to run around a photograph or graphic element.

running turn   ensuring that sentences carry on from one COLUMN to the next and from one page to the next, to discourage the reader from breaking off.

saddle-stitching   a method of BINDING magazines by folding pages at the seam and stapling.

scanner   an electronic or computer device used for converting photographs, artwork and typewritten COPY into digital form.

scanning   the process of converting photographs, artwork and typewritten copy into digital form.

schedule   a timetable of production events from the commissioning of material to printing.

Scitex   equipment used at the COLOUR house for the manipulation and enhancement of colour photographs at high resolution.

screamer   an exclamation mark.

search engine or **tool**   a program on WEB SITE used for finding things in the INTERNET.

section   a part of a magazine formed from a single sheet of paper before being stitched and trimmed.

sell   see STANDFIRST.

separations   see COLOUR SEPARATIONS.

server   a computer used for storing large volumes of material, either in the office or as part of the INTERNET.

shoot   a photographic session.

sidebar   additional material enhancing a FEATURE, often placed in a PANEL or BOX to one side of BODY COPY.

sidehead   a small HEADING in the text, flush with the left of the COLUMN of type.

slander   spoken defamation.

slug   a small HEADING at the top of a page used to define the type of material on the page beneath: 'news', 'personal view', 'industry focus', etc.

solus ad   the only advertisement on a SPREAD.

solus reader   a reader who is loyal to a single magazine.

special feature   often an AD-GET feature.

spike   a metal spike used for holding discarded copy. Now banned for safety reasons but sometimes replaced by a similarly named area in a computer system.

splash   the front-page lead story in a newspaper-format magazine.

sponsorship   generating revenue by selling one or more advertisers the right to associate themselves with some EDITORIAL area or event.

spot colour   single colour (in addition to black).

spread   see 'double-page spread'.

s/s   abbreviation for 'same size'.

standfirst   the introductory material to a FEATURE, written by editors or sub-editors.

standing artwork   graphic material used in every issue.

standing matter   text elements used in every issue.

stet   Latin for 'let it stand': an instruction to reinstate something shown as deleted on the HARD COPY or PROOF.

sting   the central and most damaging allegation in a LIBEL case.

strap or **strapline**   an additional HEADING above or below main heading and in smaller type.

strict liability   a type of CONTEMPT OF COURT that can be committed accidentally.

style   see HOUSE STYLE.

style book   the repository of HOUSE STYLE.

style-sheet   (a) a shorter version of a style book; (b) in desktop publishing programs, a stored set of type specifications to which incoming text can be made to conform.

stylist   the person responsible for organising a photographic shoot, especially if models are involved.

sub   sub-editor (sometimes known as copy-editor).

subhead   a subsidiary HEADING in small type beneath the main heading.

SWOT   Strengths, Weaknesses, Opportunities, Threats: a fashionable way of analysing a magazine's position in the market.

synopsis   a brief summary of an article.

SyQuest   an optical disk used for storing and transporting large volumes of digital material, e.g. scans and completed pages.

Teeline   a shorthand system favoured by journalists.

think piece   a ruminative FEATURE.

thumbnail   a miniature print-out or drawing of a page.

TIFF   a format for storing images in digital form.

tint   a printed area covered with dots to simulate light colour or grey.

titlepiece   the magazine's title in the typographical form used on the COVER.

TOT   Triumph Over Tragedy: an emotional story built on human suffering but with a happy ending.

transparency   a single frame of positive photographic film.

transpose   to reorder characters, words or paragraphs.

trim lines   lines indicating the printing area in DESKTOP PUBLISHING software.

turn arrow   a symbol at the end of a page of type telling the reader to turn the page.

typeface   a complete alphabet in a particular design.
typo   abbreviation for 'typographical error'.

unfair dismissal   any dismissal that is not in accordance with employment law.
unjustified   type which has not been made flush at both ends of a line.
upper-and-lower   a HEADLINE regime in which UPPER and LOWER CASE letters are used as sense requires: as opposed to 'all capitals' or 'initial capitals'.
upper case   capital letters.
Usenet   also known as 'news groups': an unmoderated INTERNET discussion area that has nothing much to do with news.

variable direct costs   costs which increase with the PRINT RUN and PAGINATION.
variance   departure from an agreed budget.
vignette   a photograph that fades away to nothing at the edges.
virus   a computer program designed to spread and damage either hardware or software
vox pop   a FEATURE or story based on short interviews and MUG-SHOTS of members of the public.

Web browser   a computer program for reading WORLD WIDE WEB pages.
Web editor   a computer program used to create WEB PAGES.
Web page   an individual document in WORLD WIDE WEB format. Will include words, photographs and graphics. May also include sound, moving pictures and animation.
Web site   a group of related WORLD WIDE WEB pages.
white space   unprinted areas used by a designer to direct the eye.
widow   the last line of a paragraph appearing at the top of a column. Best avoided.
wing copy   additional matter enhancing a FEATURE, appearing in a BOX or PANEL to one side: SIDEBARS.
womb-trembler   a highly emotional or disturbing story or FEATURE, usually involving children, childbirth or fertility.
word-rate   the fee for freelance contributions.
word-spacing   the amount of space between words. Controlled by software.
World Wide Web   a network of computer files stored according to an agreed format so that they appear as WEB PAGES when viewed with a WEB BROWSER program.
wrongful dismissal   a dismissal without proper notice.

x-height   the height of ordinary lower-case letters without ASCENDERS or DESCENDERS (a, c, e, etc.). Determines how large a typeface of a given size actually appears.

Index